⟡···· EVERY NIGHT IS ····⟡
SATURDAY NIGHT

A COUNTRY GIRL'S JOURNEY TO THE ROCK & ROLL HALL OF FAME

WANDA ★ JACKSON

WITH
SCOTT B. BOMAR

EVERY NIGHT IS SATURDAY NIGHT:
A COUNTRY GIRL'S JOURNEY TO THE ROCK & ROLL HALL OF FAME

Cover design by Becky Reiser, Rabar Productions

Book production by Adept Content Solutions

Photo Credits
Photo of author Wanda Jackson by Jeff Fasano.
Photo of author Scott B. Bomar by J. Wiley.
Photo of Wanda and Elvis Costello by Chris Holding.
Photo of Wanda and Roy Clark courtesy of Thomas Sims Archives.
Back cover photo courtesy of Third Man Records.
All other photos included in *Every Night Is Saturday Night* are from the personal collection of Wanda Jackson Goodman.

Library of Congress Cataloging-in-Publication Data available upon request.

ISBN: 9781947026018

Published by BMG
www.bmg.com

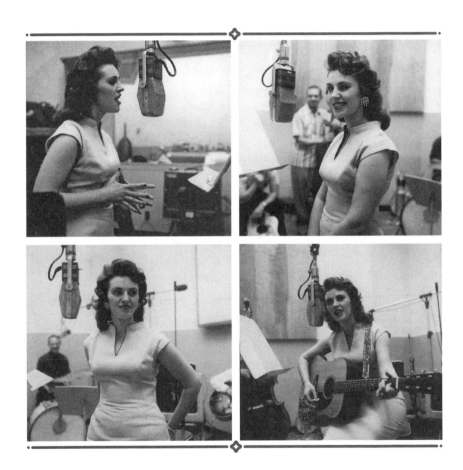

CONTENTS

Foreword v

Preface vii

Chapter 1 — Back Then 1

Chapter 2 — California Stars 11

Chapter 3 — No Place to Go but Home 21

Chapter 4 — Turn Your Radio On 31

Chapter 5 — Lovin' Country Style 41

Chapter 6 — You Can't Have My Love 51

Chapter 7 — Tears at the Grand Ole Opry 63

Chapter 8 — I Wish I Was Your Friend 75

Chapter 9 — Rock Your Baby 85

Chapter 10 — If You Don't Somebody Else Will 97

Chapter 11 — I Gotta Know 109

Chapter 12 — Let's Have a Party 121

Chapter 13 — Fujiyama Mama 131

Chapter 14 — Both Sides of the Line 141

Chapter 15 — Right or Wrong 151

Chapter 16 — You're the One for Me 161

Chapter 17 — A Woman Lives for Love 171

Chapter 18 — Santo Domingo   181

Chapter 19 — Kickin' Our Hearts Around   191

Chapter 20 — Tears Will Be the Chaser for Your Wine   201

Chapter 21 — I Saw the Light   211

Chapter 22 — My Testimony   221

Chapter 23 — Rockabilly Fever   231

Chapter 24 — Whole Lotta Shakin' Goin' On   241

Chapter 25 — Thunder on the Mountain   249

Chapter 26 — In the Middle of a Heartache   257

Chapter 27 — Treat Me Like a Lady   265

FOREWORD
Elvis Costello

The legend has it that Pete Seeger was so horrified by Bob
Dylan's electric set at the Newport Folk Festival of 1965 that
he had to be restrained from cutting through the power cables
with an axe. I have my doubts about this story, having seen a
much older Seeger, swinging a jackhammer at a railroad spike,
while singing a work song on the stage of Carnegie Hall. If he'd
intended to stop the music, he could have done so easily.

But here, in the summer of 2011, was that same erect, still
resolute frame standing just a few steps ahead of me in the wings
of the Newport stage as that darn rock-and-roll music rolled out
again into the afternoon. Did he look like he was about to do
something rash and bring the music to a halt?

Not a chance. . . .

I eased myself level with the great man and saw that he was beaming broadly at the sight and sound before him: Wanda Jackson leading her band from country ballad to rockabilly rave-up in a set that lit a fire in the sunlit crowd.

It was the music of American folk, as this is ALL American music.

That it took a few years for Wanda Jackson to be inducted into the Rock and Roll Hall of Fame was a disgrace that once cast a shadow of credibility over that little boys' club.

She's in there now where she belongs, having broken down a fair few doors along the way, and rolling out the red carpet for young women with guitars who may not even know her name.

Within these covers you'll read the names of many great American musicians: Wanda's teachers, friends, contemporaries, and acolytes along with all the incidents, triumphs, and sorrows of her incredible career in music.

The last time I sang with Wanda was on the stage of the Cain's Ballroom in Tulsa—one of America's finest musical addresses.

We gathered in the dressing room beforehand. "Just what I needed in my life, another Elvis," said Wanda's gentleman husband, Wendell, repeating a joke that he'd cracked at our first meeting regarding people's enduring curiosity about his wife's earlier friendship with The King.

We introduced Wanda to the kind of ovation that starts in Oklahoma and can be heard for states around, before singing the Buck Owens hit, "Cryin' Time."

Wanda took her bow and flashed those green eyes in my direction mischievously. As she passed behind me into the shadows, I swear somebody pinched my cheek, and I don't mean the one below my eyes.

She's just what we needed in our life, The One and Only Wanda . . .

PREFACE
Big Daddy

"Wanda? Oh, Wanda. . . . Are you tired? You need to wake up, honey!" Daddy was insistent on getting my attention, but I was silently praying he'd leave me alone. I knew he wouldn't. This was the kind of thing Daddy never let slide. It was 1956, and we were in my Pontiac Star Chief barreling down a two-lane highway between a town I can't remember and another one that's just as hazy in my mind. I was eighteen years old and had only been out on the road as a professional singer for a short time. Those days often run together in my memory as a blur of motels, dance halls, long stretches of blacktop, late-night diners, cheering crowds, friendly autograph seekers, and music, music, music.

Daddy was my traveling companion, manager, chaperone, sounding board, guidance counselor, teacher, and, in many ways, my best friend. He was also my protector. Maybe my over-protector sometimes. "Wanda? Did you hear me? It looks like you're getting pretty tired there." Daddy was driving, and I was sitting next to him in the middle of the bench seat. On my right was a good-looking young singer who was headlining the tour. When we traveled from town to town, Daddy would let guys ride with us, but I couldn't go with them. I had my car and that's the way I traveled. Daddy's rules. Sometimes I'd get sleepy, and my head would lean over onto the shoulder of the guy who was riding next to me. As soon as he saw it, Daddy would pull over and tell me to get in the backseat. "If you're tired," he'd say, "you can stretch out and get some good rest back there."

"WANDA!"

I knew I couldn't pretend any longer. "What is it, Daddy?" I tried to play innocent.

"Sweetie, I think it's time we pull over so you can get in the back. I'm sure Elvis doesn't need you leaning all over him. We want our passengers to be comfortable, don't we?"

Of course it wasn't just that I was tired. This wasn't any old musician who decided to ride along to the next gig with us. This was Elvis Presley. Several months earlier I'd never even heard of him, but now I really liked him. And not just his music. Every teenage girl liked his music. But I liked being around him. I liked the way he made me feel. And he liked me, too. Soon after, he would give me his ring and ask me to be his girl.

At that moment, though, there was no getting around Daddy's watchful eye. I couldn't put my head on someone's shoulder. I couldn't sit on a guy's lap. A lot of guys would want me to sit on their knee to take a picture after a show, but I couldn't do that, either. Daddy was very quiet, but he was always watching. If he needed to intervene, he would. If I forgot the rules, I definitely heard about it later. It was important to him that I maintain a good reputation. I learned a lot from Daddy, and I realize today how important a good reputation is. Even if I was pouting in that backseat after he banished me from Elvis's shoulder.

I've always been a lady. That was instilled in me by both my parents from an early age. But they also taught me that it's good to be different. "You don't want to be like everybody else," Daddy used to tell me as we traveled those long lonely roads through countless dark nights from one show to another. We might be sharing the bill with Jerry Lee Lewis, Carl Perkins, Johnny Cash, Buddy Holly, or Elvis at an auditorium or dance hall somewhere in Texas, Missouri, Arkansas, or wherever the work took us. As a single young woman—still in my teens and just barely out of high school—there was certainly no way Daddy was going to send me out on the road alone with the boys. That's not the kind of thing a lady did in the mid-1950s.

With Daddy by my side, I had a front-row seat to the early rumblings of what was soon to erupt as a cultural phenomenon. I sang strictly country in the very beginning, which was known as hillbilly music at the time. Boy, that term always just upset me. I didn't like it. Elvis didn't either, but he was known as the hillbilly cat. Whatever you called it, our music was mixing with the blues to give birth to the early strains of what we now call rock and roll. Daddy and I both saw that something new was happening. We heard the screams of the girls that lifted the rafters with every movement of Elvis's hips. We saw the ecstasy on the faces of young people who were beginning to feel like they had a new kind of music they could call their very own. Though I'd started as a country singer, I soon joined the rock-and-roll party, with Elvis's encouragement, and made sure I was able to rock just as hard as the boys. In recent years people have looked back on that

era and started calling me the "sweet lady with the nasty voice."
I like to joke with people when they use that term, and ask,
"Whoever said I was sweet?"

While my folks never failed to remind me to conduct myself
with dignity and class in all situations, I didn't exactly fit the mold
of the typical girl of the 1950s. Some people thought I was too
strong. Others thought I was too wild. That never bothered me
or my parents because I was taught that you can be different;
you can break away and do some crazy stuff, as long as you stay a
lady about it. And that's exactly what I did. I was like a prim little
lady, but fiery. I had a burning fire in my bones when it came to
making music, and I could not be stopped.

There are probably two Wanda Jacksons. Actually, there are at
least two Wanda Jacksons. Some of my fans might be surprised to
learn that, offstage, I'm really a traditionalist. I'm a wife, mother,
and grandmother (and recently became a great-grandmother!)
whose grandkids call her "Ma." I never thought I'd be called Ma,
but my first grandbaby couldn't say "Grandma," so that's just how
it came out. And it sure sounds awful sweet when they say it. I
was married to the same man, Wendell Goodman, for more than
fifty-five years, until he passed away in 2017. After we married,
Wendell stepped in and took over the role my father had before
him. He took care of the business, and, frankly, I've always felt like
I needed a good man to take care of me. I was never taught to
have responsibility. Daddy handled everything, and then Wendell
took it from there. Thanks to them, I actually could be the sweet
little girl (nasty voice and all) who didn't have to fight her own
battles. I would tell them my problems, and they took care of it. I
let them be the "bad cop" and be perceived as hard to get along
with, when it was usually really me all along. Because of them, I
didn't have to worry about anything but the music. I've been well
protected in that respect, and it has allowed me to successfully

navigate my way through a long career without ever really butting heads with anyone.

I've been asked if I'm a feminist, and I've been told I'm a hero to feminists. But I don't put myself in that category. People have always thought I was the woman who stood up against the man, but I was never that way. I understand that some women have to take a leadership role when their men won't, but women who just want to rule the roost and put men down so badly? That bothers me. I guess I just love and respect men. I don't want to fight them. I suppose I would if I got really mad or something, but I honestly prefer the company of men to women. Their conversations are much more interesting to me. At parties, I would always migrate over to listen to the men talk. Women would talk about their kids and their school and all that, but I didn't relate to it. The bottom line is I highly respect men, and I always depended on a man, whether it be Daddy or Wendell.

And then there's another Wanda Jackson. The one the public knows. I probably never had as much self-confidence or self-esteem as people thought, but if you watch old videos of me performing, it's the absolute picture of confidence when I'm on stage. Once I got onto that stage, I was able to become something else entirely. I almost unconsciously flipped a switch. The stage is where I'm the Queen. Always have been. I enjoyed shocking people a little bit, but that was the only place I'd do it. On the stage is where I sometimes made Daddy nervous with my sexy outfits and shaking hips. On the stage is where I would let out my trademark growl and express the raw power of music that lived deep in my soul.

When I'm onstage I hear everything the band is doing. I've always been good at that. During a show, I'll call the bass player over and say, "You're playing 4/4 time all the way through. I don't want that." Or I might tell the guitar player, "Hey, cut the

volume down," or maybe, "Turn it up!" And drummers? So many
drummers rush the beat. It's hard to find a good drummer who
will lock into the right tempo, but I push them to be their best. I
control the stage. The stage has always been mine. People couldn't
put purses or coats or drinks down on it. If some guy was sitting
on my stage, I might just step on his hand, or if people set things
there, I might just kick them off. I can't do that anymore at my
age, but I could get pretty feisty when protecting my domain in
my younger years.

The reason that stage is so important to me is because I know
that everyone who comes to see me perform wants to have a
good time. And that's what I want to give them. Every night that
I entertain people and watch them have fun, it reminds me of
being a young girl growing up in California when Mother and
Daddy would take me to Western swing dances. I'd stare up at the
stage at those musicians in their beautiful, sparkling outfits. I was
mesmerized.

I grew up thinking that music was happy and that it would
always make me feel great. I associate music with fun and laughter
and warm feelings. Going to those Saturday night dances with
my folks was a wonderful time in my life. I didn't want Saturday
night to end. I just had to figure out how I was going to live my
life in a way that made that feeling last. Sometimes I chased the
wrong things in that pursuit, but I never lost sight of throwing
a party for my fans at every show. I don't care if it's a Tuesday or
a work night, or a school night; if you come to a Wanda Jackson
show, every night is Saturday night.

I never thought of myself as a great singer, but I thought I
was good, and I knew how to entertain people. After being in
this business for over sixty-five years, I still love getting in front
of an audience as much as I ever did. Once I come down from
that stage, however, I'm not particularly outgoing. Some fans

have described me as mysterious because there are things I don't talk about, and I'm not one to assert myself too much. I guess this book is my chance to talk a little more than usual. This is my opportunity to let you a little deeper into my life.

The truth is, much of my life revolves around my career. I'm an only child, which meant I got all the attention. I was smothered with a lot of love and a lot of help when I was starting out, and that has continued all the way until today. My career wound up becoming a family affair, and it still is. Whether it was Mother designing my stage outfits, Daddy taking care of the details on tour, my granddaughter Jordan managing my social media accounts, or Wendell taking care of all my business, my life has been a Cinderella story. I even got the handsome prince!

As we all know, even Cinderella stories include a mix of challenges, joys, and frustrations along the way. I've learned a lot of things in my life about music, love, and what really matters. I've learned what it means to find peace and meaning, sometimes in the face of adversity. I've learned to find my grounding in a good man, a good family, and, most importantly, in a good God, who is the source of all light and truth. These are the influences that have allowed me to keep the musical party going for decades. I'm glad to have you at my party, and I hope you enjoy reading about my life. Just remember to have fun along the way. It is Saturday night, after all!

Chapter 1

BACK THEN

My mother was born Nellie Whitaker on December 19, 1913, in Hickory, Oklahoma. Her parents, William and Grace, both hailed from Denton, Texas, but were married in Rush Springs, Oklahoma, in 1909. They moved to the town of Roff, Oklahoma, around 1916, where my grandfather worked as a farmer.

My father, Tom, was born on March 24, 1915, in Texas. His parents, Will and Maud, were from Missouri and Texas, respectively. My paternal grandfather only made it through the fifth grade, and the Jackson family really struggled financially. Mother used to say that when she first realized how hard Daddy had it growing up, she felt sorry for him. They were as poor as people can possibly be, but one thing Daddy did have was a deep

1

love for music. He began playing guitar and fiddle from an early age.

Mother was still living in Roff as a young woman in the early 1930s, but, at some point, she traveled to Maud, which is about sixty miles east of Oklahoma City, to visit her sister, Edna. Even though my aunt's name was Edna, everyone called her Polly. That's the thing about country people. You have to work to keep up with all the various names! I haven't even told you about my Aunt Electa yet. But we'll get there eventually.

The little city of Maud was established in the late 1800s and straddles Pottawatomie and Seminole Counties in central Oklahoma. I've been told that it was on the dividing line between Oklahoma Territory and Indian Territory, and that a barbed-wire fence once ran along Broadway to keep the Indians from crossing that border. The town was named for Maud Sterns, who was the sister-in-law to the owners of the local general store. By the early 1900s there was a post office, a train station, and a newspaper. When oil was discovered in the 1920s, Maud became a boom town, and the population of a few hundred residents soon swelled to as many as 10,000. By the time Aunt Polly was living there, things had settled down considerably, and the population was less than half what it had been in its heyday.

One Saturday night Polly suggested that she and Mother go out to a dance. My daddy was the leader of a little band that was performing that night, and he spotted Mother as soon as she arrived at the dance hall. During one of the songs Daddy turned to his brother, who was also in the band. "You take over for a minute," he said. "I've gotta go meet this girl, but I'll be back soon." He climbed down from the bandstand, made his way across the room, and asked Mother if she'd like to dance. I guess that was it for both of them. Mother was a beautiful woman, and Daddy was quite a handsome guy in his younger days. They both adored music and loved to dance. It was love at first sight.

Mother and Daddy married in 1933 and made their home there in Maud. My father worked various jobs and played music on the side. He was working at a gas station by the time I came along on October 20, 1937. He soon found work driving a delivery truck for a bread company.

I was born prematurely, and my family says it was the last time I was early for anything! They tell me I live on rock-and-roll time. Mother was scheduled to have a C-section, which was pretty unusual at that time. I'm not entirely certain what sort of complications she had during her pregnancy, since people really didn't discuss those matters openly in those days. I do know that she had a very difficult time. The plan was that I would enter the world at a hospital in Oklahoma City, but when Mother unexpectedly went into labor, she had to stay in Maud. That's where I was born on October 20, 1937.

Mother wanted to name me Roberta, because my dad's middle name was Robert. He wouldn't have it. I don't know where he came up with it, but Daddy said he always wanted to have a daughter, and he declared, in no uncertain terms, "Her name is Wanda. It's got to be Wanda." Since he was set on the first name, Mother came up with my middle name, which is Lavonne. I don't know why it wasn't Roberta. Maybe she thought she'd save that name in case she had a second daughter.

But another child was not part of the plan for the Jacksons. Not only was Mother's pregnancy difficult, but natural childbirth was an extremely painful challenge for her. She was always number one for Daddy, and when he saw what a problem she had, he didn't want her to ever risk going through that kind of pain and discomfort again. He went to the "chopping block," as he called it, so there would be no chance of Mother getting pregnant a second time. And, with that, Wanda Lavonne Jackson's fate as an only child was sealed.

A lot of people have asked me over the years if I feel like I missed out by not having brothers and sisters around. I didn't know any different. Truth be told, I kind of enjoyed being the center of attention. I think being an only child helped me grow up a little faster. I wasn't real interested in kid things, even when I *was* a kid. I spent a lot of time around adults, so I was like a little adult very early on. Even though it's the only thing I ever knew, I don't think I would have wanted it any other way. Mother and Daddy put all their focus and energies on me, which is almost certainly the main reason I would later be successful in my music career.

Even though I remember very little about my early childhood, I've always thought of Maud as my hometown. In the late 1980s the city launched an annual Wanda Jackson Day. There was a parade, a carnival, food vendors, a car show, and booths with handmade crafts for sale. The festivities would culminate with a big concert in the evening, featuring some of my Nashville friends whom I'd invite to perform. Eventually, we added a talent contest. I thought maybe four or five people would participate, but we were flooded with applicants. One year we had seventy people pay the entry fee to be a part of the competition. I would typically serve as one of the judges, and we would recruit radio personalities and others to join me. The winner of the contest would get to open the show that evening, which was great exposure for them.

We celebrated Wanda Jackson Day for thirteen years, and it turned out to be a really good thing for Maud. All the profits went to the city, which allowed them to get the things they needed for their local government. My dad's sister lived in Maud and was killed in a house fire. The fire department didn't have the equipment they needed to rescue her at the time, and I'm proud that funds we raised allowed the department to obtain the equipment to assist them when entering a burning building. That was very important to me. I'm also proud that our benefit allowed the police department to purchase new cars. I'm thankful, too, that we helped Maud officials get the attention of their legislative representatives, resulting in new highways and other improvements. They even named a street after me one year. Just think, if my mother had not gone into labor early, I would have been born in Oklahoma City and might not have had the opportunity to make the same kinds of contributions to the birthplace I called home for the first few years of my life.

One of the more distinguished residents to come from Maud was Edmond Harjo, a Seminole Indian who was one of the famous code talkers who helped transmit secret messages during World War II. He received the Congressional Gold Medal for his service in Normandy and Iwo Jima, and was the last surviving Seminole code talker until his death in 2014. I'm honored to hail from the same town as an American hero, and I suppose Edmond and I have been Maud's ambassadors to the world over the years.

When I was around five years old, our family moved from Oklahoma to Los Angeles. That was a pretty common thing back then. All us Okies and Arkies and Texans couldn't find much work, so we headed west in search of better opportunities. All the images you associate with *The Grapes of Wrath* were a real thing. People were desperate for a better way of life, and California held the promise of fresh opportunities. As an only child, I had what I needed. I never suffered. Mother saw to that. But Daddy had friends in California, and he thought maybe we could go out there, and he could learn a trade that would give us more chances to make a better way in the world.

We had a two-door Pontiac coupe with a small storage space behind the front seats. Mother was quite a seamstress, and Daddy built a little frame so they could put a mattress for me to sleep on back there. One of my earliest memories is that car ride on Route 66 headed for the West Coast. There were no interstates then, so it took a lot longer to wind our way out there than it does now.

The war was on at the time we arrived in California, and the war industry brought an even larger wave of migrants than those who had come out during the Dust Bowl era. I remember seeing signs picturing Uncle Sam that talked about "the Japs." You didn't see the word *Japanese* then. It was always "Japs." I could have never imagined as a little girl that one day I would be a professional singer who would have a number one song in Japan, become a superstar there, and tour the country for weeks at a time. But that moment, of course, was still a long way away.

When we first arrived in Los Angeles, we rented a single-room upstairs apartment in a large house called Gramercy Place near downtown. Mother had a hot plate, so she could fix soups or open a can of something simple for us to eat. Built in the early 1920s, the old mansion is still there today, and is still operated as a boarding house and hostel. Mother had lived in Oklahoma her entire life, and Los Angeles was an enormous new world. She was protective of me anyway, but being in a new environment made her pretty nervous. The kidnapping of Charles Lindbergh's one-year-old baby in the early 1930s caused a lot of people to realize that the world can be an unsafe place. Bad things can happen even to children, and it seemed that these things were more likely to occur in big cities.

When we went out in public, Mother held my hand tight for fear of a stranger snatching me away. Even when we were home, she didn't like it when I was out of her sight. The bathroom was down the hall from our tiny apartment, and I would usually bathe in the early evenings when Mother was fixing supper. She'd tell me to sing while I was in the bath. She'd pop her head in and say, "Sing louder, honey. I can't hear you!" A few minutes would go by, and I'd hear her call out to me, "Keep singing, Wanda!" She was afraid I was going to fall in that tub and drown, but she knew if she could hear me singing I was okay. One time I heard her coming toward the bathroom, so I lay down in that tub real still to trick her. I about scared her half to death. That was me being a little prankster, I guess. Those must have been the genes from my dad's side of the family!

Mother and Daddy were pretty different in that regard. She tended to imagine the worst-case scenario and was somewhat of a worry wart. She was a fairly nervous person and was always in motion. My dad was more laid back. He was a joker and she was a workaholic. Even though my parents were complete opposites, they were real cute together and were affectionate toward one another—and toward me. From my earliest memories, our home was always filled with love.

By the time I started school, we had moved to a small apartment at 2727 Menlo Avenue, just east of Vermont. I attended Vermont Avenue Elementary School, which was located on the other side of the street from where we lived. Vermont was, and is, a busy thoroughfare running through Los Angeles, but there was an underground pedestrian tunnel that would take us to the other side. Mother felt it was safe and usually let me walk to school with my friends. I didn't like that tunnel, though. It seemed so dark and scary, so we would take a deep breath and run through, not daring to breathe until we got to the other side.

When I began school, I was known to everyone by my middle name, Lavonne. I'm not sure why, but that's what I wanted everyone to call me then. I was Lavonne to everyone, including my parents, during my elementary school years. That's not the only thing about me that would change later. Even though I'm known for my dark hair, I was actually a blonde when I was little. It would be quite some time before blonde Lavonne would transform into the Wanda Jackson you know today.

Both Mother and Daddy were still at work when I got home from school each day, so they hired a woman named Ma Settlage to watch me for a few hours. I went through a clumsy phase where I would knock over milk—or whatever I was drinking—all the time. I'm sure it was maddening. One time I knocked some milk over on the table, and Ma Settlage made me scoop it up with my mouth. Mother happened to walk in at that very moment to see what was going on. She was steaming mad. "You don't have her licking stuff up off the table," she barked. And that was the end of Ma Settlage.

There were about four other kids living on our block on Menlo Avenue, and since the entire country was preoccupied with the war at the time, it was only natural that my friends and I would stage pretend battles in our backyards. I also loved Tarzan. One girl's house had a balcony, so we imagined that balcony was our treehouse, and we'd make up all sorts of adventures. When we weren't playing war or Tarzan, it was usually cowboys and Indians. I had a couple of toy six-shooters tucked into holsters with a hat, vest, and the whole getup. Later on, I'd be known for introducing high heels, strappy dresses, and glamour into the world of country music. As a kid, however, I was no demure little girl having a tea party. I was running around the neighborhood like a wild banshee. And I loved it!

The other game I remember playing with the neighborhood children was "preacher." There was a Baptist church at the north end of the street where Mother attended regularly. She enrolled me in Sunday School class and took me to services pretty much every week. I'd go home afterward, line up the other kids on the stairs outside, and start preaching to them. I don't remember what

I would say, but I remember I'd be pacing back and forth and shaking my finger at them. That must have been what the pastor did at the church. I was just a little girl, but I was showing off already. I guess I had the performance bug from an early age and was already looking for my stage.

Church was always an important part of Mother's life. She was a fine Christian lady. Daddy thought her dedication to the church was great, but he didn't feel like it was for him. He never interfered, though. He thought it was wonderful that Mother enjoyed being a part of the life of the church. She wasn't the type to get involved in all the various activities during the week because she worked outside the home, but we were there every Sunday morning in little matching outfits. She'd curl my hair and treat me like a little doll on Sundays. I liked going, but as soon as I got home, I was ready to put on one of my costumes and go tearing off into the neighborhood to get into another adventure with my friends.

I don't remember much about the music I heard in church on Sunday mornings, but I seem to remember it was a little uptight. I did like the sound of the piano, but that music just didn't make much of an impact at that age. I do remember a lot about the Western swing music that was so popular on the Coast in the 1940s. Back then, church music was pretty reserved. Country music back east was fairly polite, too. It was made for sitting and listening. On the Coast, though, country music was made for dancing. Fortunately, Mother and Daddy never lost their love for dancing. They were both beautiful dancers who would go out nearly every weekend.

People didn't get babysitters very often then. They took their kids along with them. If Mother and Daddy went to a dance, I went too. There were several venues and dance halls around the city, but the Venice and Santa Monica Pier ballrooms were the most popular. They drew literally thousands of dancers to hear the likes of Bob Wills and His Texas Playboys or Tex Williams and his band. My favorite bandleader was Spade Cooley. I absolutely loved his group. He had two or three pretty girls in the lineup, and I thought they dressed so beautifully. The Maddox Brothers and Rose were big at the time, too, and were known as "the most colorful hillbilly band in America." I just thought Rose was the greatest. She was so feisty onstage! Heck, the whole family was a feisty bunch. I was paying close attention, and all this music was having a significant impact on me.

Even though Mother worried about me all the time, she always said she never had to worry about me at a dance. She knew exactly where I'd be. I would stand right in front of the bandstand staring up at the performers all night. I wasn't about to wander off! As a little girl people would ask me, "What do you want to be when you grow up?" I'd always tell them, "I want to be a girl singer." I don't suppose I really could have been any other type of singer, but that's what I told them. I knew I wanted to sing, but I also wanted to wear shiny clothes and be pretty and glamorous while doing it!

Daddy put a guitar in my hands when I was about six. He got me a little Kay brand guitar from the Sears Roebuck catalog and, like any good cheap guitar, the strings were so high off the fretboard you could barely push them down. But that's all you had to learn on if you couldn't afford a nice instrument. Every night after supper Daddy would listen to a popular news commentator on the radio named Gabriel Heatter. After that I'd get my little guitar and we'd have a lesson. He'd show me some chords and teach me to push down on those big ol' high strings. Daddy had a guitar and a fiddle and, after I mastered a few simple songs, we were able to start playing music together.

Chapter 2

CALIFORNIA STARS

Even though music was such an important part of our life as a family, Daddy didn't get into playing publicly in California like he'd done with his brother back in Oklahoma. He would play his guitar and fiddle at home, but I don't remember him ever going out or meeting up with other musicians to play gigs. Instead, he poured his energies into working various jobs to make ends meet. I can't remember what they all were now, but I know he had a laundry service at one time. He'd go to the movie studios to pick up laundry, and then come home and tell me about all the interesting things he'd seen on the sets. I was already somewhat of a dreamer, and I was mesmerized by his tales.

Mother was a workhorse and generally provided a steady income when Daddy hopped from one job to another. She could always find work wherever we went. She'd go around and knock on doors if she needed to, but she was going to give it her all. Mother was exceptionally honest, invariably serious, always meticulous, and a model employee for anyone who hired her. When we were living in Los Angeles, she went to work for Virture Brothers, which was a company that made the chrome and Formica dinettes that are now so popular with my retro-minded rockabilly fans. Mother worked in their upholstering division, and she later got Daddy a job there, too.

After we'd been in Los Angeles for a little while, Daddy decided he needed a real trade that he could depend on. I don't know where he got the idea, but he decided to go to barber school. His classes were down on Skid Row. The drunks would go in and get their hair cut, which is how the students learned. Mother and I would have to go pick him up in the evenings when his classes were finished. She would just hate to go down there where folks were passed out in doorways. It kind of scared me as a child, and it might have scared Mother even more. She took me with her because she was too nervous to leave me at home. We always stayed in the car with the doors locked until Daddy came out. Then we would hightail it out of there!

When he completed his barber training, Daddy searched around for a job in Los Angeles, but wasn't able to find anything. We had relatives who lived outside Bakersfield, about a hundred miles north, and they told Daddy about an opportunity nearby. We eventually moved up there, a few miles south of Bakersfield, where he started barbering in a little town called Pumpkin Center. In fact, the barber shop was responsible for the town's name. California's Central Valley is a rich agricultural region known for its abundance of crops ranging from cotton to fruit to almonds. Apparently, pumpkins were plentiful in the area in the 1930s when a full-blooded Cherokee barber named Lone Bush dubbed his shop the Pumpkin Center Barber Shop. Even though the area had been called Giminiani Corners previously, the name stuck, and a Pumpkin Center post office was opened in 1942.

We lived in nearby Greenfield in a little house right across the street from the Greenfield Union Elementary School. Even though we didn't live in the city, our address was Route 2, Box 536, Bakersfield. I started the second half of my third-grade year at the school in the beginning of 1947, and was still known to my family and classmates as Lavonne at that time. I had cousins close to my age—Raymond and Vernon Jackson—who lived out there. They were the sons of my dad's brother, Albert, and his wife, Electa, who lived in one of the shotgun houses in the middle of one of those cotton patches. I always thought Electa was the strangest-sounding name I'd ever heard!

I loved playing outdoors with my cousins. We'd play cowboys and Indians and run wild through the fields. Mother was much more comfortable letting me roam, since we were no longer living in a big city. I guess she thought someone would have to put in some serious effort to snatch kids out of a cotton field in the middle of nowhere. Sometimes at night I'd go stretch out in the fields and look up at the millions of stars, thinking about all the adventures that might await me out in the vast universe. I would get just as lost in my own dreams flipping through magazines and looking at pictures of the other kinds of stars—Western swing singers and icons of the silver screen who populated the California of my youth. I almost felt something down deep telling me that my place in the world was going to involve entertaining others.

Learning to entertain folks was something Daddy began unconsciously teaching me early on. The house we lived in had a long hallway that ran straight through it. I had the first bedroom, and Mother and Daddy had the back bedroom. There was a series of doors that went right through the house. I remember the floor was slick, and Daddy would run from the front room in his sock feet. When he hit my door, he'd slide through my room with his arms crossed like a genie, saying "G'night, 'Vonne," as he slid straight through, disappearing into the back bedroom. It would make me laugh every time.

When we were living in Greenfield, it was the only time in my life that Mother didn't work outside the home. She was always there, and I think back on that period fondly. I particularly appreciated it when I needed her to nurse me back to health. I had a weak ankle, and one day Mother looked out the window and saw a couple of boys carrying me home with a sprain. I wasn't real physical. I didn't play sports or anything like that, and it seemed like every time I was around a ball I got hurt. Shoot, I was just standing in the school yard at one point, after we moved back to Oklahoma, and a football came out of nowhere and hit me. Another time, as a young adult, I was walking with country star Hank Thompson somewhere on a baseball field. We had finished singing and were walking back down to the dressing rooms when a baseball went flying between my legs and nearly tripped me. Let's just say I was never at risk of going to the Olympics!

Feeling like we'd settled down in Greenfield, Mother and Daddy let me get my first pet. I wound up with this cute little black and tan hound. I don't even remember where we got him, but I named him Jeepers. I loved that dog, and he would chase me all around those cotton fields. Those are very warm and happy memories for me.

Our house was made of knotty pine, and Mother fixed it up to be really pretty. She wanted to do things traditionally and keep everything just-so. Daddy didn't much give a flip about those kinds of things. If we had a Christmas tree or some lights outside, that was Mother's doing. Daddy might help her decorate, but it was all at her prompting. He didn't mind her doing it, but he wouldn't have spear-headed it, either. I tended to be more like Daddy and wasn't as concerned with tradition or nostalgia. In later years, we were on the road a lot and were often gone for holidays. If it was Thanksgiving they might have turkey and dressing in the restaurant of whatever hotel we were staying in. But if they didn't, that was fine. We'd just have soup and sandwiches.

Birthdays were the same. If it was Daddy's big day, he'd just want to go up to the drive-in, get a burger, and go home. That would never fly with Mother. She saw to it that I had a birthday party every year. Even though she had all this other stuff to do, she made it a priority. I remember, when we were in Greenfield, she had these ribbons of crepe paper tacked up on the ceiling and then twisted each one together all the way to the table. A big birthday cake sat in the middle, and it was so festive and cute. Even when she wasn't working outside the house, Mother always had some project going. I don't really remember her ever sitting still.

As had always been the case wherever we lived, our home in Greenfield was filled with love. It was nothing for me to walk into a room to find Mother and Daddy hugging each other, or her sitting on his lap. They were very open and expressive. The three of us had a beautiful relationship. I didn't have to vie for their attention. I was smothered with it, and they both loved me very much. In some ways, being an only child kept me a baby. Mother spoiled me. When I eventually married Wendell, he did the same thing. Maybe we "only-children" are just particularly lovable!

Even though my parents were very focused on loving, nurturing, and encouraging me, they didn't let me get away with bad behavior. Not that I particularly wanted to be bad. I always hoped to please my parents—especially Daddy. The thing I was most afraid of as a child was upsetting him, because I was so close to him. Mothers, of course, are upset all the time, so I wasn't too worried about that. But, boy, I just couldn't stand it if there was any tension between me and Daddy. He didn't harp on me or speak harshly to me, but I just didn't want to disappoint him. I knew what he wanted from me, and it would just kill me to let him down or upset him. Daddy wasn't overly verbose. Today we'd say he was "cool." He didn't lavish me with praise, but when he did compliment me, it meant I'd really done something special. It was never just flattery or insincere words. If he said it, he meant it!

I had boundaries and rules as a child, and I didn't really break them, except on rare occasions. Daddy didn't like to spank me, but he would do it if I needed it. Whenever he did, I'd have to stay in my room afterward to think about what I'd done wrong. After a while, he'd come sit and talk with me, which is exactly what you're supposed to do after you punish a child. I don't think there were really books about that kind of technique then, so Mother and Daddy just stumbled into good parenting by accident.

I started noticing boys early on. In fact, there was one tall, thin boy I liked at Greenfield named Wendell. Maybe that was a little foreshadowing of my future. Unfortunately, there was a lot less diversity in those days, and I didn't encounter too many people who didn't look like me. Out of my entire class at school, there was only one African American boy. His name was James Oliver, and he would play with us sometimes. I liked his company. We had a big picture window at our house and, in the mornings,

Daddy would look out and yell to me, "Wanda? Are you ready for school yet? You better hurry up! Your boyfriend's here! It's James Oliver!" He was just teasing me. Daddy was never prejudiced. He had quite a few blues records in addition to the "hillbilly" fare, like Jimmie Rodgers and the Western swing stuff. He liked black music, but Mother would get on to him. "Tom! Can't you play something else?" She never learned to appreciate the blues—or music in general—the same way Daddy and I did. She was simply too busy!

On Saturday nights we would go over to Aunt Electa and Uncle Albert's house to gather 'round the battery-powered radio to listen to the *Grand Ole Opry* from Nashville. The adults would pull up chairs, while cousins Vernon and Raymond and I sat on the floor. We'd all just sit there and stare at the radio while the show was on. I wonder now why we thought we had to actually *look* at the radio while we heard the show, but that's what we did!

I was still playing guitar at home most nights while Daddy accompanied me on his guitar or fiddle. We would work out different songs we knew from the radio or the 78 records Daddy bought, while Mother would write them all down in a little notebook. We kept adding to it during my growing-up years, and I still have it and treasure it. All my favorites are in there: Bob Wills, Spade Cooley, Tex Williams. There are so many great old songs, like "Silver Dew on the Blue Grass," "Make Room in Your Heart for a Friend," "Along the Navajo Trail," "When My Blue Moon Turns to Gold Again," "Tennessee Saturday Night," "Born to Lose," and on and on.

They didn't have as many of the big dances around Bakersfield like they had in Los Angeles. There was a famous honky tonk there called The Blackboard that I used to hear about all the time, but that was just a little dive. Mother wouldn't go in there. A few years later a young guy named Buck Owens started playing guitar in the house band at The Blackboard. A few years after that, another young guy named Merle Haggard worked there some. Obviously, those two went on to superstardom, so there was plenty of country music that came out of Bakersfield. But that all started happening later on.

Even though Daddy and I loved listening to country and Western swing, I also listened to the pop music of the day when we were in California. I heard Rosemary Clooney and Patti Page, and that kind of thing. Because of that interest, Daddy decided it would be a good idea for me to take up piano, too. He knew that would give me an overall knowledge of how music works, in terms of harmony and basic theory. Mother found a teacher who gave his lessons in a performance space of some kind. Of course, I was just a kid, but I remember it as a grand ballroom. The teacher sat me down in the midst of all this grandeur. He showed me where middle C was and showed great patience when I started banging around on the keyboard. He set some sheet music in front of me for one of the popular songs of the day and began to teach me to read. I didn't really get it, but I was pretty good at picking up the notes he played. I mostly learned to play by ear.

I loved those piano lessons and looked forward to them each week. I probably liked the teacher because he didn't challenge me too much. He had me playing notes with my right hand, but just octaves with the left. That's the only way I knew to play, but I never dreaded having to practice the piano. We had an old upright in the house, which was the first time we'd ever had a piano in our home. As soon as I got out of school each day, I'd head straight for it. I would play a song up to the point when I made a mistake. Instead of picking it up from that spot, however, I would go back to the very beginning and play the entire song until I made a mistake again. Then I'd return to the top and start it another time. After doing that over and over Mother would say,

"Wanda, why don't you go play outside for just a little while?" That's when I knew I was driving her nuts! I still tell people today that if a kid loves music, the piano will really bring it out of them. It's easier to learn than the guitar, and it makes for a good musical foundation.

Mother and I would visit Oklahoma in the summers, but Daddy didn't always come back with us. His family wasn't particularly close. There were five kids in Daddy's family, while Mother was the oldest of three. She had one younger brother and one younger sister, and it was important for her that I get to know her side of the family. She didn't want me to grow up in total isolation out in California. I enjoyed those trips back home, but I also treasured living in the Golden State.

I look back on our time near Bakersfield as an idyllic era of my childhood, but, like all good things, it eventually came to an end. Daddy had flat feet, and they started giving him trouble. It became obvious that standing up barbering all day was not going to work for him with his feet in that condition. He would limp along and was in real pain. He'd come home and say, "Oh, I wish I had a little girl with brown hair and green eyes who would bring me a tub of water to put my feet in it." Boy, that's all it took. I loved bringing him that water so he could relax and soak. The reason we'd moved to Greenfield was for the barbering work, so when Daddy's feet played out on him, and that profession proved unsustainable, we had to figure out a new plan.

Around the same time, Mother was getting real homesick for Oklahoma. Her mother had rheumatism and was crippled. I don't remember seeing my grandmother, who I called Mama, ever actually stand. She was always in a chair. She didn't have a wheelchair, but she would lift her chair up from side to side to scoot around the house. I remember my cousin and I—they'd gotten us some little rockers for when I'd come visit in the summers—would play "Mama." Off we'd go, swinging those chairs from side to side across the floor.

Around the time Daddy was trying to figure out how to make a living, Mother was feeling really guilty about not being around to help with Mama. She didn't think it was fair that her sister and brother had to take care of their mother by themselves while we were off in California. It was actually fine, but Mother put a lot of responsibility on herself, and she felt it was her duty to return to Oklahoma to help. Daddy told her, "All right, Nellie. We'll go back, but when you have to make the gravy out of water, we're coming home to California! He loved California and I did, too. We all did. I hold that state very dear to my heart to this day, and I still draw my most enthusiastic crowds out there.

Chapter 3

NO PLACE TO GO BUT HOME

I was nine years old when we returned to Oklahoma from California. We moved in with my Aunt Flossie, who had been married to Daddy's brother, Henry. Uncle Henry and Aunt Flossie had relocated to Los Angeles when we were still renting a room at the Gramercy House, but they divorced somewhere along the way. She went home to Oklahoma City while we were still living near Bakersfield. When Mother and Daddy and I moved back, Aunt Flossie was kind enough to rent us one side of a duplex she lived in on South High Street. We shared a front room with her, and I had to put my piano in her living room so we could have two bedrooms.

With Daddy no longer able to pursue his work as a barber, he got a job driving a cab. Mother eventually found long-term work at Tinker Field, which is an enormous Air Force base in Oklahoma City. I've been told that it's now the biggest employer in the state, and it might have been back then, too. In the 1950s, Buddy Holly and his band recorded some songs at the base's Officer's Club while they were on tour, which I thought was pretty interesting. I wish I could say I was interested in Mother's job there, too, but it just wasn't my world. She did something with key punch machines and data that they stored on punch cards. She started out as what they call a GS3, and started working her way up the ranks. She was always studying at home to move up a rank or get a promotion. As you know by now, it's no surprise that Mother was focused, disciplined, and driven when it came to her work.

I started fifth grade at Crooked Oak Elementary School that fall, which is when I decided to start going by the name Wanda. I was struggling from the very start, so the principal called Mother and me in for a meeting. He expressed some concerns about my work and suggested that they put me back in the fourth grade. That was my first introduction to Oklahoma. Mother told him we'd discuss it, but I remember I was just heartbroken. I didn't enjoy schoolwork, and I certainly didn't want to have to repeat a grade I'd already finished. That just meant I would have to be in school for one more year than I needed to be. I cried and cried in the car on the way home, and all that night. I think Mother saw how upset I was and took pity on me. She went back to that principal and just begged him, "Please don't do this to her. She's just devastated. Her father and I will help her and will see to it that she studies." I guess he saw that she was sincere, and decided to give me a chance. I dodged a bullet on that one!

I'll admit that my grades were never stellar, but I wasn't dumber than the other kids. I just didn't apply myself. All I wanted to do was sing and play music, and it was impossible for me to sit still. That's a trait I picked up from Mother. To their credit, my folks really worked with me on my school lessons. Poor Daddy nearly pulled his hair out trying to teach me math. I just could not get it. Daddy would get so frustrated trying to get through to me. He'd say, "Wanda, if you've got five apples . . ." That's where he'd lose me. He'd try to break the problems down into concepts I could grasp, but it was an uphill battle for him. He'd get exasperated and say, "Can't you see how this works?" I'd shake my head. Finally, he said, "Just learn it and do it. You don't have to understand it!"

Though academics held little interest for me, I enjoyed the social aspect of going to school. It's never easy coming into a school as the new kid, but as soon as they learned I could sing and play guitar, I was in. I made friends pretty fast, including a girl named Wanda Williams, who became my best buddy. The kids all started calling her "Wanda 1," while I became "Wanda 2."

I liked boys ever since I figured out I wasn't one. I had a little boyfriend in school named Thurman. I don't even remember his last name now, but I carried a picture of him in my purse. Mother would take me and Wanda 1 up to the school and drop us off for basketball games. We'd strut around with our long hair and our collars up. We thought we were pretty cool. We had no idea what we were doing, but I was learning!

I had become a California girl, so the first time I ever saw snow was when I was a student at Crooked Oak. We were on recess and I was just fascinated. I'd hold my hand out and look at each flake. I thought it was just the greatest thing, but the other kids must have thought I'd lost it to be so enchanted by something they'd already experienced many times over in their young lives.

Crooked Oak was pretty well out in the country at the time. There weren't any swings or anything available to us when we had recess. It was just land. We had each other and our imaginations, and that was about it. One day when we got back in the classroom after playing in the field, we were hit with an awful smell all of a sudden. We thought someone had tooted or something, so we were getting tickled. It just hung in the air, but nobody would confess to the deed. Everyone was looking around the classroom when I crossed my legs and noticed a big chunk of cow dung stuck on the bottom of my shoe. It turns out I was the culprit. Boy, that stench was just running us out. I started laughing so hard. The teacher made me go out and scrape it off.

Obviously, that wasn't my fault, but I can assure you I was sent out in the hall plenty of times just for laughing too much during class. I remember, when I was in fifth grade, there was a girl in our class named Jeannette. I was looking around the room and not paying attention to the teacher, as usual, when Jeannette starting heading down the aisle to turn in a paper. She was walking along minding her own business when that poor girl's panties suddenly dropped around her ankles. I tried to be quiet but I couldn't contain myself. I started snickering. Boy, she felt it right quick, and she just jumped out of those drawers! I thought I was going to lose it. I wound up out in the hallway over that one, but I couldn't help it. I just loved laughing and having a good time. I've always loved a party atmosphere and, considering it was already starting at that young age, I guess I come by it naturally!

The school bus stopped almost right in front of our duplex on South High Street, so I enjoyed having a little autonomy to travel to and from school on my own. Since I would usually get home before Mother, she gave me my first little chore. It seems

like we had fried potatoes with supper about every night. She
showed me how to peel a potato, but she didn't use a peeler. That
would have been too easy. Instead, she used a knife. It seemed as
though Mother did everything the hard way. She would have me
peel the potatoes, and then she would slice them up later when
she got home from work. That was my job. She also had me set
the table before we ate. I think that was all she trusted me to do.
She wouldn't teach me anything else because she didn't have the
time. I don't know if my mother was a great cook, but she did
pretty good, and we all stayed fat and sassy. We had some kind of
meat every night with fried potatoes and maybe green beans or
something. She would fix a salad with just lettuce and tomato,
and then use mayonnaise for the dressing. We just didn't have
that many choices. She couldn't make elaborate things because
she had too many other things to do. Mother was always in a
hurry and wanted everything done "right now!" I do look back
on those days fondly, though. In those days, people sat down as a
family and ate together. Sadly, that's not as common anymore, and
I think we've lost something as a society by letting that tradition
go by the wayside.

Mother and Daddy eventually built their first little house at
721 Southeast 35th Street, which wasn't far from where we'd
been living with Aunt Flossie. From our new house, we could
walk down the street, take a right on Lindsay, and go a couple of
blocks up to South Lindsay Baptist at the corner of 33rd. Mother
joined the church soon after we returned to Oklahoma, and I
did, too. It would become a very important place to me and my
family over the years.

Mother was a real stickler about attending Sunday school each
week. I could occasionally skip church, but never Sunday school.
We had our little envelopes that we wrote our names on and
put our little donation in each week. I'd faithfully put my dollar

in there. Those envelopes also had little boxes to check on the back about whether or not you read your Bible every day, and if you studied the lesson from your Sunday school book. Those disciplines were ingrained in me, and I really loved the church and all the activities it provided. Baptists always give an altar call at the end of the service in case there are people there who want to surrender their lives to God. I didn't really fully understand what that meant at the time, but I kept a hot path down that aisle. I wasn't running from God when I was a kid. In fact, I was trying to run to him. It would take time, however, before I understood what it meant to accept God's love and grace for what it is, instead of trying to respond out of a misguided fear of divine punishment. But that day would come later.

Some of my closest friends were kids I went to church with, especially Beverly Wright, who became my best friend and with whom I stayed close for the rest of her life. Everybody loved Beverly. She was a gregarious, heavyset girl, and the life of the party. By the time I was around twelve years old, we'd get together for parties at Beverly's or someone's house after Sunday services. I'd carry my guitar and sing some songs or do some yodeling, which I was trying to perfect at the time. I don't know how I got it in my head, but I thought if I was gonna be a girl singer, I had to learn to yodel. I taught myself to do it by listening to it over and over on the radio. I jokingly tell people you learn to yodel by getting on a horse, getting into a good trot, and setting him loose on forty acres. That shaking will make your voice yodel right away! I remember the song "Chime Bells," by Elton Britt, which made a big impression on me. That was one I would practice yodeling with all the time. That's how you actually master it—practice! I was also very influenced by Hank Williams, so "Jambalaya" and "Kaw-Liga" became staples for me when I would sing at parties.

I mentioned before that my lack of athletic prowess guaranteed I would never grace a Wheaties box, but I was reminded of that one day while playing softball with some church friends. I was at bat, but when the ball came across the plate, I swung and missed. I swung that bat so hard that I spun myself around. At that moment, my friend Estle Wall had picked up the ball to throw back to the pitcher. Somehow, I got in the way, and that ball hit me right in the chin. I felt a sharp pain and what seemed like a ringing in my ears. I felt tears welling up in my eyes. I opened my mouth. "Am I bleeding?" I asked Estle.

She winced. "No, but it's not good," she replied. "You've broken your teeth."

Sure enough, my two front teeth were cracked. Mother and Daddy took me to the dentist and, for several years, my front teeth were gold. They didn't have much they could do back then in terms of white caps or anything like that. I remember the dentist telling my mother that, at my young age, he wanted to put something strong there that would hold up. I had those gold teeth until I saw a picture of myself. Of course, there was nothing but black-and-white film then, and that gold looked black. I couldn't stand it.

We went back to the dentist, but he discovered that I had somehow gotten an abscess in one of those teeth. I don't know why, but he decided he had to pull the gold caps off without anesthesia. Mother and Daddy and the dentist's nurse held me down while he went to work. It was excruciating. They got those gold caps off and he said, "We'll get those teeth out now." He pulled out my two front teeth and then, for no reason at all, he pulled out the two on either side of those. He said it would look better for a bridge. So, ever since I was about twelve, I've had to wear a bridge. It took me forever to learn to talk with that stupid thing. I'd wake up in the morning and wouldn't have the bridge in my mouth anymore. I would have woken up in the night and sleepily thrown my teeth across the room. I'd find them in the closet or down at the foot of the bed or something. Those fake teeth were my deepest held secret. I was embarrassed, and I didn't tell anybody about it.

Mother found me a new piano teacher within walking distance of our house, but she didn't understand the way the guy in Bakersfield had taught me to play. I had never paid any attention to that bass clef, but this teacher wanted me to start learning the left-hand parts. I just couldn't get it. I would go to her house each week for a lesson, but I didn't like her too much. I probably didn't like her because she was trying to really challenge me and teach me, but I was always trying to do things my own way. I wasn't interested in all her theory. I just wanted to know enough to get by and play the songs I liked, but she had me doing little kid stuff to try to teach me the rudiments of the instrument. She thought I wasn't really trying, and we probably gave up on each other pretty early on. She got to where her boyfriend was there every time I'd come for a lesson. She'd say, "Now practice that for a minute," and then she'd go over and they'd love on each other in the corner. It might have lasted as much as a year, but I eventually just quit. I can't even remember what her name was now.

By that point, I was probably about evenly skilled on both the piano and guitar, but I couldn't sing as easily while playing piano as I could with the guitar. Since people encouraged me to bring it when we'd have school or church parties, I increasingly gravitated to the guitar. I realized early on that's what my audience wanted!

Since I was getting a little older, Mother would occasionally let me head downtown with some church or school friends. Capitol Hill was the main area where there were some movie theaters and a drugstore where kids could congregate. I would head over to that area with Mother every Saturday so she could pay bills and do some shopping, but I was just starting to become a teenager, and was wanting to strike out on my own without her sometimes. One of my favorite things to do was meet up at the drugstore at the corner of Commerce and South Robinson Avenue to get a Coke with my friends. It was fun to feel like I was just starting to become a young lady and could enjoy a little independence of my own.

Sometimes, I acted more like a dumb kid than a young lady, however. I once shoplifted a magazine from the newsstand across the street from the drugstore and snuck out with it somehow. I loved to see look at those movie magazines with Marilyn Monroe and Elizabeth Taylor and folks like that in them. I was drawn to glamour, and for some reason I couldn't resist taking it. I felt so guilty about it that I couldn't sleep that night. I brought it back the next day and slipped it back onto the rack. Nobody ever knew, but I felt bad. I was driving by there recently with my granddaughter, who's in her twenties, and pointed out where that newsstand used to be. I said, "That's where I stole something for the first time." She started laughing. "The *first* time?" she said. "How many more times were there?" I had to chuckle about that. "Maybe I didn't word that like I meant to," I told her. "It was an isolated incident. Your sweet grandmother doesn't have a secret life of crime in her past!"

My favorite thing to do with my friends—when I wasn't taking a five-finger discount at the newsstand like a hot-handed little kleptomaniac—was listening to the jukebox at the drugstore. We'd check out the hits of the day and talk about what we liked about each song. I especially loved to hear the girl singers and imagine what it would be like if I ever heard my own voice on a record one day. It seemed as far-fetched as the idea of me winding up next to Marilyn Monroe in one of those magazines, but I enjoyed the fantasy.

Just across the street from the drugstore was a little radio station called KLPR that had a small studio inside that could accommodate about twenty audience members. Sometimes after school we'd walk to the station and watch the performers play on the air. It wouldn't be long before I would get my own chance to strap on my guitar, step up to that microphone, and beam my voice over the airwaves to the good people of Oklahoma City.

Chapter 4

TURN YOUR RADIO ON

Radio station KLPR broadcast all kinds of different programming. This was before radio stations had dedicated formats for one type of music or another, so you might hear a news program at a certain time, followed by a preacher, followed by the Top 40 popular songs. This particular station had an hour of country music every weekday afternoon that was hosted by a deejay named Cousin Jay Davis. Jay played country records for forty-five minutes and devoted the last fifteen minutes of his radio time to local talent.

When I was about thirteen or fourteen, some of my church friends kept urging me to take my guitar over to the station and audition for the show. I brushed it off the first few times anyone mentioned it, but they were persistent. They'd say, "Oh, come on,

Wanda. We'll go over there with you so you can try out. Let's do it! When do you want to go?" I would tell my friends I didn't sing well enough to be on the radio, but finally they'd had enough of my resistance and resorted to other tactics. They dared me. Now, a dare is one thing, but then they double dog dared me. I don't know what your experience was like growing up, but in Oklahoma, in 1951, if someone double dog dared you, you'd better be ready to deliver if you wanted to save face. I finally gave in.

One day, after classes at Capitol Hill Junior High School, I walked up the hill to Commerce Street with a group of my friends, including Beverly. The station was located on the second floor of a storefront building that housed the *Capitol Hill Beacon* newspaper. One of the boys carried my guitar up the steps for me. I felt like I'd brought my own cheering section. It was very encouraging to have friends who believed in my talent and thought I was good enough to sing on the air.

We waited until Cousin Jay signed off from his daily show. I wasn't quite sure how to introduce myself or what to say, but before I could figure it out, Beverly marched right up to him with her hand outstretched. "Hello, sir. Our friend Wanda here is the best singer in the world and she'd like to audition to be on your local talent spotlight." Jay smiled. He was polite, but seemed a little hesitant. I was only in the ninth grade by this point, and I'm sure he'd seen plenty of kids come through who weren't as talented as they thought. The studio wasn't very big, so he certainly couldn't avoid me. "Okay," he finally conceded while motioning for me to get my guitar. "Let's hear what you've got, young lady."

Once I strapped on my guitar, my shyness and nervousness melted away. I started singing my best rendition of Jimmie Rodgers's "Blue Yodel No. 6." Just as I was losing myself in the song, Jay suddenly stopped me midway through. I felt my face get hot. "Is something wrong, Mr. Davis?" He smiled real big. "No, Wanda, quite the opposite. You have a fine voice, and I'd be happy to have you on the local talent spotlight. Be here tomorrow afternoon and don't forget to bring your guitar." Beverly started jumping up and down. "I told you, sir," she squealed. Cousin Jay started laughing. "And be sure to bring your fan club," he added.

Before long Cousin Jay was rotating me into the local talent portion of his show once every week or two. That wound up being a very good starting place for me in terms of getting experience, singing into a microphone, responding to audience feedback, and gaining more confidence as a performer. At that time, there were a lot of local talent contests in the movie theaters on Saturdays, which were very popular and drew pretty good crowds. It wasn't long before KLPR hosted a competition of their own. They broadcast the show on the air and encouraged people to write or call in to vote for their favorite performer. The grand prize would be a fifteen-minute daily radio show from 5:15 until 5:30 each weekday for a month. Since I'd been getting a good response to my appearances on Jay's show, I decided to enter. Would you believe I wound up winning that thing? Suddenly, I was going to have my very own radio show, even if it was just for a little while!

For the next month, I would cart my guitar to school with me each day and then walk over to the drugstore with my girlfriends after class until it was time to head across the street to the station for my show. Cousin Jay was on from 4:00 until 5:00. Grant Lad read the news from 5:00 until 5:15. Then, the airwaves were mine for the next fifteen minutes. It was just me and my guitar, and I would play and sing whatever was popular on the country charts at the time. It might have been just pitiful, but somebody out there must have liked what they heard.

Near the end of the month the station manager stopped me as I was packing up my guitar one afternoon. "Wanda, your show's doing well and drawing listeners. Would you like to keep doing it?" It only took me about an eighth of a second to come up with my answer to that question, "Golly, yeah. I really like singing on the radio." He nodded his head with a chuckle. "Well," he responded, "if you can get some good sponsors for your time slot, you can keep the show as long as you want." Maybe a lot of adolescent girls would have been deterred, but I went after it with a vengeance. That was the only time in my life I've ever had to sell myself or anything like that, but I didn't mind it one bit. Daddy helped me put together some ideas for sponsors, and then I started pounding the pavement. I went to a lumber company, and they signed up right away.

That was the start of the Wanda Jackson Show on KLPR, and I treated it with all the seriousness of a regular job. The lumber company liked what I was doing, and then Davis Furniture signed on as a second sponsor. I went to Grant Lad, who was a seasoned announcer, and asked him to help me write advertising spots. He was a real professional and seemed to admire my spunk. We got along great, and he took the time to teach me how to take the facts about special deals or sales the store was offering and put it into words that were exciting to the listeners. He gave me great pointers on how long each commercial should be, and soon I was writing my own ad copy and coming up with my interesting promo spots. It was a lot of fun, and I was always grateful to Mr. Lad for taking me under his wing in that way. It seems kind of remarkable now to think about having taken on all that responsibility at such a young age, but that was just my life. All I wanted to do was play guitar and sing. I was earning a little money for my show, but if keeping sponsors happy was part of the job, I was going to do that job one hundred percent. Plus, I was having the time of my life!

Plenty of young girls pursue careers in music today, but they have something I didn't have: role models to look to. Patsy Montana had a big hit with "I Want to Be a Cowboy's Sweetheart" in the 1930s, and that was really about it for girls in country music. Kitty Wells had not yet become a big star when I was starting my radio show, so there was no blueprint or roadmap available to me. I was flying by the seat of my pants, but it didn't scare me to get out on a limb and try something brand new. I liked it.

Daddy was still driving a taxi during this period, and his cab stand was just a couple of blocks from KLPR. He usually got off work around 5:00, but he would typically wait for me to finish my show so he could drive me home. Daddy would listen to the broadcast when he could, and while we were driving, we'd talk about the songs I was singing and how I was interacting with my radio audience. He was as excited about my show as I was. He was really happy to see me have a chance to play music and, not long after it became permanent, he took me to a pawn shop to buy me my first good guitar. It was a Martin D-18 that I played for many years. Today it hangs in the Rock and Roll Hall of Fame.

Country music was not as popular in the early 1950s as it is today. There were plenty of folks who liked it, but a lot of people turned their noses up at it, too. That made some country fans kind of embarrassed. Country music had a stigma to it at that time, and some people just didn't want others to know they liked it. Everybody at school knew I was performing on the radio, but I didn't get made fun of. I guess I do remember some boys laughing sometimes when I was lugging around my guitar after school. They'd call to me, "Hey, whatchya got in that case? A machine gun?" But, other than that, nobody said much of anything. I think a lot of the kids were just proud to know someone who was on the radio.

During my radio station days, there was one country artist who was my absolute favorite, and that was Hank Thompson. I bought all his records and was a big fan of the hits he'd had at that point, including the Top 10 singles "Humpty Dumpty Heart," "Green Light," and "Whoa Sailor." The fact that he lived in Oklahoma City and had a TV show on WKY-TV made me an even bigger fan. I played and sang some of Hank's songs on my show from time to time, and thought of him as my musical idol. In fact, I always liked how Hank enunciated his words and the way you could understand all the lyrics. That was something I tried to do from the very beginning, thanks to his example.

One day I had just finished my show at the station, which I had been doing for several months by that point, when someone from the KLPR office came into the studio. He said, "Wanda, there's a call for you out here. It's some man, but he didn't give his name." I looked at my watch and figured it must be Daddy wanting to know if I needed him to pick me up. I went out to the reception desk to take the phone call. A warm and friendly voice on the other end said, "Hi Wanda, this is Hank Thompson." I just about fainted. I was tempted to think it was a joke, but Hank's speaking voice was very similar to his singing voice, and I could tell that it was really him.

Hank told me that he was driving in his car when he heard my radio show. "I pulled over as soon as you were finished so I knew I'd be able to catch you before you left the station," he explained. Maybe I murmured something back to him, but I might have been too stunned to respond. "You've got a really interesting voice and I like your singing style," he continued. "My band and I are playing at the Trianon Ballroom on Saturday night, and I'd like to invite you to come down and sing a couple of songs with us."

By this point I thought for sure I was in a dream. This was just too good to be true. I said, "Gee, Mr. Thompson, I would love to, but I'll have to ask my mother." He laughed a little, but then realized I wasn't kidding around. He cleared his throat.

"Good grief, girl, how old are you?"

"I'm fourteen," I said, trying to sound as confident and grown up as possible while praying that my newly revealed age wouldn't get me uninvited to the show.

"Fourteen? That's hard to believe," he chuckled. "I thought for sure you were much older than that. You have a very mature voice." I held my breath waiting to see what he would say next. "Well, Wanda," he finally continued, "you be sure to ask your mother and, if it's okay with her, we'll see you on Saturday night.

And you be thinking about what you might want to sing." I
thanked him profusely and hung up the phone.

I ran as fast as I could to the cab stand to tell Daddy about the
phone call from Hank. He saw me coming and got out of the car
thinking something might be wrong. "Wanda, honey, are you okay?"
I ran right into his arms and began breathlessly recounting every
detail of my conversation with Hank. He was overjoyed by the
news. "Hop in the car, sweetie. Let's get home and tell your mother.
She's not going to believe it!" Mother and Daddy both liked Hank's
music, so there was no question about getting their permission. That
Saturday night the Jackson family was going to be one place, and
one place only: the Trianon Ballroom in downtown Oklahoma City.
That was the big place in town at the time. You'd walk in at street
level and get your ticket. Then you'd walk upstairs into a great big
room with one of the best dance floors in the whole Southwest.
It was raised and had a nice wooden floor. Unlike a lot of country
nightspots, there weren't many fights at the Trianon. I think people
were afraid they'd fall down those steep steps!

Jay Davis wanted to go down to the show with Mother and
Daddy and me, so the four of us rode to the Trianon together that
night. It felt good knowing that at least I would have a three-person
support team in the audience . . . if nothing else. We arrived a little
early and I found Hank by the side of the stage. He was tuning his
guitar and I didn't want to bother him. He saw me lingering nearby
and turned toward me. "Hello there, young lady," he smiled.

"Hi, Mr. Thompson," I stammered. "I'm Wanda Jackson." He
put his guitar down and stepped toward me.

"Of course! I'm glad you were able to make it. We'll call you
up in a little while to do your songs."

"Oh, okay," I said. "When did you want to rehearse?"

He just gave me a wink and said, "You'll be fine."

That's when I discovered that bands didn't really practice
before their gigs in those days. We singers would go out and do

our thing, and the musicians were expected to be good enough to follow us. The only problem was that I had never performed with any other pickers before. My radio show was just me accompanying myself on guitar, so when Hank called me up on stage it was a mess. I started into "Blue Yodel No. 6," but I couldn't keep time properly and was breaking meter something terrible. Those poor boys in his Brazos Valley Boys band had to try to follow me. At one point the group went into a solo, and I didn't know when to start singing again. I was panicked. The musicians were behind me saying, "Okay, Wanda. Come on back in." I was so embarrassed, but when the song was over the audience applauded.

Hank stepped up to the microphone. "How about little Miss Wanda Jackson, everybody?" They clapped even louder. "Wanda, honey, why don't you do another one for these fine folks?" I gulped hard, smiled, and tried not to look terrified. I launched into "Jambalaya," which was a new song at the time, but was already very popular. I was about two bars into it before the band even realized I'd started playing. And, of course, I didn't mention to them what key I played it in. There was a little scrambling there for a moment, but Hank's band members were real professionals, so once they got a handle on what I was doing they fell into place real quick. Audiences have always loved "Jambalaya," and still do to this day, so by the time I finished that second song, I'd won them over. It probably helped that I was a cute little girl with my great big guitar and cowboy boots. A lot of them knew me from the radio, too. Quite a few people complimented my voice.

Even though I felt self-conscious about letting Hank see how green I was, he was enthusiastic. "You did real good, Wanda," he said as I left the stage. "Just don't forget to have fun." I was pretty serious about performing and I might have been a little uptight. But, then again, I was a fourteen-year-old girl onstage in a big dance club for the first time—and with my musical hero watching my every move. I'm just glad I didn't pass out or fall off the stage!

Even as bad as I was that first night, Hank wanted me to come back. He saw the potential in me and, despite having the top country band in the nation and scoring hit after hit, he was still kind enough to be interested in my career. Almost every time he was in town, he'd have me come sing with him. I was still in school, so I couldn't go on the road, but it got to where I worked with him pretty regularly when he played local shows. I'd forget my lyrics, continue to break meter, and make all the mistakes that a person makes when they're learning to work with a band. I had a lot to figure out, but Hank was gracious enough to let me make my mistakes. He gave me the space to mess up because he knew I was serious about getting good, and he knew that every misstep was a learning experience. He stuck his neck out for me by letting me get on his stage when I wasn't ready, but it was the finest education I could have asked for. Hank was a true friend and mentor, and I can't possibly overstate how much he did for me.

After performing with Hank for a while, I was becoming more confident on stage. Before long, I auditioned for Merl Lindsay, an Oklahoma City—based Western swing bandleader who had a regular Saturday radio show that was broadcast from the Palladium Ballroom. Merl wrote "Water Baby Boogie," which became a country standard. He also recorded as an artist for the MGM and Mercury labels in the early 1950s. His band, The Oklahoma Night Riders, was a popular and well-respected group in the area. When I found out they were looking for a girl singer, I decided to try out.

Fortunately, Lindsay was already familiar with who I was from my radio show, and he liked my voice. I got the job, so I started working with them regularly and appearing on their radio show. I would just sing a few songs throughout the night, but I stayed up on stage the whole time. I'd clap or dance along a little bit. One of the guys in the band taught me to play a little percussion. It was a good experience to spend entire nights on the bandstand where I could study what everyone was doing, watch how audiences reacted, and observe the nuances of how to properly interact with a crowd. I felt like I was going to country music college, but my professors were the Oklahoma Night Riders and Brazos Valley Boys. I couldn't have asked for better teachers.

Believe it or not, I'd never heard a recording of my own voice up to that point. I knew what it sounded like in my own head, but all the radio work I'd been doing was live, so I'd never had a chance to actually listen to myself objectively. Even though Merl Lindsay's show was broadcast live on Saturday nights, the radio station would replay it on Sundays. Soon after I started performing with Merl, I wanted to listen to the re-broadcast. The only problem was that it conflicted with church. One week Mother said that if I went to Sunday School first, I could go out to the car and listen to the show while she stayed in the church service.

I was out there listening to the show by myself, but when I heard my own voice I froze. It sounded nothing like I thought it did! I didn't like what I heard at all, and I began sobbing in the car. I couldn't believe it. I said out loud to nobody, "I can't be a girl singer. I'm not any good!" That experience really threw me for a loop. I thought, *Boy, what am I going to do if I can't be a singer? It's all I ever wanted.* Looking back, I don't know if I was actually bad and got better, or if it was just the shock of hearing what my voice sounded like to other people. Either way, Mother and Daddy came to my rescue. I told them I didn't think anyone could possibly like my voice, but they reminded me that all those people who listened to me on KLPR liked it. They pointed out that Merl Lindsay liked it enough to hire me, and that Hank Thompson seemed to think it was good enough to stake his reputation on. I was almost ready to quit, but my parents knew where my true love was, and they talked me through it. And I'm sure glad they did.

Chapter 5

With my first boyfriend, Leonard Sipes, who would later be known as Tommy Collins.

LOVIN' COUNTRY STYLE

In 1981 Merle Haggard had a Top 10 country hit with a song he wrote about a young entertainer who found fame as a singer and guitarist before going on to experience some ups and downs in his personal life. It was a true story. Haggard was paying tribute to his old friend Tommy Collins, who, as Merle sang, helped teach him to be a songwriter and even bought him some groceries when he was a struggling musician in Bakersfield, California. Before he was known by the stage name Tommy Collins, he was an Oklahoma boy named Leonard Sipes. That's why the song was called "Leonard." What you don't learn from the lyrics, though, is that Leonard Sipes was also my first love.

Merle started his song with the phrase, "When Leonard finally came to California . . ." In real life, when Leonard came to California he was riding with me, Mother, and Daddy. When we lived in California, Mother and I would travel back to Oklahoma each summer to visit family. Once we moved back, we'd travel out to the West Coast most summers to visit our friends and family who were still living out there. One year, Leonard decided he'd come with us.

I had first become aware of Leonard at KLPR, where he was part of the rotating cast of local talent that appeared on Cousin Jay Davis's daily show. Even before I was performing on the show, I would see him performing when my school friends and I would go sit in the small studio audience. I was just thirteen the first time I saw him, but Leonard was already a college boy studying chemistry at what's now known as the University of Central Oklahoma. He was good looking and well dressed. Almost as soon as I first spotted him at the radio station, I had a big crush on him.

By the time I was making my own appearances on KLPR, Leonard and I both enjoyed hearing each other perform. He was a step or two ahead of me in terms of his singing career, and had even released a couple of singles. Apparently, someone representing the Morgan Records label out of Fresno, California, had heard Leonard on the air in Oklahoma City and offered to sign him. I'd never known anyone who had actually made a record before, so it was pretty fun to see that label with the words "Leonard Sipes and his Rythmn Oakies." So what if the label didn't know how to spell Rhythm Okies? I didn't care anything about spelling in those days anyway. But I definitely cared about records, and, thanks to Leonard, I was quickly discovering I cared a lot about boys, too!

Eventually, Leonard asked me out for a date in early 1952. I hadn't ever been on a date before, and my parents were pretty

concerned about the idea of their fourteen-year-old daughter
going out with someone who was already in college. After Daddy
met him, he said, "Okay, Leonard's a nice young man. You can go
out with him if you want to."

I was pretty excited about getting to spend time alone with
him. I thought Leonard was funny and cute and well-mannered.
I wasn't very interested in the boys my own age, and Leonard
seemed more grown up. As I mentioned, I never felt much like a
kid, even when I was one, so the idea of dating a good-looking
guy like Leonard seemed natural to me.

On the Saturday we were scheduled for the date, I spent most
of the afternoon getting ready. I picked out a pretty dress and
took extra time to curl my hair just right. I imagined what it
would be like when Leonard arrived. I visualized him opening
the door to his nice car for me, like a proper gentleman.

My heart might have sunk just a little when I heard someone
pull up and looked out my bedroom window to see an old
pickup truck out front. It wasn't exactly a chariot waiting to
whisk me away to romantic bliss—or even a nice car—but I still
felt pretty giddy about going out on the town with a handsome
young man.

He knocked on the front door and Daddy invited him in. I
remember the two of them sat in the living room talking and
laughing. It was probably just a few minutes, but it felt like an
eternity. I was ready to get out of there and throw myself into
the exciting world of dating. I kept thinking, *Come on, Daddy.
Can't you just let us go already?* But, of course, I just sat and smiled
politely while they chatted.

Eventually Leonard said we better get going. He shook
Daddy's hand, thanked Mother for the glass of water she'd
given him, and we headed outside. He helped me up into that
old truck, which I pretended was a Cadillac for the sake of my

fantasies about the glamour of dating. We drove over to Capitol Hill, near the radio station, and saw a movie together. I don't know why he would have even wanted to go out with me, since I was still so young, but we had a good time talking about movie stars, music we both liked, and other topics I can't recall because I was too distracted thinking about how handsome he was.

Before long, Leonard was coming around the house pretty frequently. Not only was he my first boyfriend, but he also became a good friend to our family. Daddy and Leonard talked a lot and had a good time together. Leonard and I dated for several months, and I learned a few things about being a young lady as part of that experience.

In those days people didn't talk much about sex. Mother and Daddy never explained the birds and the bees to me, and it wasn't something that was discussed in school at that time, either. Whatever you knew you either picked up from other kids or figured out by stumbling into it on your own. My body began to develop pretty early, but I knew nothing about puberty, or what it meant to transition from girlhood to young womanhood. It was Aunt Flossie who finally sat my mother down and said, "Nellie, get that girl a brassiere!" Mother didn't even want to think about it. "She's only eleven years old," Mother shot back. Flossie just shook her head. "I don't care how old she is. She needs it, and she can't keep going around without one!" I guess the message must have gotten through because I got my first bra soon thereafter.

You can imagine that if my mother didn't feel comfortable talking about bras, she certainly didn't know how to discuss menstruation with me. One day I was in class during middle school when I almost doubled over in pain. I had the most awful cramps, and they kept hitting me in waves throughout the day. I went to the school nurse, who gave me an aspirin, but that didn't help. I was pretty sick, but I had no idea what was wrong with me. After school, I boarded the bus for home, feeling terrible the whole way as waves of pain gripped my midsection. When we arrived at my house, I began walking down the aisle of the bus toward the exit when I heard snickering behind me. I turned around to see kids pointing and laughing at me. I wasn't sure why until I looked down and saw that I had blood all over me. I ran off that bus with tears streaming down my face. I was embarrassed, but I was even more concerned that maybe I was about to die.

I fumbled for my key and finally got into the house as the bus pulled away from the curb. It seemed like I could still hear that laughter echoing in my head, even though the bus was rapidly pulling away from ear shot. I ran to the phone and dialed Mother, who was still at work. I was crying hysterically. I told her I was dying and needed her to come home right away. "Calm down, Wanda," she said softly. "I think I know exactly what's going on. You're not sick and you're going to be just fine. Get yourself cleaned up and we'll have a talk when I get home." When Mother got to the house that evening, she took me into her bedroom, where Daddy wouldn't hear us talking. She explained a few things that I immediately wished I'd known earlier that day!

You can imagine that, by the time I started dating Leonard, I was still pretty innocent about the world. But he taught me some things I needed to know. Sometimes we might be parked alone somewhere, and we'd get to kissing and making out a little bit. His hands would start wandering, but then he'd stop after a few minutes.

"Wanda! You shouldn't have let me do that," he'd say.

"Oh, really? I didn't know," I'd say. And he'd nod his head.

"You don't let a guy do that. That's just not the thing to do for a young lady."

He said he was trying to teach me about how to behave. Of course, I see right through that excuse now! I think he might have wanted to do a little something more than help me learn to behave, but he felt conflicted about it. A few years later, he wrote and recorded a major chart-topping single called "You Better Not Do That." It was about trying to resist "a cute little gal," and I always wondered if the inspiration might have gone back to those moments with the two of us alone in his Cadillac—I mean pickup truck.

Even though I dated Leonard for a good while and cared for him deeply, we ultimately wound up more like close friends than a typical couple. Excluding the aspect of our relationship I just mentioned, the dynamic between us was kind of like a big brother and little sister. He looked out for me and helped me understand more about how the world worked. We also enjoyed listening to music and playing our guitars together, which is something I'll always cherish.

One time Leonard was at the house, and we were telling him how we traveled to Bakersfield just about every summer. He was always talking about wanting to go back to California. I think he'd been there briefly during a short stint in the Marines before he was honorably discharged following a shoulder injury. He didn't know where in California he wanted to go, but he figured one place was as good as another. Daddy invited him to join us on our vacation and ride out there with us.

I don't remember much about the drive, but once we got to California we stopped in Los Angeles first. Leonard and I both performed on radio station KXLA in Pasadena. There was a popular DJ at the time named Squeakin' Deacon who had us on his show. We also appeared on cowboy singer Doye O'Dell's TV program on KTLA, which was a huge thrill. Probably the most exciting thing for me was getting to go visit Nudie's Rodeo Tailor, the outfitter to all the Western stars of the day. There was no way either Leonard or I could afford to purchase one of Nudie's dazzling rhinestone-encrusted outfits, but I remember

Leonard paid five dollars, which was no small sum in those days, for one of Nudie's neckties. I looked at all the beautiful clothes and dreamed about having my own custom Nudie outfit one day.

When we got to Bakersfield, Leonard went off by himself one night to a dance hall called Rainbow Gardens. The singer and band leader who performed at the club every weekend was named Terry Preston. He later became a successful country star using his real name, Ferlin Husky. During one of the breaks, Leonard went up to Ferlin and introduced himself. Before the night was over, Leonard was onstage with the band. Ferlin could see his talent immediately and talked him into staying in Bakersfield to join his stage show and play with his group.

Even though he had planned to return to Oklahoma City with us at the end of our trip, Leonard and his fancy Western tie remained in Bakersfield. He didn't even go back home to collect his things. He rented a room from my Aunt Electa, who had moved from the cotton patch into town and took in boarders to help make ends meet after Uncle Albert died in 1950. I was sad that Leonard didn't return home with us, but I was happy knowing he was still part of our family out in California.

What was supposed to be a two-week trip for Leonard turned into twenty years. He got a job as a chemist with Richfield Oil Company and continued to write songs and perform. Ferlin was already signed to Capitol Records and introduced Leonard to his producer, Ken Nelson. Ferlin started recording his songs, and then Faron Young, another Capitol artist, recorded Leonard's "If You Ain't Loving, You Ain't Living," which became a big hit.

Soon Ken Nelson signed Leonard to Capitol Records, where he changed his name to Tommy Collins and recorded his first major single, "You Gotta Have a License," in 1953. The lead guitarist on that recording was Ferlin Husky. Within a few months Ferlin and Jean Shepard, another Capitol Records country artist who was signed by

Ken Nelson, found massive success with their duet recording of "A Dear John Letter." The song hit number one on the country chart and even reached the Top 5 on the pop chart. It made major stars of both Ferlin and Jean. Ferlin moved out of Bakersfield soon after.

With Ferlin gone, Tommy recruited Bakersfield's Buck Owens for his next recording session. It wouldn't be long before Buck and Merle Haggard would make Bakersfield famous as the country music capital of the West, but it was Tommy who helped pave the way for their success. In 1954 and 1955, Tommy landed half-a-dozen songs in the Top 15 on the national country charts, and I couldn't have been more proud.

If Daddy hadn't invited Leonard Sipes to join us on our family trip to California, he might have never met Ferlin Husky, gotten signed to Capitol Records, or given Buck Owens his first real gig as a studio musician. He might not have met Merle Haggard, who always credited Tommy with helping him learn how to be a great songwriter. Of course, Tommy could have just gotten out to California some other way. He was so talented he was destined to make a name for himself. And Buck and Merle almost certainly would have found their way to fame, too. There was just no denying how good they were! It seemed like there was something in the water out in Bakersfield when it came to great music. But sometimes I like to think that maybe the Jackson family had a hand in setting the wheels in motion that gave birth to the Bakersfield sound!

In the fall of 1952 I started tenth grade, which meant leaving junior high and starting a new adventure at Capitol Hill High School. Now that I'd had a real boyfriend, the floodgates opened up. Mother used to say, "Wanda put down her doll, and the next day she started dating boys." I guess to her it must have seemed that way, but I just enjoyed spending time with Leonard, and I enjoyed getting dressed up to go out. I was fourteen years old and, I was coming down with a bad case of boy craziness.

In many ways, I was turning into a stereotypical teenager. I remember that Mother could not get me to hang my clothes up. I'd throw them on the bed or lay them across a chair or whatever. She was such a "type A" personality that it just drove her nuts. She'd tell me to do it, but when I didn't she'd come along and hang them up for me. She spoiled me in that way. Daddy finally told her to stop doing that. He said, "Just let it pile up. Let her see how bad it can get." But I still didn't hang them up. Then some crisis moment would come where I couldn't find a particular white blouse I needed to go with a particular skirt or something. Mother would say, "Well, look in that pile," and I'd find it all messed up and wrinkled. She would keep harping on me to just put the clothes away. Daddy would finally say, "Wanda, go in there and do what you're being asked to do." He started by speaking to me about it firmly, but finally had to spank me to get me in line again. He said, "You WILL hang your clothes up. Your mother can't follow you around all your life." Daddy was trying to teach me responsibility and help me for the future, but Mother would have just taken care of me and babied me if it was up to her. I don't know why I was so rebellious about that one particular matter, but that was the last time Daddy ever spanked me. I guess I was rapidly leaving the little girl stage and becoming a young woman.

With Leonard Sipes on his way to becoming Tommy Collins in California, I found myself another Leonard. Literally. My second boyfriend was a guy in school that I'd had my eye on, and his name was Leonard, too. We went out several times and I really liked him. He ended up asking me if I'd be his girl, and he gave me his class ring to wear. That lasted for a little while, but my boy craziness started flaring up, and I got to wondering about my options.

Maybe I was restless or maybe I'd gotten bored, but my time with the second Leonard had run its course. I was tired of him, and I knew it wasn't right to keep stringing him along if I wasn't really serious about our relationship. I decided to give him back his ring.

I made up my mind to do it after school, and I remember waking up that day just sick to my stomach. I don't like confrontation, and I can't stand the idea of somebody being mad at me or me being mad at them. I felt queasy and anxious all day. I told Beverly about my plan to return the ring. I said, "I just can't stand having to do this and break poor Leonard's heart. I promise I will never wear another boy's ring again." She liked to remind me of that promise a few years later after I met a young man named Elvis Presley. But that's another story.

I always liked older guys, so once I started high school, if I dated anyone they were usually a senior. That meant I went to three different proms. As a tenth-grader I was invited to the senior prom by a boy named Billy, whose ill-fitting suit was just about falling off him. He must have borrowed it from his father. I still have photos of myself as a teenager going to all these events with different boys. These were usually just school friends or boys I went out with once or twice. I was too wrapped up in my music and too boy crazy to pay attention to any one young man for very long.

That's not to say I didn't have a handful of steady boyfriends for short periods of time. I remember a young man named Ronnie Bruce that I enjoyed talking with. He was so cute and was very athletic. There was another boy named A.G. Lane who I really fell for. He was a steel guitarist who was very talented, and I used him on some performances sometimes. We dated for a little while and we went to his senior prom together in 1954. Then there was Raymond Brooks, who was my date to my senior prom in 1955. I went out with him for a while because he was such a good dancer!

I even went to a Christmas dance with Harold Taylor, who was better known as Jody Taylor around Oklahoma City. Jude and Jody were performers who also worked in the furniture business later on. Jody ended up marrying country singer Norma Jean, who was a very close friend of mine. But that was okay because I ended up marrying someone Norma Jean had dated. But that, too, is another story.

Chapter 6

YOU CAN'T HAVE MY LOVE

I think back often to the day I got that phone call from Hank Thompson when I was working at KLPR. It was probably the most memorable day of my life. That was a real turning point for me, because it was Hank who set me on a path toward becoming a professional entertainer. Had it not been for Hank Thompson, the world might never have heard of Wanda Jackson.

Since I already sang with him at the Trianon Ballroom and at various other public appearances in and around Oklahoma City, Hank soon invited me to appear on his local television show. Soon after that, KLPR launched a UHF television channel, and I landed a thirty-minute TV show where I'd perform, as well as do my own commercials promoting furniture stores and different things. There was a local country duo named Wiley and Gene who were nationally popular, and they managed the KLPR TV studio. I worked with them quite a bit on television and on their live shows. There was a little group of us, including Anita Bryant and a kid named Doyle Madden, who were popular on local TV.

That exposure, combined with my radio work, was creating a good bit of local buzz for me as a teenage country singer. As I became better known around Oklahoma City, I'd start to get recognized when I'd go out. I was becoming a minor celebrity and didn't have as much privacy as I once did. People would sometimes ask me for my autograph. I loved it! Entertainers are all just big kids and, no matter what some of them might tell you, we like attention. I enjoyed it then, and I guess I have to admit I still do. In later years, if I ever did complain about it, Daddy would remind me that I was a public figure and that it was part of my job to greet the public. Of course, I never quite got that concept. Visiting new places, meeting new people, and getting to make music never felt like much of a *job* to me. It felt like a party!

Thanks to Hank's mentorship I was getting more polished and professional every day. Even though I was still a high school student, Hank thought it was time to push my career to the next level. In 1953 I went to his pink house on May Avenue to cut a demonstration recording with his band. Hank had professional recording equipment and a bar set up in his garage, which made for a neat little home studio arrangement. He and his wife, Dorothy, didn't have a large house, but it was a nice place. Hank set up microphones for the band in the front room, but since he used quite a few musicians, it spilled over into the dining room, too. We recorded several songs that day, which Hank planned to use to help find me a record deal. One of them was "Heartbreak Ahead," which had previously been recorded by a singer named Charline Arthur. I used to go to the Big D Jamboree fairly often, where Charline was a regular cast member. She wasn't pretty by any stretch, but she was little, and you talk about feisty! She was quite a fireball. She played a big ol' upright bass and wore pants, so she was really a ground breaker for me. I just loved that song of hers, so I learned it and started doing it. When Hank wanted me to record, I knew I wanted to do that one.

Hank was trying to get a recording contract for both me and Billy Gray, who was his band leader. There weren't as many little oddball record companies back in 1953 as there would be after the rock-and-roll explosion, so if you wanted to record, you usually needed the help of a big label. Ken Nelson, who signed Tommy Collins to Capitol Records in Hollywood, was also Hank's producer and A&R man at Capitol, so that seemed like the best place to start. Ken listened to the demos and decided they weren't interested in Billy, but he liked my voice.

"She's good," he told Hank after hearing half of the first song. "How old is she?" Hank told him I was sixteen. "Oh, heavens no," Ken shot back. "When she's an adult I'll be willing to have a talk with her. We've already got an underage girl on Capitol that's giving me fits and causing all sorts of legal problems."

I assume he was probably talking about Jean Shepard, who was not yet of age when she and Ferlin Husky had their hit duet with "A Dear John Letter" a few months earlier. From what I understand, they had to go to court to finalize her contract and then have Ferlin assigned as her legal guardian for the pair to travel out of state on tour. The label certainly wasn't looking for any more of that drama.

"Besides," Ken added, "girls don't sell records!"

Ken's line about girls not selling records has become a well-known part of my story in interviews over the years. It's usually interpreted as the gauntlet that was thrown down and the challenge I was determined to overcome. That's partially true, but it's also true that Ken wasn't exactly wrong, either. There were only a small handful of exceptions. Other than Jean Shepard, the only recent success for a girl singer would have been Kitty Wells. She had a major smash with "It Wasn't God Who Made Honky Tonk Angels" the previous year, which was *Billboard's* first number one country hit by a female country solo artist. Before that, you have to go all the way back to 1935 when Patsy Montana became the first female country artist to sell more than a million copies of a single with "I Want to Be a Cowboy's Sweetheart." That was one of the first songs I ever learned, and I was thrilled to death when I got to meet Patsy in Nashville one time. I recognize that Ken wasn't being sexist, so much as he was thinking about business. But it still gave me a little nudge to prove him wrong! It would just take a little time before I'd get that chance.

When things didn't pan out with Capitol, Hank approached Paul Cohen, who was the head A&R man at Decca Records. Hank was thrilled that Decca was interested in signing both me and Billy Gray, and called the house to tell me the good news. I still remember when the Decca contract arrived in the mail one day. I was sitting on the couch playing my guitar when Daddy pulled it from the envelope and held it out for me to see. I flipped that guitar over on my lap, turned it into an impromptu table, and signed that contract on the dotted line. The next day at school they announced over the loudspeaker, "Congratulations to our own Wanda Jackson, who has signed a recording contract with Decca Records." Beverly said you could hear the applause and cheering all down the hallways.

Everybody at school supported me except for one teacher. I can't even remember his name now, but he was my history instructor. When it came time to record my first songs for Decca in March of 1954, Mother and Daddy and I took the week off school and work to drive out to Hollywood for the session.

When I came back everybody was thrilled, but this man didn't think that was right for me to take a week off school to make a record. He made it pretty hard on me after that. I passed his class, but he gave me a D, which I couldn't believe. We were assigned a project that I completed beautifully. I wrote a detailed report and recruited a friend, who was a great artist, to illustrate each of my points with a unique drawing. We took everything, placed it in a folder, and bound it perfectly. After all that hard work, that guy still gave me a D. I hate to say it, but he was a horse's heinie!

Any disappointment I might have felt about my history grade, however, was more than offset by the thrill of having the opportunity to record in a professional studio for the first time. After two and a half days of recording sessions at Capitol's studio, Hank brought his whole band over to the Decca facilities on Melrose Avenue for back-to-back sessions with Billy Gray and me. I was scared to death on that first session, but Mother and Daddy were there, and I knew the guys from the band, so it was a little more comfortable. I'd do what they call positive self-talk to get the courage up to give it my all. It seemed like everyone was on my side and they were pulling for me, so it was a real mix of fear and excitement.

When it came to choosing songs, I had full reign. Neither Hank nor Decca really intervened, which I now realize was pretty unusual for a new artist at the time—especially one who was a junior in high school! Of course, there wasn't too much to do for the backing band in those days. Arrangements were a lot simpler then, and it was easy to breeze through several songs in a single session. There wasn't that much to do! I recorded four songs that day, including "If You Knew What I Know," which was one I'd written myself, as well as "The Right to Love," which was written by my old boyfriend, Tommy Collins. Tommy was just having his first hit with "You Better Not Do That" at the same time, but I had learned "The Right to Love" from him back when we were spending a lot of time together, and I always thought it was a cute song.

I assumed I would just be recording my four selections, but when I finished there was still time remaining. Hank said, "I'll tell you what, guys, let's lay down that 'You Can't Have My Love' song."

My heart sank. Hank had received the song—a duet—at his publishing company, and had already mentioned wanting me and Billy Gray to record it together. It was as cute as can be, but I didn't like it at the time. I didn't want to launch my career as part of a duo. I wanted to do things on my own. Hank knew I didn't want to record it, but he tried to smooth it over by treating it very casually.

"It'll be all right, Wanda," he said. "We'll just do it real quick and then we'll have it recorded."

"Oh no, Hank, I'm tired. Let's call it a day."

He just smiled. "No, we're gonna give it a try."

I don't know why, but when I get mad I cry. I said, "I don't want to do this. I'm NOT going to do it!" Tears were welling up in my eyes, and I was prepared to dig my heels in. I kind of kicked at the pricks on that one. Daddy had to take me aside and talk to me. He reminded me that it was Hank who made it possible for me to get a record deal in the first place, and that if Hank wanted me to do the song, then I should respect his request.

I finally agreed to record "You Can't Have My Love" with Billy, but only to please Hank. I can still kind of hear the anger in my voice on that record. That probably actually helped my performance, because the girl in the song is telling the guy off. It gave me a little attitude on the recording. That's not because I was great at adopting the character so much as it is because the whole time I was seething and thinking, *Okay, I'll sing that damn song, but it won't be very good!* Looking back, Hank bringing up that song at the last minute was probably the plan all along. He knew he would get resistance from me, but he also thought the song could be a hit. Maybe he figured that would be the easiest way to get me to go along with it.

I was disappointed when Decca released the duet of "You Can't Have My Love" as my first single, but it turned out Hank was right about the song after all. By late July of 1954, it was making its way up the *Billboard* country chart. Decca thought it would be a good idea to record another duet with Billy as soon as possible to capitalize on the success of the first single. Hank wasn't scheduled to record in Hollywood, so we hastily assembled a session at his home studio there in Oklahoma City.

Billy and I recorded a song called "If You Don't Somebody Else Will," which had just been released on the Chess label by a country duo called Jimmy & Johnny. Comprised of Jimmy Lee and Johnny Mathis (not to be confused with the pop singer of the same name), the duo were regulars on the *Louisiana Hayride*. Even though "You Can't Have My Love" was doing well, I still didn't think I needed a duet partner. I wanted to be recognized for my own talents, and I thought the boys might not like me as much if I was always singing with the same guy. They might think Billy and I were together and lose interest in me!

As it turned out, this was the song that actually got me out of having to be a duet act. The hit version went to Jimmy & Johnny, who already had the jump on us. Theirs had come out first and, even though Decca was a bigger label than Chess, radio audiences made the original version a Top 5 hit, while ours didn't gain much traction. I secretly breathed a sigh of relief. If Billy and I had kept having hits together, I might have been stuck recording duets forever. Billy was a great guy and I had a lot or respect for him, but that's just not what I wanted for my career.

Hank, perhaps recognizing that I wasn't enthused about recording duets, suggested that I record a solo number that day at his home studio. I decided to record an original called "You'd Be the First One to Know." It was actually the first song I'd ever written, and came to me one day when I was in the ninth grade. I never did care much for school. I was so restless and always felt like my spirit just wanted to fly away. My mind was focused on my career, or maybe sketching out a design in my notebook for a new dress to wear on stage. I was constantly going to sharpen my pencil just to get out of my desk and look through the window at the world beyond the prison of the classroom. I was standing at that pencil sharpener one day when I thought to myself, *I wonder what it would be like to write a song of my own?* I went back to my desk and came up with that idea in my head.

The thought behind the lyric was, "If I ever break up with somebody, I want him to be the first to know. I don't want him to hear that it's going to happen from someone else. I'll be the one to tell him." It was actually a bit of autobiography. As I mentioned, my second boyfriend named Leonard had given me his ring. I wanted to break up with him, and I was going to have to give it back to him. I was glad I went to him first because I would have hated for him to find out via other means. I knew I was doing it right, but I don't like confrontation, and it was probably the hardest thing I'd ever had to do up to that point in my life. After school I raced home to the piano to see what it was going to sound like.

I was pretty excited to have come up with something like that by myself. Looking back, it's not a very good song, but in terms of structure I accidentally got it right. Hank later told me that the first verse of a song is where you tell what the story is. The chorus is where you go in depth, and the verses after the chorus tell the present and the future. He helped me understand song structure and the various rhyming patterns, such as ABAB or AABB. Fortunately, I stumbled upon it even before I understood the rules.

That second Decca session at Hank's house was in August of 1954. By September, I was starting my senior year of high school with a Top 10 hit, thanks to "You Can't Have My Love" climbing all the way up to number eight on *Billboard's* national country chart. Take that, Mr. History Teacher!

My classmates seemed to like me, even if they weren't big country music fans. Country wasn't that popular yet. It was just a small group of people who listened to it. Mother or Daddy used to talk about how you'd go up to a house and hear country music playing on a record or over the radio. If you knocked or rang the doorbell, they'd turn it off or change the station before answering. Given that country music wasn't the coolest thing at the time, I attribute much of my popularity at school to my one true blue friend, Beverly Wright. She was so genuine, and such the life of the party, that people just loved her. She was my greatest cheerleader, and the fact that she was always championing me and promoting me contributed to my popularity.

I would often sing in school assemblies, and the kids really liked the Hank Williams songs, like "Jambalaya" and "Kaw-liga" that were already staples of my performances. The one they loved the most was "Hot Dog! That Made Him Mad." I was always looking for songs to add to my repertoire and often found good material through movie musicals. I was a film buff and would go to the theater every chance I got. In fact, I'd take a little note pad and jot down song lyrics or, as color movies became more common, I'd make notes about color combinations and plans for dresses based on what I'd seen. I always wanted to meet Elizabeth Taylor. Marilyn, too, of course. I loved Esther Williams, Betty Grable, and all those starlets of the silver screen. I don't remember

the name of the movie, but I heard "Hot Dog! That Made Him
Mad" at a matinee one Saturday and was knocked out by it. The
singer was Betty Hutton, who was a pop artist on Capitol, but she
also sang and danced in the movies. When I heard it I thought,
Man, I'd sure like to sing that. I called Mother and asked if I could
stay to watch the movie again just so I could hear the song once
more. She agreed, and soon after, I hunted down the single and
learned how to play it.

The girls at school just loved "Hot Dog! That Made Him
Mad" because there weren't many songs out about getting back
at a guy. It got to where anytime I played for a school assembly,
I had to do that song. One day I was called into the principal's
office.

"Wanda, I'm sorry, but you can't sing that 'Hot Dog' song
anymore," the principal said. "It's entirely too suggestive." But it
actually wasn't! I never got that.

"All right, Mr. Higgins," I said. "I won't sing it anymore." The
next time I was asked to perform at an assembly, Mr. Higgins
introduced me. The minute I started walking across the stage
the kids started chanting, "Hot Dog! Hot Dog! Hot Dog!" They
wouldn't stop. I figured, "Hot dog, it might make 'em mad, but
to heck with school. They can throw me out if they want, but my
audience wants this song." I found out later that the chanting was
a lot of Beverly's doing. I had told her what the principal said to
me, so she spread the word and orchestrated everything with the
students. Even Mr. Higgins couldn't say much after that. He had
to let me do my thing.

Even though I was in no danger of becoming the
valedictorian, I did find a few ways to make high school more
bearable. I had been a twirler with the band in middle school, and
became the Capitol Hill band queen in high school. It sounds
more glamorous than it is. The job of the band queen was to pass

out the music, call roll, and march next to the leader. It was a lot of fun, and at least I was around music.

Another highlight of senior year was when I had my one and only chance in life to do some acting. I got the lead role of Reno Sweeny in Cole Porter's *Anything Goes,* which was our high school musical that year. I always wondered how I got that role when I was so country, but Ms. Munday, our speech teacher and the director of our play, said, "Wanda, you should try out for this." I found a boy I knew who could play piano by ear, and I worked with him to prepare for the tryouts. I auditioned with Marilyn Monroe's "Diamonds Are a Girl's Best Friend," and I think that was the song that let them see I could do something besides pure country. As we got into rehearsals, Ms. Munday would always say, "Stop everything! Stop it! Wanda, you can't tap your foot! Please stop tapping your foot to the music!" I didn't even realize I was doing it. When I heard music I just felt it, and that's what happened. When we performed the play, it was done at the Municipal Auditorium in downtown Oklahoma City. It was quite an affair, and I really enjoyed the chance to stretch my musical boundaries.

Though I enjoyed my school friends, and I have fond memories of my various activities, the only thing I really wanted to do was sing. I was still working with Hank, but he hardly paid me anything. I don't blame him. He was the one who was doing most of the work, but I craved it like you wouldn't believe. Daddy would drive me to wherever we were performing. We didn't do many out-of-town gigs, but we were playing at plenty of contests and other little shows locally. I begged him to let me quit school, but Daddy was a stickler. "No," he told me. "No matter what, you have to get your diploma."

Chapter 7

With fiddler Tommy Jackson and Daddy at my first recording session in Nashville.

TEARS AT THE GRAND OLE OPRY

By early 1955 I was traveling with Hank Thompson to a handful of dates in Indiana, New Jersey, Maryland, and Texas, but I wasn't able to go on the road as much as I would have liked. Daddy, of course, was very rigid about me attending school and would only rarely let me miss classes to perform. I was making twenty dollars per night on Hank's show, but it wouldn't have made a bit of difference to me if I was making two dollars or two thousand. I was just happy to be on a stage. Sometimes getting to that stage was a challenge. They didn't exactly roll out the red carpet for us country stars in those days. I remember one gig where the dressing room situation was so pathetic that I had to go to a gas station to change before the show. I went in to discover that the lady's room had flooded. Beverly was with me, and she had to help me get up on the toilet seat just to get my hose on without touching the floor. I'm sure we were quite a sight!

In March, Daddy and I headed down to Nashville for another Decca recording session. It was my first time to ever travel to the budding country music capital, and I was pretty excited. Even though I was building a career in country music, we didn't consider moving to Tennessee. Mother had lived out of state when we were in California, and it just would not have gone over for her to leave her mother and siblings again. Plus, she had a good government job, so it's not something we even discussed. As a result, there was something about Nashville that always remained mysterious to me. I was part of the industry that built the city, but I was never really part of the music community there.

When Daddy and I checked into the hotel on that first Nashville trip, the phone kept ringing in our room. I would answer and Daddy would hear me say, "No thank you, but I appreciate you calling." Finally, after this happened three or four times, Daddy said, "Who keeps calling so much?" I said, "They're all black songwriters who want me to record their material, but I sing country, not blues. I don't know why in the world they're calling me!" As it turned out, the word had gotten out among the songwriting community that I was in town to record. The folks who were calling were actually white country writers, but the white Tennessee accent sounded like a black Oklahoma accent to me. There's no telling what A-list country songwriters I turned down when they called my room. I could have used a hit, so I should have paid more attention!

My first Nashville session was held at Owen Bradley's recording studio on 16th Avenue, where more timeless country songs have been recorded than anyone could possibly list. I remember that Chet Atkins played guitar. The steel guitar duties were handled by Jerry Byrd, who played on many classic recordings, including Hank Williams's "I'm So Lonesome I Could Cry" and "Lovesick Blues." Of all the musicians there that day, however, Daddy was most excited about Tommy Jackson. Tommy's fiddle appeared on so many wonderful recordings by Red Foley, Webb Pierce, Ray Price, and others, but he was also pretty well known for his square dance albums that he recorded in the 1950s. He was an idol to country fiddle players, and Daddy loved his style.

The session was produced by Paul Cohen, the man who signed me to Decca Records. It's funny, but since the contracts were sent in the mail, I hadn't actually met Mr. Cohen in person until that day. My connection with Decca was really through Hank. I didn't actually know anyone there. Mr. Cohen was very friendly and welcomed us warmly when we arrived at the studio. I always sang with my guitar onstage, so I brought it with me to the studio thinking I would play along with the band. We kicked off the proceedings with a waltz called "It's the Same Old World (Wherever You Go)." We got about halfway through the first take before Paul stopped everybody and came out of the control room. "Wanda," he smiled, "we're getting an awful lot of your guitar on your vocal mic. Why don't we try having you play with a felt pick so it's not so loud?"

We started again, but we didn't get very far into it before he stopped us a second time. "Wanda, honey, I'm still hearing a good bit of that guitar. Why don't we try one without you playing along?"

It's funny that, even with that felt pick, they couldn't get me to play soft enough. I guess I was just banging away, which would serve me much better in the years to come after I discovered rock and roll. At that moment, though, it just wasn't working. I agreed to stop playing, but I was pretty nervous about the next take. I had never sung without that guitar in my hand. It was my crutch and my security blanket all rolled into one. "Could I just hold it if I promise not to strum?" I asked.

"Of course, sweetie, that'll be fine," Mr. Cohen answered.

After that, I knocked out three more songs in that two-hour session without any trouble at all. Later on, some of the guys started calling me "One Take Wanda" because I was able to record a song correctly the first time. I could do it again for them if they wanted, but it wouldn't be any different. Quite a few of the songs I've recorded over the years were done in one take if the band got it right. And, of course, when we were recording with some of the best musicians in Nashville—or the world, for that matter—it was an easy process. Those guys were amazing, so everything moved very fast. Today artists might hole up for months to record a new album, but we used to go in and get at least four songs in the can during a three-hour session. There was nothing painstaking about it. It was quick; it was easy; and it was fun!

One of the things that surprised me about recording in Nashville, however, was the difference in the sound from what we were doing out West. I was used to Hank Thompson's band. Even Merl Lindsay's band had horns, so I was accustomed to a pretty full sound. There just weren't many instruments used on Nashville recordings at the time. It was the sound of commercial country music of the day, so I didn't ask for drums and all the extra stuff I was used to. I probably could have requested it, but I didn't know to ask.

One of the songs I recorded at that first Nashville session was called "Tears at the Grand Ole Opry." It was written by a guy named Cowboy Howard Vokes, who was known as Pennsylvania's King of Country Music at one time. He got into writing songs during a lengthy hospital stay following a hunting accident.

Apparently, he was shot in the ankle with a high-powered rifle and nearly lost his right foot. Howard booked a lot of country music shows in his home state, and I think "Tears at the Grand Ole Opry" was a song he passed along to Hank Thompson somewhere along the way. It found its way to me and I agreed to record it.

I got my name on the writer credits for the song somehow, but I wasn't really a writer on it. Even though I wrote plenty of my own material, in those days it was pretty common for artists to tell up-and-coming songwriters they would record one of their tunes in exchange for half the writer credit. In later years, Webb Pierce used to joke around onstage, saying "This next song is one Mel Tillis wrote for me, and I liked it so much I let him keep half the writer credit." It's kind of funny now, but that was the norm in those days.

Daddy was actually the one who encouraged me to record "Tears at the Grand Ole Opry," but I never did really like it all that much. He thought it was commercial. The idea was kind of cute, but I've wished for years I hadn't pulled that stunt of putting my name on something I didn't really write. I believe we reap what we sow, so maybe it was no coincidence that two days later I would be crying actual tears when I made my debut as a guest on the real *Grand Ole Opry*.

The *Opry* began as a radio show in 1925 and was broadcast from several different venues in the early days. When I appeared there on March 26, 1955, it had been based at Nashville's Ryman Auditorium for well over a decade. The hallowed space, known today as the Mother Church of Country Music, held a powerful mystique—even back then. Anyone who was anyone in country music played the *Opry*, and being invited to sing from the same stage that hosted Hank Williams, Roy Acuff, and Ernest Tubb was the greatest thrill of my life up to that point. In fact, Ernest

Tubb was the host of the segment on which I would appear, and I couldn't believe I would be introduced by my fellow Decca recording artist, who was already a legend by then.

Everyone in country music in those days—especially the Grand Ole Opry stars—had their stage clothes made by Nudie Cohn, the famous "rodeo tailor" I'd first visited in Hollywood with my folks and Tommy Collins in tow. Those Nudie suits were decked out with all the rhinestones and were beautifully embroidered. I got my first one when I was about sixteen. It was a Western-style shirt with matching pants that had fringe down the side. It wasn't made especially for me, but was created for a girl who never returned to pick it up. Nudie put it up for sale, and it happened to fit me, so we bought it for $100. He made me a custom outfit not long after, but when Mother found out we paid $150 for it, she put a stop to that! She said, "Why are you paying him all that money? I can do that!" She was a very talented seamstress, and began making my stage outfits. The first one we designed was pretty country. It had rhinestones around the neck, and Mother bought a big piece of suede leather that she cut into fringes with a rhinestone at the end of each one. There's a picture of me and Billy Gray together where I'm wearing that outfit, and it's pretty impressive! Mother did all the intricate piping and everything. Everyone assumed they were professionally done, so I guess she was giving the famous Nudie a run for his money!

For my Opry debut, Mother and I carefully designed a new dress that she sewed. It was white and tight-fitting, but still had a "cowgirl" look. There was red fringe at the bottom with a sweetheart neck at the top and rhinestone-studded spaghetti straps that were like a halter. I paired it with some red-and-white boots that Nudie made for me, and I was looking good, if I do say so myself. I've always preferred to get dressed in my hotel room rather than changing at the venue where I'm performing, so I put my dress on just before Daddy and I made the drive from the hotel over to the Ryman. The schedule was taped to the wall backstage when we got there, so I was paying careful attention to the show to make sure I was ready for my cue.

I was standing backstage with my guitar on when Ernest Tubb himself came from around the curtain and began walking toward me with a big smile on his face. "Are you Wanda Jackson?" he asked.

"Yessir," I nodded.

"Okay, honey, you're next on the show. I'll introduce you, so go ahead and get ready."

"Thank you, Mr. Tubb. I'm ready," I said. He looked kind of startled, and his big smile melted away.

"Oh no. My goodness, honey," he stammered. "You can't go out on the stage of the *Grand Ole Opry* like that!"

I could feel my ears getting hot. "Like what?" I asked. He took a step back.

"You can't go out there with your shoulders showing like that."

I could not believe it. Here I was in the dress that Mother and I had spent so much time designing. I had on those boots, and I looked so cute with my big guitar on. I said, "Well, this is the only thing I brought. I wore it to the show."

"I don't know what to tell you," he said. "You're gonna have to cover up or you can't go on."

Since it was still March, and the Nashville air was cool in the evenings, I'd worn a white imitation leather jacket with fringe on it in case it got chilly. I ran back to the dressing room, grabbed that jacket, and put it on over my dress. I strapped my guitar back on just as Ernest Tubb introduced me to the audience. I walked onto that *Grand Ole Opry* stage, but instead of feeling like a queen, I felt like a kid who'd just been reprimanded. It just broke my heart to have to cover that cute dress. I had a bad taste in my mouth, to say the least.

As the audience clapped, however, I made a decision that I wasn't going to let Ernest Tubb, *Opry* rules, poor communication, or whatever had caused the misunderstanding about the dress to ruin this moment. I stepped up to the microphone and launched into my first song, which was an Autry Inman tune called "I Cried Again." I don't think we rehearsed, so it surprised me to hear the sound of the *Opry* band. I had gotten used to singing with Hank's Brazos Valley Boys, which was the nation's number one Western swing band. We had drums, horns, twin fiddles, electric guitar, piano, upright bass, and sometimes twin steel guitars. It was a very full sound. I got out there on the Ryman stage, and it was just the bare lineup of bass, guitar, fiddle, and maybe a piano. But that was okay. Things might have gotten off to a rocky start, but this was the *Grand Ole Opry,* and I was going to savor the moment!

In those days most of the regular cast members stayed out on the stage during all the performances. They would sit on hay bales and other props during the entire show. It seemed like the audience was having a great time, but halfway through my song, I realized they were craning their necks to see *around* me. During an instrumental section I turned around and saw that two of the show's comedians, Minnie Pearl and Stringbean, were cutting up, laughing, and doing all kinds of silly stuff behind me. They were kind of egging on the other cast members by kidding around during my song. I'm sure it was all intended as good fun, but I couldn't keep the attention of the audience. How could I with those two carrying on behind me? I mean, they *were* funny, so that made it pretty hard to compete.

Maybe I wasn't in the best of moods because I didn't get to show off my beautiful dress, but I sure didn't like feeling like I'd been upstaged. As soon as I was through performing, I walked offstage and found Daddy. I said, "Help me get my stuff rounded up. I'll never come back here again." And I didn't. At least not for a very long time.

Since then I've heard that Elvis had the same experience. I don't mean that Elvis tried to perform on the *Grand Ole Opry* in a dress that showed off his shoulders, but he wasn't exactly embraced when he performed there. They weren't ready for Elvis and they weren't ready for Wanda Jackson, even though I was singing pure country. They didn't boo me, but the whole experience was off-putting. It was really just a lack of communication, but I decided that night that the *Grand Ole Opry* scene was not for me.

I tell that story often and, over the years, I've come to realize that, in some ways, it's a story about how important my stage outfits were in defining my persona as an artist. I always loved beautiful dresses. Even my senior prom dress was a hot pink form-fitting design with lace over satin. The other girls all wore the big full skirts, but I was pretty daring in my younger days. I stole the design from a movie featuring Betty Grable in something similar. Let's just say it would not have passed the Ernest Tubb test!

A love for beautiful clothes is something that drew Mother and me close together. Mother was always what I call "put together." She wasn't necessarily fancy, but she always matched and had nice shoes with a matching handbag. She was pretty, and had a good eye for style. I think she learned to sew out of necessity, but along the way, she discovered that she really enjoyed it. She made most of my stage clothes, as well as my streetwear. We really enjoyed designing and working on dresses together.

Once my body developed and I got a waistline and bustline, I looked good in my clothes. Of course, that just made Daddy nervous. There was a couple who lived next door to us over near South Lindsay named Mr. and Mrs. Cox. Sometimes I'd forget to pull the blinds, and I'd go walking through the house almost naked. Daddy would get so put out with me. He'd roll his eyes and say with a sarcastic tone, "Wanda! Open up those blinds a little more; I don't think Mr. and Mrs. Cox have gotten enough of a look yet!"

Daddy didn't love it when I started lying out in the front yard to sunbathe. We had a little boy named Donny who lived in the shotgun house across the street and, once I started doing that, he started hanging out around our house more often. I remember one time he was over there talking Daddy's ear off, when he suddenly jumped up and ran outside. Daddy just kind of shrugged his shoulders and said, "Well, I guess ol' Donny had to go home." In a minute, he sauntered back into the house as if nothing had happened. Daddy said, "What are you doing?" Donny just grinned. He said, "I had to fart, so I ran outside." I laughed so hard at that. I guess he was learning that he liked to look at pretty girls, but he hadn't yet mastered the art of how to talk around them!

It's no surprise that Daddy kept a pretty close check on what I wore. If Mother and I were working on something, he'd want to see how short it was or how low cut it was before it was finished. He could be pretty strict and wanted to make sure that my outfits weren't too revealing. Many times Mother would be fitting me for a dress, and Daddy would come in and ask how it was going.

"Oh, we're coming along real good," Mother would say.

He'd try to act real casual about it and would say something like, "Good . . . That neckline there. Let's bring that up some."

I'd get so mad. "Daddy! Stop it!" I'd say. We'd get into a little spat about that and he would get more firm.

"Take it up!" he repeated.

Mother would be the peacemaker in these situations. She'd say, "Okay, Tom. That's okay. We'll take it up about an inch." When he'd leave the room, she'd say, "All right, Wanda, now where do you want it?"

"I want it back down where we had it," I'd say. She would just kind of smile.

"We'll keep it how you want it."

Daddy and I were very close, but Mother and I had a special bond with each other when it came to fashion.

It came in handy when I played Reno Sweeny in the high school play. She was a very flamboyant character, so the director, Ms. Munday, took me downtown to find some clothes. We went to all these stores, and I tried on and tried on and tried on. Nothing seemed to be exactly right. We got one real pretty blue suit, but Ms. Munday couldn't find anything that she thought was just perfect for the role. Finally, I said, "Well, I've got some clothes at home we could try." She came over to the house and loved what she saw. We wound up using my own clothes for the character, because the stores just didn't sell anything as flashy as what Mother and I were making!

Maybe the reason I got crazy about looking good was because I was crazy about boys. And the only other thing I was crazier about than boys (and looking good) was my music. As these interests converged, my visual image on stage took on a different tone. My experience at the *Opry* didn't prompt me to change my ways. In fact, after that, I doubled down. It occurred to me that if I could wear glamorous dresses and high heels to a formal dance, I could wear them onstage, too. I didn't need those heavy boots and a cowboy hat with Western pantsuits covered in

fringe weighing me down. I'd put on all that garb and feel like
I was about to fall over backward! Mother and I started putting
together my new style with long earrings and spaghetti straps.
My look was increasingly influenced by Marilyn Monroe. I didn't
want to look like a cowgirl anymore. I wanted to be glamorous
and sexy. I loved to give a little shock to an audience. Whether
they liked it or not, I just wanted to get their attention.

I was the first female artist in country music to wear sexy
clothes and adopt a glamorous image. Before that, the girls would
wear those old dull and dowdy farm girl dresses that were just
as boring as could be. My friend Colin Escott likes to say that
I broke the "gingham barrier." Of course, I didn't know I was
blazing a trail at the time. I was just trying to be me. I haven't
gotten much credit for it, but I hope that I made it a little easier
for gals like Dolly Parton, Tanya Tucker, Lorrie Morgan, Faith
Hill, and Shania Twain to embrace their femininity and recognize
that it's okay to be sexy and be a good country girl at the same
time.

Chapter 8

I WISH I WAS YOUR FRIEND

Daddy and I pulled into the KTOC radio station parking lot in Cape Girardeau, Missouri, on a hot July afternoon in 1955. When a traveling artist was scheduled to play a show in those days, they'd make sure to arrive in town a few hours early to appear on the local airwaves. Radio stations weren't bound by a particular format then, so you had to time your arrival to coincide with when the country programming was on the air. The idea was to have the DJ play your record, ask you a few questions, and give you a chance to invite the listeners to that night's show.

There was another reason why those radio appearances were so important. It's no secret that many of the legends of country music used to like to have a good time. And often that good time

was accompanied by a few drinks. As a result, some of them—
Hank Williams was one of the first—earned a reputation for
being, shall we say, less than one hundred percent dependable
when it came to showing up for a scheduled performance. Heck,
George Jones even came to be known as "No Show Jones" back
in his younger and wilder days. So going on the radio not only
gave us artists a chance to promote our live shows, it also gave
advance ticketholders the assurance that we had, indeed, arrived
in town and would be appearing that night as advertised.

My show in Cape Girardeau was to be a package show,
meaning several artists were on the bill. One of them was a
young singer who was rapidly gaining a strong regional following
throughout the South. I had been told that he would also be
joining me for the interview. As you know from my response to
dueting with Billy Gray, I've always kind of enjoyed having the
spotlight to myself. But this guy *was* headlining the show, so even
though I'd never heard of him or his records, I decided not to let
it bother me.

Daddy and I arrived at KTOC first. We headed inside and
were greeted by a friendly young woman at the front desk. Just as
I was introducing myself, the door opened behind me. I turned
around to a bright blast of summer sunshine streaming around
a silhouette in the doorway. The door closed behind him, and it
took a moment for my eyes to adjust. When they did, the first
thing I noticed was that this guy was pretty cute. He flashed a shy
smile. "Hi there," he kind of half mumbled, "I'm Elvis Presley."
He moved toward me with his hand extended. I wish I could
say the heavens opened and I heard angels singing, but it wasn't
anything quite that dramatic. Still, I have to admit; it did seem as
if a presence had entered the room.

Of course, I recognized right away that Elvis was handsome,
but I was actually a little taken aback by his outfit. He was wearing

black slacks and a black shirt with a yellow sport coat. I'd never seen a yellow sport coat in my life! In 1955 that just wasn't the kind of clothing a typical man would wear. But I guess he wasn't a typical man. He also had curly hair that day, which I later found out was because he'd gotten a perm. I thought that was pretty funny, but there was no question that this guy was magnetic.

I took his hand. "I'm Wanda Jackson," I smiled back. "I'll be playing on the show tonight." Our eyes met for a few seconds. Elvis suddenly broke his gaze and glanced at the floor.

He seemed almost fidgety as he replied, "Oh, yes ma'am. I've heard your records and I know we'll have a good time tonight. You've got a very nice voice and I look forward to working with you."

My smile widened. Suddenly Daddy was standing right next to me.

"I'm Tom," he announced as he held out his hand toward Elvis. "I'm Wanda's father."

"Nice to meet you, Mr. Jackson," Elvis replied. "It's a real pleasure. You've sure got a talented daughter here." Suddenly, Daddy was smiling, too.

Over the years I've been asked about Elvis Presley more than any other topic you could imagine. If I'm honest I have to confess there have been moments in my career when I've gotten a little tired of the Elvis questions from well-meaning interviewers. I certainly understand why people are fascinated by the King of Rock and Roll, and I know why they want to hear about him. It's not an understatement to say that Elvis changed the world. But there have been times I've wanted to scream, "There's a lot more to Wanda Jackson than my experiences with Elvis Presley!"

With time, however, I've come to embrace my history with Elvis. Not only did he change the world, but he changed *my*

world. It was Elvis who believed that I could sing rock and roll
before I believed it myself. It was Elvis who took the time to help
me understand the new musical revolution that was exploding
all around us. And it was Elvis who, for a short time in the mid-
1950s, won my heart as I was just beginning to understand what
it really meant to fully embrace my femininity and express myself
as a young woman. Today I very much enjoy talking about Elvis
and reflecting on the warm memories that had such an influence
on my life and career.

When I first met Elvis, I was seventeen years old and had just
graduated from Capitol Hill High School a few weeks earlier. As
you know, graduation couldn't come soon enough for me. It was
hard to devote myself to my studies when I was putting records
on the charts and playing at the legendary *Grand Ole Opry*. Even
if it hadn't exactly been an ideal experience, it was still a big
deal. I earned $1,126.56 that month alone from record royalties,
publishing income, and a handful of live shows with Hank. That
was some serious money for a seventeen-year-old girl in 1955.
We're talking about what would be the equivalent of more than
$10,000 by today's standards.

I knew the only thing I was interested in was being a singer,
and I bring up those accomplishments only to make the point
that I seemed to be finding success doing just that. I didn't see
much reason to be in school, considering that my career was
already well underway. I never stopped begging Daddy to let me
just drop out and hit the road for an extended tour, but he wasn't
having it. He said, "You graduate first." That was so important
to him. My dad's father was a sharecropper and their family was
almost literally dirt poor. Mother's people had a farm, where they
raised pigs, grew gardens, and pretty well provided for themselves.
Daddy finally earned his high school diploma at the age of
twenty-one after having to regularly take time off school so he

could work picking cotton to contribute to the basic survival of his household. With that kind of background, you can bet he wasn't about to let his only child throw away an opportunity for an education. But that didn't stop me from asking, begging, pleading, whining, pouting, and stomping my feet. I wanted out.

I can remember several of my girlfriends crying on graduation day because they felt like the best years of their lives were over. I loved my friends, so I hugged them tight and did my best to console them. Inside, however, I was bursting with joy. I was finally free to make music without any other responsibilities to hold me back. Sure, I would miss seeing Beverly and the girls every day, but so many adventures were calling me, and I couldn't wait to get started.

Now that I had my diploma firmly in hand, Daddy was as excited as I was to hit the road and help me take my career to the next level. He was a wanderlust at heart, and was ready for whatever adventures awaited us on the road. By that point most of my professional work had been with Hank Thompson. I had appeared as a single performer on a handful of out-of-town gigs, but not many. One that stands out in my mind is the famous Big "D" Jamboree, which was broadcast on KRLD from the Dallas Sportatorium every Saturday night. The facility was best known for hosting professional wrestling matches, and the round wrestling ring in the center of the arena doubled as the stage for the Jamboree shows. They drew thousands of audience members every weekend, and it was a thrill to perform for those loyal country fans. I enjoyed being the focus of the audience on that stage, and I knew that if I wanted more experiences like that, I would need to become more than the girl singer with Hank Thompson's show.

Daddy knew it, too. What we didn't know was how to get a manager, or what a manager even did. There was no roadmap in that era for how to build a country music career, but I knew that's what I wanted to do, and Daddy knew he wanted to help me. Soon after I graduated, he went downtown to the newsstand and picked up a copy of *Billboard* magazine. Don't worry, we paid for it. My criminal days were long behind me by that point! *Billboard* was the premier source of information about the entertainment industry back then, and it continues to be well known today for its charts that track the popularity of music in various genres.

Daddy brought the magazine home and was thumbing through it at the kitchen table when he spotted an ad for the Bob Neal Talent Agency in Memphis, Tennessee. "I think I'll just give him a call and see if he'd be interested in booking you," Daddy shrugged as he got up and moved to the living room. I followed, watching him closely. I sat at the edge of the couch, pulling my legs up underneath me without breaking my gaze on Daddy's face as he picked up the telephone receiver.

"Mr. Neal? My name is Tom Jackson and I'm calling from Oklahoma City regarding my daughter, Wanda Jackson, who records for Decca Records." I studied Daddy's expression as I tried to imagine the other side of the conversation. "Oh, you're familiar with her? That's great. The truth is we're looking to book some more shows for Wanda, and we thought you might be able to help." Daddy reached for a pencil and a piece of paper and began scratching down some notes. "Elvin Presley, you said? Oh, I'm sorry. Elvis. . . . No, I can't say I'm familiar with him. . . . Next month? That sounds good to me. . . . Yes, that will be fine. We'll see you then, and I thank you, sir."

Daddy set the receiver down with a straight face and pretended as if nothing had happened. He liked to tease me like that. "Well, Daddy, what did he say?" He finally gave me a wink.

"Good news, honey. You've been getting some good airplay in Memphis, and Mr. Neal knows who you are. He said our timing is perfect because he's booking a young man who is apparently getting popular really fast down there. He was actually already looking for a girl singer to join the bill on a few of his performances, so we're gonna meet up with them in Missouri for a show on July 20th."

"It sounded like you said his name was Elvis," I laughed. Nobody around Oklahoma knew who he was because they weren't playing his records there yet.

"Yeah, that's it," Daddy smiled.

"Well, that's just about the strangest name I ever heard," I giggled.

"It's a little different," Daddy nodded. "But they're gonna pay you $50 for each show, and that's more than twice what you're making with Hank. I think this could be a good thing."

Daddy wasn't about to let me go out on the road with a bunch of guys. He said, "Wanda won't take care of business, and she's got no business being out there with a bunch of men going to a different town every night." Mother and Daddy put their heads together. She had the better job at home. Daddy was still driving a cab, but he gave it up to become my manager and driver. I don't know how they made it work financially in those early days, but I didn't care. As long as I got to sing and play guitar I was happy. Daddy took a percentage, but he didn't rob me or anything. I always had the money I needed, and we were in it together.

Cape Girardeau, Missouri, is about six hundred miles northwest of Oklahoma City, so Daddy and I set out in the very early morning before the day of the show. This was before we had interstate highways, so road trips were kind of slow going in those days. It was still dark when we left the house, so I lay down in the backseat as Daddy headed out of town on Highway 62. I catnapped for a little while, but I remember waking up as the sun began to appear on the horizon. I felt happy. I had my guitar. I had my daddy. And I had an audience on the other end of that road that was going to listen to me sing my songs. It's funny now to think we'd drive hundreds and hundreds of miles on those old two-lane state highways to earn $50 for sharing the bill with a singer with a funny name we'd never heard of. But Daddy and I felt like we were living our musical dream.

After a long day of driving, we stopped for the night in Pocahontas, Arkansas, to get some rest. The next morning Daddy was up early. He slipped out of the room to grab a newspaper and came back with a cup of coffee from the diner next door. I like to stay up late at night, so I've never been a morning person. I was already on rock-and-roll time before I ever knew there was such a thing as rock and roll. "We'd better get on the road pretty soon, Wanda," Daddy said quietly. I pulled the covers over my head and groaned. "Here, I got this for you," he chuckled as he set the coffee cup on the nightstand. "You're gonna have to develop a taste for it if this is the life you've chosen. Now come on and let's get moving."

It probably sounds old fashioned now, but in those days there was just no such thing as rolling out of bed, throwing on sweatpants and flip flops, and shuffling to the car half-asleep. Daddy certainly would have never allowed it, but I wouldn't have allowed it for myself, either. Presentation was—and still is—very important to me, both on and off stage. I really do believe that a lady should always look her best. I see some of these gals go onstage today wearing an old pair of jeans and a T-shirt, and I just can't help but wonder if they're getting ready to entertain an audience or if they forgot to change clothes when they got done cuttin' the grass! I guess things are just different now than they used to be, but I still kind of like the old way of doing things.

Daddy headed out to the car to read the paper while I got ready. I applied a fresh coat of fingernail polish, put on my makeup, and slipped on the three-quarter length yellow skirt I'd laid out the night before. I had a cute matching yellow short-sleeve blouse, which I accented with a black rose pin. I strapped on my heels and opened the door to the motel room to let Daddy know I was ready. "Finally," he smiled. "I think the show's already over by now!" I rolled my eyes and flashed him a big smile.

Four hours later I was standing in that radio station lobby shaking hands with the humorously named new singer. Once all the introductions were made, Elvis and I headed into the studio for our interviews while Daddy went out to the car to listen to the broadcast on the radio. Thanks to my daily show on KLPR back home, I probably had more live radio experience at that point than Elvis had. I wasn't nervous as I answered the deejay's questions, but I was a little distracted. It was hard for me to take my eyes off this new singer from Memphis. I found him very attractive, but he also seemed a little strange in a way that fascinated me. I was certainly drawn to him—and I hadn't even heard a note of his music yet! He had an undeniable charisma, but he wasn't like anyone I'd encountered before. He seemed like a confident man, but also had a boyish charm and slight shyness about him that made for a peculiar mix.

After the radio appearance Elvis and I headed out to the parking lot and said our goodbyes. I told him I'd see him at the show later and headed across the parking lot. I slid into the passenger seat of our Pontiac where Daddy was waiting. I pulled the door shut, but Daddy didn't say anything. He was staring straight through the windshield shaking his head from side to side. "I ain't never seen nothin' like that," he clucked as I followed his gaze and spotted Elvis, with his yellow coat and funny hair, sliding behind the wheel of a bright pink Cadillac. A man driving a pink Cadillac in 1955? This was before there was such a thing as Mary Kay Cosmetics, and nobody had ever so much as *heard* of a pink Cadillac. Elvis might as well have been getting into a rocket ship! Daddy just about drew the line there. "You might should stay away from that one, Wanda," he said flatly. "I think this Elvis character could be a nut!"

Chapter 9

ROCK YOUR BABY

My first show with Elvis was at the Cape Girardeau Arena
Building, and was a benefit for the Southeast Missouri Chapter of
the United Cerebral Palsy Fund. Tickets were only a dollar each.
Dancing started at 8:30, with the stage show scheduled to start
at 10:00. Several of us were on the bill, including Little Willie
Bryan, Johnny Daume and the Ozark Ridge Runners, and Bud
Deckelman. The building held a few hundred people, and it was
pretty crowded by the time I took the stage. I went on just before
Elvis closed the show. At the time, it was just Elvis on rhythm
guitar, Scotty Moore on lead electric guitar, and Bill Black on the
upright bass. This was before DJ Fontana joined them on drums.
Based on his instrumentation I figured Elvis was probably just

another good-looking country singer, even if his style was a little eccentric.

I wanted to hear Elvis's set, but when I left the stage I headed back to the dressing area to freshen up and rest for a moment first. Daddy and I were alone back there when suddenly we heard all this screaming and carrying on. It was like the whole place was in upheaval, and it pretty well scared us half to death. Daddy said, "My gosh, Wanda. I wonder if there's a fire? You gather your things up and sit tight, but get ready to go quick if we need to get out of here. I'll check it out and be right back."

A couple of minutes later Daddy came back with a grin on his face. He leaned against the wall and started laughing. "What is it, Daddy," I asked, "Is there anything wrong?"

He shook his head. "Wanda, you are not gonna believe this. Come on, you've gotta see for yourself."

I followed him out the door, but it seemed like the screams had gotten louder. Daddy led me to the edge of the stage, and I suddenly realized that there was, in fact, a fire. But it wasn't a literal fire consuming the building in flames. It was the heat of Elvis Presley drawing the girls from that audience into the fiery furnace of rock and roll that he was inventing before their very eyes. Those girls were pressed up against the bandstand as Elvis moved and gyrated across the stage, keeping each and every one of them right in the palm of his hand. He knew how to flirt with his fans, and I was fascinated. On top of that, he had such a great voice!

I immediately understood why Elvis made those girls feel the way they felt, but it was still quite amazing to witness it in person. We hadn't seen anything like that before. Frank Sinatra was a heartthrob, but the girls in his audience just fainted. They didn't lose their minds and fling themselves in a hysterical fit toward the stage. My jaw dropped in awe of both Elvis's performing style and the reaction of the crowd. I stayed on the edge of that stage and listened to every last note of the rest of Elvis's performance. His uncanny and seemingly contradictory mix of swagger and shyness cast a spell on everyone. It was almost as if he knew his natural tendency to be bashful was attractive, so he mustered up the courage to harness it with confidence. There was nobody else like him. *Performing with this guy is going to be really nice,* I thought to myself. I couldn't wait to get to the Silver Moon Club in Newport, Arkansas, where I was scheduled to appear with him again the following night. I glanced over at Daddy standing next to me. He didn't look as excited as I felt.

The next day we set out on the three-and-a-half-hour drive from Cape Girardeau down to Newport. The radio was on and neither of us had said much. I was just beginning to doze off somewhere around the Arkansas–Missouri state line when Daddy's voice jolted me awake.

"That boy's got to get his show in order," he stated confidently.

"What boy is that, Daddy?" Of course, I knew exactly who he was talking about.

"That Elvis. He's all over the stage messin' around. And he's got to stop slurring his words, too. Nobody can understand him."

I smiled. "Well, I can understand him." Daddy just shook his head. I don't think they had a term for it yet in those days, but it was on that car ride that I first understood the concept of a generation gap.

Newport, Arkansas's Silver Moon Club was a honky tonk, but it was a nice one. They had an elevated stage that could hold well over a thousand people. The place sold out that night with a crowd that was even larger than the one we'd played for in Cape Girardeau. Once again the girls screamed, squealed, and swooned. It was almost kind of frightening to experience, but seeing what kind of power a performer could have over a crowd intrigued me. Something was stirring within.

When I got home after those first two appearances with Elvis, I was just like every other teenage girl in America who was quickly coming down with a severe case of Elvis fever. I immediately went out and bought his records, and started counting down the days until I'd see him again.

On the first day of August, I was back on the road playing a series of shows with Elvis that had been packaged by Bob Neal. Elvis fever was spreading rapidly. In fact, he had spent the previous week on a tour through Florida headlined by comedian Andy Griffith. There were several other country performers on those shows, including Marty Robbins, Ferlin Husky, Jim Reeves, Jimmy Rogers Snow, and my old boyfriend, Tommy Collins. There's a line in that song Merle Haggard wrote about Tommy that says he once followed Elvis Presley. That's the truth, but you can bet nobody wanted to follow Elvis by the end of that week!

Three days before I saw him again, Elvis was mobbed for the first time at a baseball stadium in Jacksonville. The audience busted through police barriers and chased him to the locker room, managing to get away with his shirt, coat, shoes, ring, and watch. All he was left with were his pink pants, and even those were pretty well ripped to pieces! The Andy Griffith tour wrapped up in Tampa the night before Elvis and I played together once again. That Tampa show was where they took the famous picture of him and his guitar onstage that you see on the cover of his first album for RCA. It's the one that says "Elvis" in pink lettering down the left side and "Presley" in green letters across the bottom. If you can picture that image, then you know exactly what Elvis looked like the day after it was taken when we reunited once again. And if you can't picture it, I'll just tell you. He looked good!

The first show of our package tour was in Tupelo, Mississippi, which was Elvis's hometown before the Presleys moved to Memphis. It was the first time he'd played there since his recording career began, but the headliner for the tour was actually country star Webb Pierce. Elvis received second billing, above Red Sovine and then me. There were a half-dozen or more additional performers on the bill, including Bud Deckelman, who'd been with us in Cape Girardeau, Charlie Feathers, and quite a few local and regional acts. Elvis was dressed in black pants and a light-weight pink coat. He was probably only on stage for about twenty minutes, but we were playing at the fairgrounds, and the crowd was enormous. By the time Webb Piece took the stage to close the show, most of them were gone. And the ones that were left were too excited to concentrate on anything else but what they'd just seen. Webb had been drinking and he was a little off his game that night. But it hardly mattered. He'd already lost that crowd before he started. When Webb finished his set, he made it clear that he would never follow Elvis again. As far as I know, he never did. The remaining four shows we played on that tour all concluded with the rising king of rock and roll closing the proceedings.

The next day, we traveled down to Sheffield, Alabama, to play a couple of shows, and a new artist named Johnny Cash joined us for those appearances. The audience didn't seem too interested in headliner Webb Pierce, and that made Webb, a bona fide country legend, a little mad. I think he left before the show was over. We headed on to Arkansas to play in both Little Rock and Camden. I know most of the crowds were coming out to see Elvis, but I was getting a good reception, too. By the time we got to Camden, I was going on just before Elvis's closing set, and we were both getting multiple encores.

It was after one of the shows on that tour that Elvis asked me out after a show to get a Coke. Of course, I had to ask Daddy. I didn't like all his rules, but I knew he was looking out for my best interest. Daddy said that it would be all right and, after that, he was pretty good about letting me go on a drive with Elvis or catch a movie or something with him if we got to a town early for a show. Daddy didn't mind if Elvis or any of the other guys ever rode with us, but of course I never could ride with Elvis from town to town.

Elvis, Scotty, and Bill usually rode in Elvis's Cadillac. They were just starting to get air conditioning in cars at that time. Up until then we just had to roll the windows down and let it blow. I used to have an Uncle Henry who kept the windows up in the sweltering summer heat because he wanted to impress folks by making them think he had air conditioning! Elvis really did have it, but he wouldn't use it at first because he said it closed up his throat. I don't know if it was because his bandmates threatened to kill him, but I think he got used to it pretty fast.

We usually went out to eat after our performances. I still do that. I've never been able to eat right before a show. A lot of times a group of us would head out together for hamburgers or whatever. One night after a show we went out with Elvis, Scotty, and Bill. The three of them were in the backseat, while Daddy was driving and I was in the passenger seat up front. Elvis liked to tease me, so he started horsing around in the backseat and flipping my ponytail back and forth. That's when we girls were just starting to wear hair pieces. My hair wasn't long enough at the time to make a pretty ponytail, so I got a fake one on a comb and set that over my real one. Of course, we didn't let the guys know our beauty secrets back then, so Elvis thought he was just flipping my hair around. He started coughing and gagging and carrying on.

"Wanda," he joked, "don't you ever wash that ponytail?"

I reached up, yanked it off, threw it in his lap and said, "Here, *you* wash it!" That gave him a pretty good shock. He hadn't ever seen anything like that before, and we all had a big laugh over it.

We finished up the tour playing for several thousand fans at the Overton Park Shell in Memphis. Most of the acts we'd been playing with all week were there, but several others joined us, including Sonny James and Carl Perkins. That afternoon, before the show, Elvis picked me up and took me to his house where he lived with his mother and father. I'm surprised Daddy let me go, but Elvis had pretty well won him over at that point. Though skeptical at first, Daddy had come to see that Elvis was a sincere and polite young man. It doesn't matter who you are, if you were around Elvis for very long, he would win you over. He had a childlike innocence about him and was very respectful. He always said "ma'am" and "sir," and had those Southern manners that fascinated people even back then. I think Daddy got to where he really liked Elvis.

When I arrived at the door of his house, Elvis introduced me to his mother before taking me down the hall to his bedroom. He had a record player and a lot of records stacked up next to it. He had been telling me all week that I should start singing this new kind of music he was doing, but I didn't think I could pull it off. He began playing different records to help me get a grip on the feeling of what he was doing. He told me I needed to let loose and have more fun. That's the same thing Hank Thompson had told me way back at the Trianon Ballroom. I didn't realize I was being uptight on stage, but maybe I was.

Elvis would play an R&B record and then pick up his guitar and say, "Look, instead of playing country style by plucking each individual string, you need to strum all of them at once like this." I had actually started out playing that way, but Daddy said not to do it like that. He taught me to pick the strings, and didn't like me strumming them all at once. After the episode with the felt pick during my recording session in Nashville, I'd done my best not to play so heavy. Elvis wanted me to unlearn. That was my real introduction to how to play rock and roll. Elvis's career was really booming, yet he was still concerned about me and my little career. He knew I loved it so much, and I think he sensed that I would be around for a while in the business. It meant a lot that he took an interest and encouraged something he saw in me that I couldn't yet see for myself.

I've been asked several times over the years what the records were that Elvis played for me that day. Give me a break! I was a seventeen-year-old girl in Elvis Presley's bedroom. Do you honestly think I was paying a lick of attention to remembering what exact records I was hearing? I was just trying not to jump out of my own skin or pass out on the floor like all those girls at his shows. You know how Elvis on stage could drive a young woman to hysterics? Try getting a private concert from him in his bedroom when the physical attraction between the two of you is palpable. I felt like I'd died and gone to heaven. At one point we were interrupted when Elvis's mother tapped on the door and poked her head in.

"Honey, I'm going to the store now," she said. "What would you like for supper?"

Elvis thought about it for a second and said, "I think I'd like some weenies and sauerkraut."

She nodded. "Okay, that'll be fine. I'll be back shortly."

I kind of smiled to myself thinking about how much his family was like our family. The parents' lives were wrapped around their child as they did all they could to support those musical dreams.

Suddenly Elvis and I were alone again. He ran his fingers nervously through his hair. Elvis always seemed to be full of kinetic energy and couldn't stop fidgeting no matter where he was or what he was doing. His restlessness sometimes made me feel a little nervous. He got up from the edge of the bed and removed the needle from a record that was still playing. The room was suddenly silent. It was the first time we had ever been together with no distractions, and the thought of being alone with him made my heart pound so loudly in my chest I wondered if Elvis could hear it. He reached over and shut the door before slinking over to the chair where I was sitting by the record player. He took my hand, interlocking his fingers with mine as he leaned in close. You know what happened next? Well, I'm a lady, and a lady never kisses and tells.

I didn't play with Elvis again until a week-long stint through Texas in mid-October. He was the advertised headliner by that point, and our traveling show included Johnny Cash, Porter Wagoner, Jimmy C. Newman, and Bobby Lord. After a show at the Memorial Hall in Brownwood, we went on to Abilene, Midland, Amarillo, and Odessa.

I wouldn't see Elvis again until April of 1956. I met up with the tour in Denver, Colorado, and we played twelve cities in thirteen nights, usually two shows per day. By that point we were drawing crowds of 5,000 to 10,000 people per show. I remember the third stop on that tour was in Lubbock, Texas, where we staged two performances for a capacity audience at the Fair Park Coliseum. There was a local singer who opened the show, and someone said we should watch him because he was really good. Elvis thought he was just great. He seemed like a nice kid, but he wasn't handsome. I have to admit I was into handsome in those days, so I didn't really appreciate this young man named Buddy Holly until later on. Truth be told, I had eyes for Elvis and that was about it. I didn't yet have the maturity to know what to look for in an artist, and I didn't see the raw talent. I was still kind of boy crazy. Or at least pretty Elvis crazy!

I'm embarrassed to say that Johnny Cash didn't make much more of an impression on me than Buddy did at first. Johnny always seemed like kind of a loner to me. Any time I saw him he was off by himself leaning up against a wall having a cigarette. I didn't go out of my way to try to talk to him, since he was a bit older than me and was already married with a family. To be honest, I didn't really care that much for him at first. Daddy and I both thought he was trying to copy Elvis because he had the same three-piece band configuration Elvis did with a lead guitarist and upright bassist behind his rhythm guitar and vocal. Elvis saw his talent before I did. Any time we were all playing a package show together, Elvis would find me and say, "Come here! We've got to watch Johnny!"

"Oh, I don't even like him, Elvis," I'd say.

He got on to me one time and said, "Johnny's a great talent. I predict he's going to be the biggest name in country music. He'll be a legend."

I would stand there and watch Johnny's show from the side of the stage, while Elvis would squat down with a big smile on his face, just totally engrossed in what Johnny was doing. Maybe I was just too focused on Elvis to see it at the time, but of course he was right in his assessment of Johnny. I came to understand what a powerful entertainer he really was in later years, and we became great friends.

Early in the tour Elvis got word that "Heartbreak Hotel" had officially become his first single to sell more than a million copies. Everything was accelerating for him during that time, and it seemed as if he was on a merry-go-round that was spinning faster and faster with each day. Midway through the tour we played two shows in Amarillo, Texas. Late that night, Elvis and his band jumped on a plane and flew to Nashville for a recording session the next day. I believe they recorded "I Want You, I Need You, I Love You." That gave us one night off, and Elvis and the boys returned in time for the next set of shows in San Antonio.

Somewhere along the way we played both a matinee and an evening performance. I remember it being a Sunday. Between the two shows Elvis asked me if I would step outside with him for a moment. We were in the parking lot next to one of his pink-and-white Cadillacs. "You know I really like you, Wanda," he said as he leaned against the car.

"I like you, too, Elvis," I smiled. He took my hand.

"I was hoping that maybe, if you want to, that you'd be my girl."

Of course, I said "yes" right away. I don't know if he'd even gotten the words out completely, but I wasn't about to hesitate. He was wearing a ring with some itty-bitty chip diamonds in it. He pulled it off his finger.

"I'd be honored if you'd wear this," he said.

Of course, the minute I got back to the motel room that night, I took a simple gold chain from my jewelry box and proudly put that ring around my neck.

I was thrilled to be Elvis's girl, and I was thrilled when we had the chance to play in Oklahoma City near the end of the tour. Apparently, some city officials were warned that Elvis's hip gyrations at the previous night's show in Tulsa were vulgar. The Chief of Police dispatched dozens of officers with orders to stop the show if things got out of hand. That kind of thing really hurt Elvis. He would tell me, "They're taking something fun and trying to make it into something dirty. That's not what I mean by any of it." It would make him pretty angry when he heard that kind of talk because, to him, what he was doing on stage was just dancing and feeling the music. He was angry that they couldn't see that the young people just wanted their own music. Elvis told me what the headlines were in Tulsa. He said, "If they think Tulsa was bad, wait until they see what I do tonight." But, fortunately, the show came off without incident.

The auditorium in Oklahoma City was on the second floor, and when Elvis was coming down the back stairs after the show, it seemed like girls appeared out of nowhere chasing him and trying to touch him. When he finally got in the car he was kind of rumpled up. He had to get his coat back on because they had been pulling at him. Later Mother said, "That poor guy! He's not going to be able to go anywhere." Daddy just shook his head. "Elvis is creating a monster, I'm afraid."

Chapter 10

IF YOU DON'T, SOMEBODY ELSE WILL

When we weren't playing dates with Elvis, Daddy and I were usually out on the road doing country package shows or one-nighters anywhere we could book. To save money we always shared a motel room. These days it would be really frowned upon for a teenage girl to stay in the same room with her father. It *sounds* awful, but we never thought a thing about it. Our family was close, and we'd always lived in cramped quarters. We worked it out so we both had privacy. Daddy stayed dressed, and he didn't really see me dressing, either. He'd wake up before I would and go get breakfast and a newspaper. He'd return to the room, wake me up, then go off and read the paper somewhere while I got ready.

We kept up a pretty aggressive schedule, and Daddy was very helpful to me in those early days of traveling. I appreciated that he always gave me honest feedback about my performances. He didn't just rave about everything or tell me I was great when I wasn't. He could see things that I needed to change, but he knew how to give constructive criticism in an encouraging way. I listened to him because I knew that any suggestions he offered came from a desire to push me to be the best I could be. I valued the fact that Daddy didn't give empty flattery, and that when he gave a compliment he really meant it. If he thought a show went well, he'd come in that night, sit on the foot of the bed, and tell me what a good job I'd done and how proud he was of me.

I've been asked over the years how a little person like me wound up with such a big voice. I can thank Daddy for that. When I started singing there wasn't really any place to perform but honky tonks and dance halls. I'd come offstage and Daddy might say, "I couldn't hear you very well. You've got to sing louder and get in that microphone. I want the guy who's sitting all the way in the back to be able to hear you perfectly clearly." So that was my aim. I learned to really belt it out and sing with power. That wasn't the way the demure ladies of country music did it in those days, but I didn't care. I was never interested in trying to sound like anybody else. Daddy always told me to do it my way and to be who I am. I got a lot of encouragement from him on that.

Daddy wasn't a big talker, but when he did speak, everyone listened. He was a sweet and jovial man, and everyone liked him. As we spent more time on the road together, he began to open up more during our conversations in the car. We'd tell jokes and stories and talk about the music business. We listened to the radio and analyzed the songs together. Our relationship deepened in those years, and I came to really value his insights. Daddy had

what country folks call "good horse sense," and was a bit of a
philosophizer. He had a gift for cutting through all the fluff and
getting to the heart of a problem. Maybe that's just the difference
in the communication styles of men and women. Mother and
I would talk, talk, and talk some more about some issue. Then
Daddy would simply say, "Well, here's the basic problem and what
you can do to fix it." I still find myself saying, "Daddy always
said . . ." I appreciated his input and instruction, and I feel like I
gained a lot from his wisdom.

I always had good crowds because I worked hard. During
every intermission I would walk around and greet people to
get to know them a little bit. That didn't come naturally to me,
but that's what Hank Thompson did. I'd seen him make a point
of working the room every time I performed with him at a
dance hall, and I recognized that the fans loved it. Here was *the*
Hank at their table having a drink or taking pictures. Daddy also
recognized it was an important strategy for connecting with fans
and making sure they'd come see you the next time you were
in town. It wasn't always easy because I'm actually a bit of an
introvert. I didn't always feel like doing it—especially if I was
suffering with menstrual cramps—but Daddy always reminded
me it was part of the job. "This is the job you chose," he'd say.
"You don't have to get up at seven in the morning and punch a
time clock and stand on your feet all day, but this is part of the
responsibilities of your chosen career." I always made sure to
make my way around the whole room and to do it early before
the crowd got to drinking too much. I'd shake hands and see if
there were any song requests, and that kind of thing. As long as I
was in that club, I was "on" and I appreciated Daddy for helping
me stay focused.

Another thing he emphasized was presentation. Daddy wanted
me to dress nicely and conduct myself appropriately any time

we were in public. He liked to see me in those fancy dresses and looking like a star. He was always reminding me to keep my legs together on stage and to remember to carry myself with dignity and class. He had a little pity on me during those long road trips at least. I was young so I could go without makeup. I'd wear my hair in rollers or pin curls, and wear jeans, pedal pushers, or long pants when we were in the car. At least I didn't have to make three-hundred-mile road trips in tight dresses and heels!

I trusted Daddy completely. He couldn't understand why, on the rare occasions I would do a show without him, I would forget to get paid. I just never had a mind for business, and I didn't think about that stuff. I couldn't get interested in anything but music. I can remember several times Daddy would say, "Wanda, don't you want to know how much money you have in the bank?" I'd say, "Well, no, not as long as you know." I figured I was the talent and he was the brains. Together, Daddy and I were Wanda Jackson Enterprises. Mother was our silent partner, holding down the fort at home and working so hard on my stage costumes. They even built me a room off my bedroom that was like a den. I had my record player and my piano in there, as well as a little desk to sign autographs and mail letters and things. My parents were so accommodating and supportive. It was always a family business.

In July of 1955 I performed on the *Ozark Jubilee* for the first time. Hosted by Red Foley in Springfield, Missouri, the *Jubilee* aired on ABC-TV, and was really the only national country music program on television at the time. Broadcast live on Saturday nights, it was a popular show, thanks largely to the strong reputation Red Foley had earned as the host of the *Grand Ole Opry* segment that was carried on the NBC radio network each week.

I was invited to join the cast of the *Jubilee* the following month, which I immediately accepted. The show was less strict than the *Grand Ole Opry* in terms of requiring cast members to be there a certain number of dates per month. Regardless, I was there as many Saturday nights as I could be. It was nearly a three-hundred-mile drive between Oklahoma City and Springfield, but we would generally try to book a show or two nearby when we made the trip.

The *Jubilee* had its own booking agency called Top Talent, which put together package shows of both *Jubilee* artists and stars from Nashville. They began scheduling shows for me across the U.S., but they didn't book me exclusively, so sometimes the schedule could get hectic. I began the month of October, 1955 with an appearance on the *Jubilee,* before heading out for a series of one-nighters that Top Talent booked in Oklahoma City, Tulsa, Witchita Falls, Ft. Worth, and Lubbock. After just one night at home in my own bed, I was back in Springfield to play the *Jubilee* again, before shooting straight back down to Texas for a six-day tour with Elvis booked by Bob Neal. Two days after that Texas whirlwind wrapped up, I was due in Denver to begin a series of one-nighters booked by A.J. Bamford that took me to Salt Lake City, Reno, five cities in California, two cities in Arizona, and a final date in Albuquerque. Two nights after that I was back in Colorado for a date with yet another booker, and then right back to Farmington, New Mexico, three nights after I'd played in Albuquerque. The next morning I was on a plane to Springfield to put in my third *Jubilee* appearance of the month. Daddy and I racked up over 8,500 miles on the car that month alone, which was not atypical during that period. In fact, the following month, we put another 10,000 on it!

When I headed out on the road, I'd work hard and sing hard, so I perspired on stage. I was pretty hard on my clothes, so I'd have to take enough dresses to cover me for the trip. I learned early on that fringe doesn't wrinkle, or at least if it does it doesn't

really show, so fringed dresses became a staple of my wardrobe. I'd
lay out a piece of tissue paper, roll a dress up in it, and pack my
suitcase that way. When we'd come home Daddy would take the
clothes to the cleaners, but there were some that Mother insisted
on hand washing. She said they didn't get them clean enough at
the cleaners. We were often only home for a short period of time,
so it was like a race car driver pulling in for a pit stop. All hands
were on deck, to turn us around and get us back out there in
record time!

One rare morning when I was at home, I poured myself a
bowl of cereal, but I wasn't as hungry as I thought I was. I had
some left over in the bowl.

"Aren't you going to finish your breakfast?" Daddy said.

"No I think I'll just give the rest to Jeepers," I told him. I
called the dog but he didn't come. Daddy kind of raised his
eyebrow, but I couldn't figure out why. "C'mere, Jeepers," I called
a couple more times.

"Well, this is unbelievable," Daddy muttered.

"What is it, Daddy," I asked.

"Wanda, we got rid of Jeepers three months ago, and you just
now missed him," He said.

I felt awful. I really did love that dog, but I wasn't there to take
care of him. My grandmother was staying with us at that time,
and Mother had enough on her plate between her job, keeping
the household going, making my stage outfits, and caring for her
ailing mother, who wasn't able to get around on her own. Jeepers
had been my responsibility since I first got him in California, but
Mother didn't need yet another responsibility.

Later on, my grandmother told me about the day they came
to get Jeepers. Mother had called the dog pound, if you can
imagine. It makes her sound so hard-hearted, which she wasn't,
but we didn't really know any better then. Mama said when the

people from the pound came, she could hear Jeepers barking and squealing. "It was so hard for me to sit there, knowing I couldn't move or get out of my chair, when they took Jeepers away," she told me. That tells you how wrapped up in my career I was and how little I was home to not even realize for three months that my little buddy was gone. I was heartbroken when I figured out what happened, and I never had another pet until many years later.

In December of 1955 I returned to Nashville for another Decca session. It had been over a year and a half since my hit with Billy Gray, and I hadn't been successful in getting another record on the national charts. I was getting great exposure on national television and drawing good crowds at live shows. I was even voted "Best New Female Singer" by *Country and Western Jamboree* magazine's 1955 Reader's Poll, but, for whatever reason, I was struggling to find success on the radio.

That finally changed the following year when I was back on the charts once again. But it wasn't a song from my Decca session in December. In fact, it wasn't even a song I'd recorded. Instead of finally getting to the charts as a solo artist, I got there as a songwriter when Bobby Lord had a Top 10 country hit with a tune I wrote for him called "Without Your Love."

Bobby was a fellow *Ozark Jubilee* cast member who was close to my age, and we became good friends. Columbia Records had signed him in the early '50s and, like I would soon be doing, he cut both country and rockabilly material. We were scheduled for road shows together pretty regularly by Top Talent, and Bobby would ride with us sometimes to help Daddy with the driving. We had a lot of fun. Bobby was just crazy and funny, and we all had a great time together. Daddy trusted Bobby, too. Sometimes, if we had a short trip that was just a quick out-and-back, Daddy would say, "Get in touch with Bobby. If he'll go with you and look out for you, I think I'll sit this one out and stay home for a little break."

Bobby and I were out on the road together one time and got into a conversation about songwriters. I don't think he had ever really applied himself to try to write songs of his own at that point, so I issued him a challenge. I said, "I'll tell you what, Bobby. When I write a song, I like to have somebody in mind that I think would sound good singing it. I'm going to write a song that hopefully you'll like and, if you do, you can record it on your next session. And maybe you can write one for me."

"Okay, it's a deal," he said. "I'm gonna try to write one for you, too."

The next time we saw each other at the *Jubilee* we played our songs for each other, and they were both good. He cut "Without Your Love," and it became the only Top 10 hit that Bobby ever had. Even though everyone liked him and he was a good entertainer, Bobby never got really big. His voice didn't sound real country, and he just didn't reach that "big star" status. I always wished he had. Even though the song he wrote for me, "Did You Miss Me," didn't become a hit, I was proud to have had a hand in encouraging him to write.

The *Jubilee* cast included, at various times, Webb Pierce, Porter Wagoner, The Browns, Leroy Van Dyke, Sonny James, Carl Smith, Hawkshaw Hawkins, Jean Shepard, and Brenda Lee, who was just a ten- or eleven-year-old kid when she joined the show. Because it was such a high-profile TV program, every major country star wanted to work on the *Jubilee.* From Eddy Arnold to Patsy Cline, Lefty Frizzell, George Jones, Little Jimmy Dickens, Faron Young, Ray Price, and just about any other name you can name, I got to stay right there in one place and work with them all! I was never shy about a fan or another artist taking a picture with me, but for me to ask someone else if I could take a picture with them would make me so nervous. I hated to ask Daddy to snap a photo of me and another performer. That's why I only have very few snapshots of all the legendary artists I worked with over the years.

I was meeting at least as many performers playing package shows on the road, and was always eager to watch others' shows to see what I could learn. The country music community was more like a family in those days, and people tended to help one another more often. I remember I was doing a show with Ferlin Husky one time, when he gave me a bottle of Avon's Ambush perfume. He said, "Wanda, you're a young lady now, and you need to wear nice perfume. Don't ever wear that cheap stuff." He said, "Here's something to start with. This isn't a real expensive one, but it's better than what you're using." That just endeared him to me, and I appreciated his honesty. I got to pay that forward with a girl in Sweden several years ago. She was a very good-looking young lady who sang like a bird, but talk about body odor! A lot of Europeans still didn't wear deodorant at the time, so I got her some and said, "Trust me. You need to use this." Another time I had a French photographer who smelled so awful I didn't know if I'd get through the shoot. In that case, I was too scared to even take enough of a breath to make the suggestion!

We'd do these package shows and be out for two weeks at a time, so the guys liked to entertain themselves by pulling practical jokes and getting into trouble. It wasn't ever anything too bad, just nonsense to keep themselves entertained. I remember one time Top Talent sent several of us out for a tour supporting Marty Robbins. Marvin Rainwater, who was a fellow *Jubilee* cast member, decided to pull a joke on Marty on the last night of the tour. During his portion of the show, Marvin told the audience his plan. He said, "Just go along with me." What he did was he got a big card and wrote "laugh and applause" on one side and "quiet" on the other. When Marty came out to do his set, he started delivering his onstage one-liners that usually got a great response. Instead, everyone was silent. Little did Marty know that Marvin was poking his head out from that back curtain holding up his sign. When Marty would say something serious, everyone would break into applause. He didn't know what to think!

The boys could get pretty silly, but most of the time I didn't know what all the jokes were about because I didn't hang out with them much. Daddy would know. He loved to joke and was playful, but he kept me away from all that for the most part. I wanted to be where they were telling jokes, having a drink, swapping stories, and having a great time, so sometimes I felt a little left out. I remember in the early days when we were traveling with Hank Thompson, it was pretty unusual to have dressing rooms large enough to accommodate his band. Instead, they would all hang out on the bus until it was time for the show. If there was a matinee we'd all stay at the theater until the evening. I'd want to go hang out with everybody, but most of the time I didn't get to. Daddy was very protective of me. A man knows men, and I was smart enough to know that. If Daddy said something about some guy, it was probably true. He knew what the guys were talking about when I wasn't around, and that's why he wouldn't let me into the dressing rooms. There were some men that Daddy didn't mind me being around because he knew they were upright guys and more settled. Autry Inman and Charlie Walker come to mind. Sonny James, who was with me on the *Jubilee,* was another one. He was very responsible. But there were only a handful on Daddy's strict security clearance list!

Precisely because of the national exposure I was getting on the show I was offered some opportunities for jobs that would have forced me to leave the *Jubilee.* At one point, Ernest Tubb wanted to hire me as the girl singer with his band. Despite our previous run-in at the Opry, it was tempting. Ernest was a legend

and always drew huge crowds. I would have worked more and
made more money, plus Daddy thought it was a pretty exciting
opportunity. I kept thinking about it. It was getting closer to
the time I had to make a final decision, but every time I'd think
about leaving the *Jubilee* I would just cry and cry. It seemed like
the Nashville people had a clique, and it was easy to feel like
an outsider. At the *Jubilee* we were a smaller group and, gosh,
if somebody got a hit, we were just tickled to death for them.
It seemed that Nashville was more competitive and there was
more jealousy going on, while the *Jubilee* cast was a family. One
time Daddy saw me tearing up in the car and asked, "What's the
problem?"

"I don't want to leave the *Ozark Jubilee,*" I said. I was just
having so much fun and making good friends there. "Daddy,
when I think about leaving it makes me so sad."

Daddy looked at me and said, "Well . . . then don't."

Simple as that. That was his way of cutting through the drama
and getting to the heart of a problem. I needed that kind of
clarity that he brought to my career planning.

In the summer of 1956 Jim Halsey became my booking agent.
He had founded his company with Hank Thompson as his first
client in the early 1950s. I was his second. Over the years, The Jim
Halsey Company would become the largest country music talent
agency in the world, representing a roster that included Roy
Clark, The Oak Ridge Boys, Tammy Wynette, Merle Haggard,
Waylon Jennings, Leon Russell, Reba McEntire, Clint Black,
The Judds, Dwight Yoakam, and too many more to name. Halsey
became so successful he eventually sold his company to the
prestigious William Morris Agency in 1990. Back when I started
working with him, his vision and tireless promotion skills were
the boost that I needed. Daddy had been working with various
bookers on a piecemeal basis, but Halsey was able to consolidate

the efforts and negotiate better fees. Where I had been getting about $75 for a booking, I was now getting $150, $200, and, in some instances, as much as $500 for a single show. At the end of 1955 I'd made a little more than $7,600. With Halsey's help, I doubled my income in 1956, earning over $15,000 by year's end. That doesn't sound very impressive now, but that's the equivalent of nearly $135,000 in today's dollars. I wasn't exactly living in the lap of luxury, but I was working hard, living my dreams, and making a very good living—especially considering I was still a teenager.

Chapter 11

With Capitol Records A&R man, Ken Nelson.

I GOTTA KNOW

My recording contract with Decca Records was a two-year deal with the option for an additional year when the time came. Of course, it's always the *company*'s option, not the artist's option. Even though I hadn't had much luck with them, Decca was interested in extending the agreement. Paul Cohen was a nice man, but he wasn't a musician, and I never felt like he really understood me or did a whole lot for me. I knew from the response I was getting on the road and from my appearances on the *Ozark Jubilee* that I was connecting with audiences. It seemed like my label just wasn't sure how to capitalize on that momentum. I didn't have a lot of faith that things would change on that front if they hadn't already changed after two years. I don't remember the details, but somehow Decca was willing to forego the next option and release me from the contract. Since I wasn't having hits, it probably wasn't too difficult to convince them to let me go.

It was no secret that I'd wanted to be on Capitol Records from the very beginning. To me, that was just the ultimate label. I had been talking with Hank Thompson about it, and he took it upon himself to go back to Ken Nelson, reminded him about me, and let him know that I was eighteen years old and contractually available. It didn't hurt that nearly every single one of Hank's releases became a Top 10 hit, so he had a lot of clout with the label. Ken trusted Hank's instincts, and also liked what he'd seen of my performances on the *Jubilee*. Ken really believed in my talent and my potential, and he thought we could have greater success than I'd had with Decca. In 1956 I became a Capitol recording artist. That made two record deals that Hank Thompson made possible for me.

By the time I traveled to Los Angeles for my first Capitol session in June of 1956, Elvis and I were drifting apart. We hadn't worked together since a two-week stretch of dates through the southwest in April. After the tour Elvis would call me regularly. Mother used to laugh in later years and say, "You used to break your neck to make sure you were home every day at four o'clock when Elvis would call!" He might not have called *every* day, but Elvis did call faithfully. Amazingly, we never exchanged any letters. He was moving around too much, and I was working and traveling to different dates. I wish we had swapped at least a few letters, as that would be a fun memento from that era to have today.

With time, however, Elvis started making movies and was spending more time in Hollywood thanks to his manager, Colonel Tom Parker. Elvis could have been a great actor, so when he got the chance to be in a movie he jumped at it. He did a handful of pretty fun movies before getting drafted. He was stationed overseas in Germany for a couple of years. When he returned, his career took a strange turn. I didn't care much for Colonel Parker. He had Elvis wrapped around his finger, and I never understood that. The Colonel eventually stopped Elvis from doing live shows, and just about ruined his career signing him up for one bad movie after another. They just started churning out the same basic B-movie over and over with Elvis playing himself in different settings. By that point, I was completely out of touch with him. I don't remember telling him goodbye or anything. I think it just sort of fizzled out between us. Thanks to Mother I still have the ring he gave me. After a year or so I didn't know where it was, but she hung on to it and I have it today.

That ring might bring back a few good memoires, but the lasting thing to emerge from my relationship with Elvis, of course, was my awakening to rock and roll. Elvis had been nurturing it ever since I'd first begun touring with him the previous year, and he seemed determined to convert me since that day in his bedroom in Memphis. Elvis was always explaining to me and Daddy that most entertainment was aimed at adults or married couples, but this new kind of music appealed directly to young people. He'd say, "I'm telling you, they have some money now and they're buying the records. They're the ones calling the radio stations requesting songs, and they can make or break you. You need to aim your songs at that audience if you want to sell a lot of records."

I didn't feel confident that I could pull it off. "I don't know if I have the voice for it," I'd tell him, "and, besides, I'm a girl. How would people react? I don't think I can do that kind of music!" But Elvis would always say, "Yes, you can, Wanda. You can *do* this. You'd be great at it." It was Elvis who gave me the courage to try.

My first Capitol session was recorded in the famous Capitol Tower near the intersection of Hollywood Boulevard and Vine Street. The building had just recently been constructed, and I was fascinated by the iconic round design. Now we're used to seeing it in every movie that's set in Los Angeles, but a round building in 1956? It seemed like something from a futuristic science fiction story!

We recorded four songs at the session, three of which were typical country fare of the day. The other selection—"I Gotta Know"—gave me a chance to dip my toes in the rockabilly waters for the first time. The song's intro sounds as country as cornbread with plenty of fiddle, courtesy of Bakersfield's Jelly Sanders, and steel guitar, thanks to the legendary Ralph Mooney, who pioneered the distinctive West Coast country sound popularized by Wynn Stewart, Buck Owens, and Merle Haggard. Then I sang the first note, "Well . . ." With that, the band picks up into a bouncing rockabilly rhythm for the verse, but slows back down into a twangy country waltz for the choruses. Coming out of the second chorus, virtuosic guitarist Joe Maphis played a fantastic rockabilly solo that's probably my favorite part of the record.

Joe was a big influence on a lot of West Coast musicians, and I just loved him. He played on a lot of my early Capitol sessions. He played lead guitar faster than just about anyone in the world, but he was so laid back. One time he showed up to record and was wearing his house shoes! You didn't see that kind of thing in the '50s. He'd sit there. He'd have a cigarette in his mouth, and the ash would get so long on it while we were recording. After a while, he'd look around for an ashtray and would just casually flick the ash in the general direction of the closest one. Someone would finally get an ashtray and put it next to him. He was quite a guy! It's a shame I didn't realize how wonderful these musicians were that I was having the opportunity to work with. I recognize it now, but at the time I was pretty young and just took it for granted. At the time, I was wanting Joe to play more like Scotty Moore or Luther Perkins, who, respectively, gave Elvis and Johnny Cash their distinctive guitar sounds. But now I listen to some of the parts Joe was playing on my records and my jaw just drops. I had one of the best guitarists who ever walked the earth!

"I Gotta Know" was written by Thelma Blackmon, who lived in Oklahoma City. I went to school with her daughter, Vicki. After I started performing on KLPR, Vicki's mom would bring me some songs from time to time. I thought she was really good and I liked the stuff she wrote. She was also tall and dark with black hair and was just a really pretty lady. She was the kind of woman I looked up to. I had recorded a couple of Thelma's songs on Decca, including "It's the Same World (Wherever You Go)" and "I'd Rather Have a Broken Heart." But this one was something special.

At some point I told Thelma about Elvis encouraging me to try my hand at rockabilly music, but I confessed that I didn't really know how to get into it. I had a dilemma because I wanted to venture into a new realm, but I didn't want to lose my country fan base. Unbeknownst to me, Thelma took it upon herself to go off and write a song that blended the two styles together. When she brought me "I Gotta Know," I said, "This is it!" The verses are full of references to "boppity-bopping," "knocked-out music," and "rock and rolling," but it always came back to that country foundation. It seemed like a great way to keep the country fans and attract some new fans, too. It would be a natural segue. I had already jumped into the male-dominated world of country, so it was only natural to take the plunge into rock and roll, too.

"I Gotta Know" was released in July as my first single for the Capitol label. It started climbing the country charts in October and got all the way up to number fifteen in *Billboard*. It's kind of funny that Ken Nelson signed me as a country artist, but we got a hit right out of the gate with a song that incorporated a lot of rock elements. You have to remember, though, that rock and roll was a new thing in the mid-1950s, so it took some time for people to realize it was a category unto itself. Sure, there were plenty of blues and R&B elements in rock, but there was a lot of country, too. It wasn't uncommon for artists like Elvis, Carl Perkins, Jerry Lee Lewis, and The Everly Brothers to place the same song on the country, pop, and R&B charts at the same time. In fact, even though I was embracing rockabilly, I was named the Best New Female Singer for 1956 in both the Deejay and Readers Poll in *Country and Western Jamboree* magazine. The best New Male Singer honors went to Elvis.

After "I Gotta Know" became a hit in the fall of 1956, I was invited to join the cast of the *Grand Ole Opry*. I was faced with yet another decision about whether or not to leave the *Jubilee*, but this time it was just no contest. I wasn't interested. I liked being on television, and I loved my *Jubilee* family. And I have to admit that it felt kind of good to turn the Opry down after my experience there!

In the wake of the song's success, Thelma Blackmon went on to record a few songs as an artist for the MGM label in 1957. And I would go on to immerse myself in rock and roll, but would continue to record country music as well. Ironically, I wouldn't get a single on either the country or pop charts in the US for the rest of the 1950s. I would, however, cut some of my most enduring records and unwittingly create a legacy that, though not commercially successful at the time, would earn me generations of fans and plenty of accolades decades after the fact.

When it came time to return to Hollywood for another Capitol session that fall, we started with a newly written song called "Baby Loves Him." When I say "newly written," I mean that I literally wrote it on the way to the session because I only had three songs ready, but needed a fourth. That was the first rockabilly song I ever wrote. It was the same session where I recorded "Honey Bop" and "Hot Dog! That Made Him Mad." I knew from the reactions I got from my fellow students back in our high school assemblies that my audience would love that one. Ken wasn't sure about it, but I knew that the girls like to hear that type of song where the girl's taking charge. The message was basically telling a guy, "You think you're so hot? I'll show you." There weren't many songs written like that, and I believed in it. Ken conceded and let me do it.

If you search online you can find some grainy footage of me singing "Hot Dog! That Made Him Mad" on a show called *Ranch Party* that was filmed in Los Angeles. The cast was made up of some of the biggest stars on the West Coast country scene, including Johnny Bond, Tex Ritter, Rose Lee Maphis, her husband, Joe—who played guitar on most of my Capitol sessions in the 1950s—and several others. What you'll notice about that performance is that when I get to the title line—what they call the hook—I deliver it with a rough growl.

That's how I intended to sing it on the original session, but it didn't quite come out that way. Ken had called for a quick break just before we recorded that song. They had a little break room there at Capitol, so I went in with the other musicians. Everybody was drinking coffee, but I got a container of milk. I was chugging that milk when Ken came through the door.

"Wanda," he exclaimed, "what are you doing? Put that down! Put down that milk!"

I couldn't figure out why he was so worked up. Did he think the milk was bad or something? It tasted fine to me. I lowered it from my lips kind of sheepishly. I said, "I'm sorry, Mr. Nelson, but I don't understand. Why?"

"Milk ruins your throat for singing," he said. "You won't be able to get your voice to do what you want it to."

And, boy, was he right! By the time we got back in the studio and started recording, that line came out as a rasp instead of a growl. That could have been the day I unleashed the full Wanda Jackson rockabilly growl on the world, but it would have to wait. You can bet that was the last time I drank milk before singing!

Even though a lot of rockabilly musicians were appearing on the country charts, a growing number of older country fans didn't care for the new trend. Rock and roll threw the music industry for a loop. It was like a whirlwind had started, and there I was right smack in the middle of it. There was definitely a backlash, and we artists had to tread that line carefully. I always thought it was kind of silly. Good music is good music no matter what you call it! Whether it be country, rock, blues, or pop, give me a good song and I'm going to love it. You have to feel kind of sorry for Ken Nelson and Capitol Records, however, in terms of knowing what to do with me. They signed me thinking they had a girl country singer, which they did, but then here I was showing up to my second session with all these rockabilly songs! The great thing about Ken, though, was that he signed artists for their talent and then trusted their instincts. He gave good advice, but he didn't try to control me or turn me into something I wasn't. I'll always be grateful to him for that.

The one country song we did record that day was "Silver Threads and Golden Needles." That's one that's been recorded many times over the years. A British group called The Springfields had a Top 20 pop and country hit with it in 1962. Linda Ronstadt took it to the Top 20 in 1974. It's been recorded by The Everly Brothers, Janis Joplin, Dolly Parton, Dusty Springfield, and many others. My version, however, was the first. I included the original second verse that most other versions didn't preserve. I'm not sure why they didn't, but maybe it's because that's how it was done on the best-known version that others began copying. Hank Thompson had that song, which is how I got it. He thought it was a hit, but since it was written for a female, he passed it along to me. Hank was right. It was a hit. Unfortunately, it just wasn't a hit for me.

My second Capitol single had "Hot Dog! That Made Him Mad" on one side, and "Silver Threads and Golden Needles" on the other. For whatever reason, we just couldn't get airplay for either one. Both songs have always gotten great reactions from audiences, and I still perform them to this day. When I do a country-oriented show now, I use "Silver Threads" as the opening song. Even if most folks know it from other recordings, I'm still glad I recorded it and I still think it's a great one.

When I got into recording rock and roll, I never abandoned country. I thought of them as different branches of the same tree, and Capitol really latched onto the practice of releasing one of my rockabilly songs on one side of a single and a country song on the other. I give Ken a lot of credit in being open minded to let me try different things. Because of that I was usually willing to try things that he brought to me, even if I was a bit skeptical. Sometimes, however, there were some things I was really unsure about.

One of those songs was "Don'a Wan'a," which honestly, I "don'a wan'a" anyone to ever hear again. There was a small window of time when calypso music was very popular, thanks to the success of Harry Belafonte. He scored some big hits in the '50s with songs like "Jamaica Farewell" and "Day-O." And, of course, whenever one artist gets a hit with something unique, everybody else then tries to do the same kind of song. "Don'a

Wan'a" was written by Boudleaux Bryant, who was one of the greatest country songwriters of all time. This is probably proof that even the great ones have an off day. I don't know how Ken Nelson got the song, but he wanted me to record it to try to get in on the Calypso craze. He suggested I adopt an islander accent, but it sounded like I was mocking that kind of music. I didn't want to do it at all. I said, "Ken, I feel silly, so it's bound to *sound* silly." I was horrified by the whole thing. Capitol wasn't great at rushing to get releases out, and by the time they did, the record got no attention. I'm not kidding you, it was almost like the day that song was released was the day calypso died. I don't know for sure, but I may have been the one who killed it!

Capitol was still trying to figure out what to do with me, but they maintained faith that I could have strong potential in the teen market. One of the singles they released with that aim in mind was "Cool Love," backed with "You Missed Me." Neither song had much of a country sound. "Cool Love" was one I'd written with Vicki Countryman, my friend who was the daughter of Thelma Blackmon, who wrote "I Wanna Know." There was a fairly short period of time that I went to high school with Vicki. I had to walk home pretty often if the weather was decent and I didn't have a radio show that day. I'd usually walk with some of the kids I was friends with from church and, if I was with them, Mother didn't worry about me too much.

One day it was just me and Vicki, and I had this idea for a song called "Cool Love." We couldn't write anything down while we walked, so we would throw out lines and memorize them as we went. When we got home I sat down at the piano and came up with the melody. That was one of the most unusual songs I ever wrote. It was kind of pop-oriented and just different from the things I usually came up with. When we recorded it, we goosed it up a little bit with a bluesy boogie-woogie-meets-

rockabilly approach with Buck Owens on lead guitar. It didn't
do a thing at the time, but I've recorded that song in Germany
and France, so it turned out to be a good one for me in the long
run. The flip side was "Did You Miss Me," which was a doo-wop
influenced record, and the song that Bobby Lord wrote for me at
the same time I wrote "Without Your Love" for him.

One of the country things I released in that era was "No
Wedding Bells for Joe," which was written by Marijohn Wilkin.
She was another of my friends from the *Jubilee.* Marijohn
later moved to Nashville, where she wrote massive hits such as
"Waterloo," "The Long Black Veil," and "One Day at a Time." I
wasn't able to get a hit with one of her songs, but I'm proud to
be one of the first artists to record her material.

The B-side of "No Wedding Bells for Joe" was "Fujiyama
Mama." I'd wanted to record that song ever since I heard the
original version by a black blues singer named Annisteen Allen.
Her record came out in early 1955 when I was in the final stretch
of my senior year of high school. I met up with some girlfriends
at the drug store in Capitol Hill one day to hang out by the
soda fountain and listen to records on the jukebox. Someone
played "Fujiyama Mama" and I fell in love with it. There was a
good record store in Capitol Hill and they had it in stock. Oddly
enough, Annisteen's version was released on Capitol. I bought it,
took it home, and taught myself to play it immediately.

When I told Ken I wanted to cut the song, he was a little
worried about me singing those words. For one thing, the lyrics
brag about drinking a quart of Japanese wine, smoking dynamite,
and shooting out the lights. That wasn't exactly the kind of thing
people expected from a young girl who was best known for
singing country music. The sexual innuendo was not only strong,
but referenced the destruction of the atom bomb and mentioned
Nagasaki and Hiroshima by name. The war was still fairly fresh in

peoples' minds and Ken was concerned. He didn't think it would be a good thing, but I talked him into letting me do it.

Once we began recording, Ken wanted me to sing it differently than I was doing it. I can't remember if he wanted me to deliver it softer, or maybe change a line or what. Either way, I was getting pretty frustrated. Daddy finally came into the studio. He usually stayed in the control room with Ken, but he came in there and called me aside. He said, "Wanda, this is *your* song. You're the one who wanted to do it, so you need to do it your way. Now you get back over to that microphone, and you just rare back and sing that damn thing the way you want to!"

Daddy's words gave me the freedom to completely let go. I don't know where that growl came from, but I tell people the songs themselves bring out things in our voice we didn't know we could do. Without a carton of milk to thwart me like it had for "Hot Dog! That Made Him Mad," and with Daddy's encouragement, I finally unleashed my full voice in the studio that I'd been bringing to the stage. And it worked! That record has become a classic and is the one I think of as the start of the fully unbridled rockabilly version of Wanda Jackson that fans know me for today.

Chapter 12

LET'S HAVE A PARTY

In April of 1957 I set out on a month-long tour with Johnny Cash, Carl Perkins, Jerry Lee Lewis, and Onie Wheeler, who was recording for Columbia Records at that time. We started off in Des Moines, Iowa, before making our way up into Canada for a series of ten one-nighters. We appeared in Billings, Montana, working our way back down South, where we all appeared on the *Big D Jamboree* in Dallas. Forget about the stage, the real show was going on after-hours with Johnny and Jerry Lee. Those guys would tear up hotel rooms like you wouldn't believe!

Jerry Lee, in particular, was a wild man. If you didn't watch him, he'd rip up everything in sight! I remember one time we got to a job in the early afternoon. Jerry Lee always went in early to check out the piano. He'd get so mad if it hadn't been tuned or if a key was stuck or something. We didn't have riders in our contracts then, so you had to wait until you got to a gig to find out if they'd supplied everything you needed. I was there listening to him try out this one particular piano, and, boy, was he mad. It was an old upright that had seen better days. He said, "Who would bring a piano like this and expect me to play it? I'll tear this thing up before my show's over so nobody else will have to use it. I'm gonna put it out of its misery." And he did, too, boy. He kicked the bottom of it in, put his feet up on those keys and busted as many of them as he could. He kind of frightened me. I didn't want to be around Jerry Lee too much.

Somewhere along the way on that tour we did a Sunday matinee and didn't have an evening show. I had seen a little church close by where we were staying. I told Daddy I'd like to go to church that evening, but he wasn't interested. I said, "I'll ask if anybody wants to go." I'm sure he probably laughed to himself at that one since those boys weren't exactly big churchgoers at that time.

"Okay, but hold on a minute," he said. "Let me go let them know you have something to ask them."

He went back where all the guys were hanging out and drinking and doing whatever else those boys were doing that Daddy did his best to shield me from. He cleared the way and made sure everyone was dressed.

"Fellas, Wanda wants to ask y'all something," he said.

I went in to a dressing room where they were all hanging out. I said, "I'm gonna go to church tonight. Who would like to go with me?" Dead silence. I said, "Well, okay. I just wanted to let y'all know in case anyone wanted to come along." Everybody looked at the floor. I turned to go. As I was walking away I heard a voice behind me.

"Hold it, Wanda, hold it." I turned around. Jerry Lee was getting up from his chair. "I'd like to go to church with you," he smiled.

I didn't know what to say as we walked down the road to that little church. I was kind of hoping maybe several of the boys would have come along. The prospect of being alone with Jerry Lee was pretty scary to me, but once we started walking, he was a perfect gentleman. We slipped into the service a little late and sat in the back. We shared a hymnbook and sang those great old songs together that had been part of both our formative years. It was really sweet, and that memory is very dear to me. Of all the people, it was Jerry Lee who went to church with me. We've since become good friends, and I always enjoy seeing him. We're about the only two left from that group.

Not too long ago Jerry and I were booked for a show in London in one of the old theaters that had recently been refurbished. The dressing rooms were on the second floor, and they didn't have an elevator. I'd been having problems with my knees, so there was no way I was going to get up those stairs. They started hustling around, trying to figure out what to do. My husband, Wendell, said, "We don't need anything fancy. She just has to have a little room where she can leave her jacket and her purse, and so she has some place to go." The manager had this little cubby hole of an office on the first floor. It was tiny, but it was better than nothing. They set me up in there, and even put a sign with my name on it on the door for me. We hadn't been in there too long when the door opened and Jerry Lee stuck his head in. He said, "Wanda, can I share the dressing room with you? I can't get up those damn steps!" We had a good laugh over that one. It's a long road from kicking the piano to pieces to not getting up the stairs. That day was probably the most I ever talked to Jerry Lee over the years.

Jerry Lee's sister, Linda Gail, was with him at that show. She told me I was the one who gave her the courage to start singing, and even to work with Jerry. She said she always loved the music her brother did, but assumed that since she was a girl she couldn't do it. She said, "You were working with Jerry somewhere and I saw you perform. It was such a thrill because I said, 'Okay, I can do it.' I thank you for paving the way." I guess I was taking the hits for the other gals so they could get into rock music, too. It certainly wasn't always easy.

By 1958, a lot of country fans were giving us rockabilly people a hard time. It was becoming obvious that country and rock were moving in different directions, and I just flat out could not get my records played on the radio. I guess the rock deejays thought I was too country, and the country deejays thought I was too rock. Plus, a lot of people did not think a girl just moving from her late teens into her early 20s should be shaking her hips in silky clothes and singing that "nasty" music. There were plenty of folks who thought rock music was straight from the devil! Sure, some of the songs were suggestive, but gosh, if you listen to those traditional country songs, they were all about cheating and drinking. They didn't exactly have the moral high ground over rock and roll.

Even though I was innocent about the world in a lot of ways, I knew that some of the rock material I was recording was a little racy. That didn't bother me. When you're singing a song, it's similar to an actor playing a part. You get into the character, and you embody that story. I knew exactly what I was doing. I wanted to be the Marilyn Monroe of country music who could bring that rockabilly energy and sex appeal into the genre. All I had to work with was my voice, my body, and my outfits. I liked being that person, and I liked the control it gave me. People look back now and say I was a fireball onstage in the '50s because I brought raw energy to my music in a way that women weren't really doing at the time.

I don't remember either one of my parents having a problem with rock and roll like so many parents did back then. Mother had a very simple mind-set. She didn't go very deep in terms of why someone would do one thing or another. She didn't overthink it too much. She thought the songs were cute, and she always liked my up-tempo material. And Daddy, of course, understood the business aspect of it. He knew rock and roll was popular, so he encouraged me to pursue it. He probably thought it was a little controversial, but he knew that getting people talking was an important thing in building a music career.

I had that idea of being a lady drilled into me, and I liked that aspect of my personality. But I had this other side that was kind of raging and wanting to get out. The stage was my outlet. I felt so comfortable onstage unleashing this other side of myself. I just wish I had fought a little harder for some of the things I wanted. There was so much more I wanted to do on stage, but they were things that were unheard of at the time. I wanted to have staging with the band on risers. I wanted to come down a stairway onto the stage like Marilyn in *Diamonds Are a Girl's Best Friend*. I wanted fans blowing my hair like Beyonce does now, but nobody would have even entertained that concept all those years ago. Even if they did, there was no way to transport those kinds of props at the time when we were traveling from city to city in a four-door sedan.

I did what I could with what I had, but nobody else did much of anything. I would have been considered feisty if I'd done nothing but tap my toe, never mind moving my hips like a female Elvis. Kitty Wells just barely breathed. Same with Jean Shepard. Those were the only two girls who were popular. I was the third one to come along and, even though they both did better in country music than I did, neither of them had rock music to fall back on over the years. Country music has taken some dives, and there have been times when it wasn't popular at all. Those have been the moments when my rockabilly fans have stayed loyal. I'm proud that I was forging a path in both fields, and it served me well in the long run.

In retrospect, I've been called the first sex symbol in country music. I'm proud of that. I've often thought, *Well, they didn't know it at the time. They didn't recognize it for what it was. They tried to hush me up, but I stayed steadfast and hung in there even when I couldn't get a hit. I remained true to my own voice and my vision, and I stuck to my guns.* Daddy liked that I didn't copy anyone else, but it probably limited me at the time. It took a lot of years before folks looked back and appreciated what I'd done to pave the way without reaping any immediate benefits.

Perhaps that's why I've always been a bit of an outsider in Nashville. Looking back, I realize I didn't really play shows in the deep South very often back in the 1950s. Even though I was very country, I had more of a West Coast sensibility about my music. Maybe that was a good thing, because I didn't feel constricted by Nashville's rules, but I think my career probably suffered somewhat. The truth is I couldn't have been put in that narrow box. I wanted to push boundaries and try new things.

My wide range of musical interests was making it trickier for Capitol to know what to do with me. Ken decided I should record an entire album, along with a handful of singles, over the course of four days in April. The album that would become my self-titled debut included pop material, such as "Let Me Go Lover," which had been a hit for Patti Page, and rock covers like "Long Tall Sally" and "Money, Honey." Most of it, however, was country. One of the songs I cut was "Heartbreak Ahead," which is the song I'd cut on my original demo when I first recorded at

Hank Thompson's home studio in 1953. I guess Ken figured we'd keep throwing darts and see what stuck.

Another song we recorded for the *Wanda Jackson* LP was "Let's Have a Party." I wasn't planning to do it, but we had a little extra time on the recording session and were trying to figure out what to cut. We thought about it and thought about it, but nothing came to mind. Finally, I said to Ken, "This isn't really country, but how about 'Let's Have a Party?' I've been opening my show with it recently and people really like it."

Even though Elvis had included the song in his movie *Loving You,* that's not how I knew it. In fact, I didn't even realize Elvis had recorded it. I became familiar with "Party" through Larry and Lorrie Collins, who performed as The Collins Kids on *Town Hall Party* in Los Angeles. Though it was just a local TV program broadcast from Compton's Town Hall, the show was extraordinarily popular on the Coast. It was the *Grand Ole Opry* of California, but it embraced an edgier and more rockabilly-oriented sound than the country music community back east. The *Town Hall Party* cast was always good to me. The house band, led by Joe Maphis, was fantastic and worked really hard to get the songs right. I always felt welcome when I was there, and felt a kinship with Lorrie Collins, who was one of the only other girls singing rockabilly at the time. She was dating Ricky Nelson. I guess we had something in common as females making our way in a male-dominated genre while dating guys who were a big part of creating the blueprint for rock and roll. I always liked Ricky's music, but I only ever worked one show with him, which was down in Houston. I wish we'd had the chance to work together more often.

Ken listened to "Let's Have a Party" and said, "I don't know. It doesn't really fit with the rest of the album." He was right. I basically screamed my way through the song, which didn't make a lot of sense on an album of predominantly country material. But we didn't really have a lot of other ideas. Finally, he said, "Okay, go ahead and do it." We were getting close on time, so I think we did it in one take. It's all we had time for.

Once we finished up the album, we spent a day recording a handful of songs intended for singles, including my rockabilly originals, "Mean Mean Man" and "Rock Your Baby." Though I had recorded a couple of originals since getting into rockabilly, those were country songs I came up with and later adapted to the new style. I hadn't really focused on trying to write songs from scratch that were specifically formulated for rockabilly. I finally had to do it out of necessity, since there just wasn't much material available for a girl rocker. I could change the gender on some of the guys' songs, but I was always trying to find another "Fujiyama Mama," or something a girl could do. I knew I wasn't going to get a hit copying Chuck Berry, Little Richard, or Elvis, but I wasn't sure where to turn.

One day Daddy said, "Wanda, you've been writing country songs for a long time. Since we can't find any material, why don't you just write some rock songs?"

At first, I thought he was crazy. I said, "I can't write that kind of stuff."

"Well, I've listened to these songs and they sound real simple to me," he said. "Most of them are just three chords. I think you could write one real easy. I even have an idea to get you started. Write one about a mean boyfriend doing something you don't like, but you think you love him anyway."

He showed me the beat he had in his head, and that got me started. Pretty soon, I realized I could do it.

"Mean Mean Man" was my first one, but "Rock Your Baby" was written soon after. Honestly, I didn't really ever consider myself a songwriter, but if I got a good idea for how to say something, or if I thought of a good title, I would write a song around it. I love words. I love rhyming and stringing words together, even if there are folks who are a lot better at it than I am. I never had the discipline to say, "Well, next week I'll sit down and write songs for my new album." For me, the songs that come in quick bursts are the only ones that are any good. If I have to work on a song for a couple of days, that means I'm laboring over it. That's when I know there's probably nothing there. A lot of times those were the songs where I would just toss them. For a song to work it has to just flow out of you. Those are the ones that are rare, but they're also the ones that have the most power.

My rockabilly records are considered classics among fans of the genre today, but after "I Gotta Know," the rest of the 1950s were a commercial dry spell for me in terms of getting a hit. Capitol released a dozen singles before the decade was out, but we weren't having any success. In fact, they didn't even schedule any recording sessions for me at all in 1959. I guess Ken Nelson had plenty in the can, and they likely weren't looking to invest more time and effort in an artist who wasn't proving particularly successful compared to some others on their roster.

At the very same time the Capitol Records executives were scratching their heads over what to do with me, I was finding international success in the unlikeliest of places. I landed my first number one hit in 1958, but not in the US. Would you believe that my first chart-topping hit and taste of superstardom actually came from halfway around the world?

Chapter 13

FUJIYAMA MAMA

In January of 1959, Mother and Daddy and I moved from our house on Southeast 35th Street in the South Lindsay neighborhood of Oklahoma City to a bigger home about two miles away at 525 Southwest 42nd Street. Daddy was always very careful with money and refused to buy anything we couldn't afford to pay for with cash.

The idea of avoiding credit was drilled into my head at an early age. I forgot how old I was, but I was already working and making ten or twelve dollars here and there. Daddy opened up a savings account for me, and that's where all that money went. Hope chests were a big thing back then. You had to have that hope chest before you got married. There were some dishes I liked and I was showing Daddy, saying, "Look here, there's all these pieces and it's just three hundred dollars."

"Do you really want them?" he asked.

I was sure about it. I said, "Oh, yeah, I want 'em. And I can pay for it for just five bucks per month."

"No, we don't work that way," he said. "You've got a little over three hundred dollars in your savings account, so if you want them you'll pay for them outright, but that will take almost all your money."

I realized I didn't want them that bad after all.

Daddy's financial cautiousness caused some friction between him and Mother because she really wanted to move somewhere with a two-car garage. That would have cost more money, so Daddy refused. Mother said, "All right, Tom. That's fine. If you'll only agree to a house with a one-car garage that's okay with me. But I get the garage!" And that's what happened. Mother really liked to keep her car looking good and shiny, and Daddy knew it was a serious matter for her. He built a carport onto the side of the house for the second car. When she wanted to build a laundry room, Daddy wouldn't splurge for that either. He said she was fine doing the wash in *her* garage!

It was a stressful time to move. Just a few days after we relocated to the new house, I had to pack for my very first trip overseas. Despite the worries Ken Nelson had about the song offending people, the Japanese branch of Capitol Records issued "Fujiyama Mama" with a picture sleeve that showed my photo next to a cartoon drawing of Mount Fuji. After my record hit number one in Japan, Daddy and I were invited for a seven-week tour starting in Tokyo. I always loved Oriental style, and Japan was the only foreign country I can remember ever wanting to visit when I was growing up. My bedroom was decorated with Japanese furnishings, including a beautiful privacy screen. I just loved that look and was fascinated by the culture. We had to leave poor Mother at home to unpack all the boxes, but she was so organized and had her particular way of doing things that she was probably glad to have us out of her way!

On January 27 we flew from Oklahoma City to Los Angeles to change planes. At that time a lot of the airline gates were outside, so you might not even go into the terminal when you were traveling through a city. This was when airplanes were powered by propellers, but when we landed at LAX and were headed to another gate to catch our next flight, we noticed there was a buzz going around and people seemed to be gathering for something. They were saying there was going to be a jet airplane landing soon and everyone was really excited. "A jet plane," Daddy whistled, "I'd sure like to see that." We headed over to where everyone was congregating. While we were watching the jet descend, there were a couple of guys standing behind us.

"Man, how does that thing fly?" one of them asked. "It's got no propellers!"

"Yeah it does," the other one said. "They're just going so fast you can't see 'em."

We just couldn't imagine how a plane could possibly fly without propellers!

Once we left Los Angeles we took another flight to Hawaii, where we changed planes once again and flew from there on to Japan. It was pretty late when we finally landed in Tokyo. We were rolling along the tarmac when Daddy said, "Boy, they're going all out for somebody here." I looked and saw a lot of people gathered on the observation deck waving, as well as a bunch of photographers. I thought maybe they were hoping to spot a jet airplane landing there, too. Daddy said, "There must be some kind of dignitaries on our plane." Once we got up to the gate, they opened the door and I stepped out onto the stairs. Daddy was right behind me when he leaned over and nudged me. "Baby, you better start smiling. I think this is all for you!" That's when I realized they were calling my name, and all those flashing cameras were snapping pictures of me! I knew that "Fujiyama Mama" had been a success, but I had no idea I was a big star in Japan. We didn't have the global media then that we have today, so I had no way to know.

The pictures of me coming off that plane are kind of funny compared with today's standards for travel attire. Even though we'd just spent thirty-two hours flying, I was wearing a nice red dress, high heels, a mouton fur coat, and a half hat with little feathers. We had to have our hats! And, of course, gloves and a big purse. I was so put together. I wouldn't dress like that for thirty-two hours of flying anymore, but I was sure glad I happened to be dressed up at the time. I would have never imagined that I'd be getting the most attention of my life the moment those plane doors opened.

Once we got inside the airport we were greeted and welcomed by the promoters who booked the various shows I would be doing across the country. Someone said they had set up a press conference for me, but I barely even knew what that meant. "Oh, you don't mind, do you?" they asked.

I told them I'd be happy to do it, but I had to ask, "Will somebody be there with me to translate?" Here I was about to give a press conference for the very first time for members of a press who didn't even speak the same language I did. It was all quite overwhelming! They assured me I would have an excellent translator and that everything would be fine.

When the interviews began, someone from the press would ask a question in Japanese. My translator would convey it to me in English, I would respond, and he would then give them my response in Japanese. Someone asked a question and the translator kind of hesitated. He said, "You may not understand this question, but they want to know if you mind people throwing things at you when you're on stage." I must have looked a little horrified. He said, "Just smile, I'll explain it to you later, but it's all right." He made up an answer for me and then we moved on to the next one. I forgot to come back and ask him what they were talking about, but I would find out soon enough.

One of the first jobs we worked in Japan was at a Tokyo military base. We were driven there by Japanese promoters who spoke English. The three of them got in the front seat of the car while Daddy and I rode in the back. After some polite conversation, they began speaking to one another in Japanese. They were talking so fast and, of course, we didn't speak the language, so Daddy and I had no idea what was going on. Finally, Daddy tapped my leg and whispered, "Hey, Wanda, let's have some fun." He started talking to me in Pig Latin and I responded in kind. We were going back and forth as fast as we could when those guys up front all started looking at one another. When they realized we weren't really speaking English, one of them said, "What is that you're speaking?" Daddy and I had a good laugh. We tried to explain what we were doing, but it's hard to explain something like Pig Latin! I don't think our humor translated.

I didn't take any musicians with me for the trip. They had arranged for a group of Japanese players to travel with me, and they were really good. I have pretty high standards when it comes to backing bands, and these guys were solid. I didn't even take a guitar, figuring they would certainly make one available. I had only ever played acoustic guitar, but all they could round up for me was an electric. I'd never played one in my life, but I guess the notes are all in the same place, so I made do. After a couple of shows I was pretty comfortable with it.

After performing at some military bases and dance clubs in Tokyo, we headed to Osaka for a weeklong run at the Daigeki

Theater. The first night was such a strange experience for me as I learned about the difference between Japanese and American audiences. There was a walkway that jutted out into the audience. I was out there singing when, all of a sudden, different girls from the audience started to come up on the stage to bring me small gifts. I remember a little net with tangerines in it. Others brought some dolls, and one even brought a handkerchief with embroidery on it. I didn't quite know what to do. I'd never had fans climb onto the stage with me before. I'm very protective of my stage, so I didn't know what to think at first.

I noticed the audience didn't applaud very much, but they seemed very appreciative of my performance. I was singing a song near the end of the show when a small object suddenly fell at my feet. It seemed like it came from the balcony. Then another one appeared. Before long there were all these unraveled streamers everywhere. I asked my translator about it when we got offstage. "Oh, yes," he said. "That's what they were asking about at the press conference when someone asked if you liked having people throw things at you when you're on stage. That's our way of showing acceptance and appreciation. If you can reach out and hold one, then do so, but if you can't that's all right." I thought that was really interesting. They might not have clapped, but these little crepe paper streamers were their way of connecting with the performer. They would hold on to one end, and you could kind of play tug-of-war with them. I had certainly never encountered anything like that in an Oklahoma honky tonk, but once I understood it, I really enjoyed it.

After a week in Osaka we went on to Nagoya, Toyama, Kanazawa, and back to Tokyo. We took trains to a lot of these different places, and the Japanese people really endeared themselves to me along the way. They were so interested in me, and I just loved them. I remember going to a department store to get some things I needed. I was walking around trying to find something and noticed there was a small crowd following me. Every time I looked back the crowd was getting bigger. They didn't disturb me; they just wanted to see what I was doing. They were taking pictures and watching my every move. I had never experienced anything like it. When we played the military bases, they were American audiences, but when we performed in theaters I don't know if the Japanese audiences could really understand anything I was saying. It was a complete mystery to me why they liked me so much, but I'm glad they did!

Somewhere along the way, Daddy and I went to a little club that featured country music. I can't remember if I was working there or if we just decided to go, but it was amazing. They couldn't speak a word of English, but were singing American country songs phonetically and doing a great job. I got up at one point to go to the restroom. When I walked through the door, it was men on one side and women on the other. I went to the women's side, but when I walked out of the stall, there were all these men in there! I thought, *What in the world is this?* They started moving toward me and saying, "Autograph? Autograph? Autograph?" I just had to laugh. It gave me a little glimpse of what Elvis must have gone through every single day. It was fun to live like a superstar for a few weeks, but I don't think I would want that to be my life every day.

After a couple of days back in Tokyo, we took a train down to Okinawa. There was an American military base there, so we got acquainted with some of the soldiers. We were doing a theater show in Okinawa for a couple of weeks, and it was nice to get a little taste of home. The guys would come out to where we were staying, have drinks with Daddy, and listen to his stories. He always kept people laughing, and I think he really enjoyed creating an environment around us that was more familiar to him.

I thought Japan was an exotic wonderland, but Daddy was just a farm boy from Oklahoma, and I think he felt like a fish out of water sometimes. He was just big enough that we'd go in these little tea houses and he'd be knocking everything over with his knees. And he had a terrible time remembering to bow when greeting someone. He used to say, "I don't know how many people I gave a black eye to when they went to bow and I accidentally extended my arm to shake hands at the same moment!"

Daddy always liked to eat a good breakfast. I remember we were at one of the Japanese hotels one morning when he headed down to the restaurant while I slept. When he came back he said, "I had the damndest time I've ever had trying to get something to eat. I wanted rice, so I figured they could get me a bowl of rice and some milk for sure. Well, it wasn't easy at all. First, they brought out a big ball of rice on a plate. I told them I wanted it in a bowl, but then they brought out a bunch of little tiny bowls of rice. I didn't know what I was gonna do!"

Eventually, one of the promoters met him at the table, and Daddy finally got him to understand what he wanted so he could translate. The waiter brought a large bowl of rice to the table, with a glass of milk and some sugar. "Well, I poured that milk over the rice and mixed in the sugar," Daddy continued, "and that promoter practically gagged. He made the funniest face. He'd never seen nothin' like that before! He sure didn't know what to make of this ol' boy!"

The next day the promoter told us that he'd explained to his kids how he'd seen Daddy pour milk and sugar over rice, and they insisted on trying it. "It was pretty good," he told us with a wink. I don't think it's too uncommon for people to eat that in Japan today. Maybe Daddy is responsible for introducing them to a little Oklahoma country breakfast tradition!

I'm sure it wasn't easy for Mother to be working every day and settling into a new house while her family was halfway around the world in Japan for more than a month and a half. I appeared on several TV shows while we were there, and one of them worked it out to call Mother so I could talk to her on the air. That was a lot of fun and it was good to hear her voice. As great a time as we were having, I think that made me and Daddy a little homesick.

One of the things I did in Japan to feel more connected to home was reignite my interest in photography. I had taken a course in high school for a half credit, and it was probably my favorite class. I just loved learning about the camera's settings, F-stops, and the differences in various lenses. I even developed my own photos by turning the bathroom of our little house in South Lindsay into a makeshift dark room. It wasn't until Japan, though, that I got my first really good camera. I bought a Pentax, and this Japanese guy who was traveling with us showed me how to use the settings. He took some photos of me to demonstrate what a good, clear picture it could capture, and I was amazed. There's one of me jumping in the air, but the shot was crystal clear. Of course, today I have a camera on my phone that probably takes even better photos than that, but at the time, it seemed like a miracle. For the rest of the trip I was taking photos and practicing with that camera. Had I not been a singer, I think I would have enjoyed being a traveling photojournalist.

We finished the tour back in Tokyo for a six-night run at the Kokusai Theater, which held five thousand people. There was a huge mural outside one of the theaters with my picture on it. I'd never seen a photo of myself that large before, so it was exciting and strange.

These final Tokyo shows were the most elaborately produced of the whole trip, with choreography and a few costume changes. We spent considerable time rehearsing the day before the show began. The promoters had some very definite ideas about the presentation, and I pretty much went along with whatever they wanted since I was working for them. For "Fujiyama Mama" they had me enter the stage on a rickshaw. We had elaborate backdrops, dancers, and the works. They even put me in this cowgirl outfit

I didn't want to wear. If they'd let me design it, there would have been more fringe and less material! I was horrified when I saw it had matching gloves and everything. I probably said I wouldn't wear them, but Daddy likely talked me into it.

The Japanese dancers on the show taught me how to put a robe around my shoulders to wiggle in and out of costumes when guys might be around backstage. That was a helpful skill I would use many times in subsequent years. They also taught me that if you put a little sparkle right along the edge of your lips, it makes them look wet when you're onstage. This was before lip gloss and all the tools we have at our disposal now, so I brought that tip home with me, too.

Another beauty tip I picked up in Japan was how to back-comb my hair. I got my hair done while we were there, and this woman was ratting it with her brush. I thought, *What in the world is she doing?* Of course, we couldn't communicate with each other, so I just let her do whatever she was doing. When she combed it over, I was amazed. My hair looked so big! At the time, you needed to have big hair if you were gonna be a girl singer! I was thrilled.

Despite being a big star in Japan, I think I was only paid $100 per show. If I remember correctly, I believe I performed thirty-six shows while we were there, so you can do the math to figure out that the glitz and glamour of show business isn't always what people imagine. But, of course, I would have done it no matter the pay. It was such a wonderful trip, and I look back on it as one of the fondest memories of my life. I always joke that I loved playing in Japan because it's the only time I was the tallest person around. Of course, the real reason I loved it is because the fans were so wonderful to me and made me feel like the most special person in the world. I think it rained every day we were there, but I recall everything being beautiful, thanks to the radiance of the people. I will never forget their kindness. That wonderful nation holds a very special place in this Fujiyama Mama's heart!

Chapter 14

With my band, Bobby Poe and the Poe Kats, and other musicians.

BOTH SIDES OF THE LINE

When I got back from Tokyo in April of 1959, I did a three-week run of shows at the Showboat in Las Vegas with Bob Wills and the Texas Playboys. Not only did they play their own sets, but they also served as my backing band when I did my part of the show. Bob even stayed out on stage with his fiddle and trademark cigar. I was really excited to have the chance to play with Bob and his legendary band. After all, this was the group I was so impressed with as a child when Mother and Daddy took me to those dances in Los Angeles. It's not an exaggeration to say that Bob's band played a big role in planting the seed in my mind that I wanted to be a girl singer one day.

As exciting as the idea of performing with The Texas Playboys might have been, the reality was not exactly ideal. Those guys were an amazing Western swing band, but they couldn't get the feel for "Fujiyama Mama" or "Hot Dog! That Made Him Mad" to save their lives. It was awful. I wish I could sugarcoat it or put a positive spin on it because I wanted it to be amazing. But it was just absolutely terrible. That was the moment I decided it was time to do something about my stage show.

During those first few years of touring, I played with pickup bands wherever I performed. Sometimes, if I was on a package show, there was a house band that performed with us at the various tour stops. Other times, the regular band at a nightclub where I was playing might step in to back me up. In some instances, the show's booker might put together a group of players from the local musicians' union. I met and worked with some great players in those years, but you never knew what you were getting until you arrived at the venue.

I remember one time I arrived at a club for a rehearsal with the house band before that night's show. When we pulled up the guys were out having a cigarette in the parking lot. They told me they were all set up, had tuned their instruments, and were ready to go when I was. I was impressed by their professionalism and decided I liked these boys immediately. We started swapping stories like musicians do and, for some reason, I wound up saying, "I'll tell you one instrument I just can't stand, and that is a dang accordion!" Everybody laughed and we went on talking for a few minutes.

Finally, the leader of the group said, "Well, let's head on in and get started."

"That sounds great," I said, "but I didn't even get you boys' names and what instruments you play yet."

They went around the circle, and the last fellow said, "My name's Chet and I'm the accordion player."

Whoops. Like I said, you never knew what you were going to get. That was a good band, and ol' Chet was a good accordion player, but it just never was my thing.

Even though I ran into some really good pickers, I just as often encountered some real disasters. Sometimes we couldn't get into town in time to rehearse, but there were plenty of instances where we were stuck with a group that just didn't *want* to rehearse. It's embarrassing to me to go onstage with a band that's not any good. My audience has paid their hard-earned money to see a good show, and I want to give them the very best.

By late 1957 I was getting tired of the endless gamble of using pickup bands. Daddy and I talked to my agent, Jim Halsey, who suggested I find a good group and take them on the road with me. The challenge was that I needed guys who could play both country and rock and roll, but he said he knew of a band that played extensively around Kansas and Oklahoma that would fit the bill. Halsey introduced me to Bobby Poe and the Poe Kats, and we hit it off. They started touring with me and opening my shows. Then they would back me up for my set.

In addition to Bobby Poe, the band included teenagers Vernon Sandusky on lead guitar, Joe Brawley on drums, and a black piano player named "Big" Al Downing. This was a time when you hardly ever saw interracial bands outside of the jazz world. I wasn't raised to be prejudiced, and it didn't bother Daddy at all. Mother, however, was from a different time and a different mind-set. She was a good-hearted person, but there wasn't much of an opportunity for cross-racial interactions in her world. She was polite, but she didn't really know what to make of this new situation, which was pretty unusual in 1957. I remember the first time the band came by the house for a rehearsal. Mother was a little horrified that the neighbors might see Al coming in and out of our house. With time, however, she came to love him, and she was able to move past some of those unfortunate attitudes of an earlier time.

It wasn't always easy for Al when we were out on the road as a mixed-race band. America was a segregated country in the 1950s, and he often couldn't eat in the same restaurants and cafés where the rest of us did. He'd tell the other guys what he wanted to eat, and they'd bring his food out where he'd eat in the car. He couldn't use the same restrooms or drink out of the same water fountain. It was heartbreaking for me to get a glimpse into a world I hadn't really had to think much about before. It made me mad to think that this great guy would be treated so disrespectfully for absolutely no reason but the color of his skin.

I worked at quite a few NCO clubs on military bases in that era, and I recall a particular show we were doing up in Montana or Wyoming. We didn't have any kind of road manager or anything, so the guys in the band set up all the speakers and gear before opening the show with at least a thirty-minute set before I came out. The manager at this one NCO club hadn't paid any attention when the guys were setting up and doing their set, but when I went on he came out to see how it was going. That's when he noticed Al at the piano. Before long, this guy worked his way up to the bandstand and got my attention.

"You'll have to get the black boy off the stage," he said. "We don't allow that."

His comment really startled me. I said, "What do you mean?"

"I mean niggers aren't allowed on this stage," the guy said. "Not on my watch!"

By this point, the crowd had gotten quiet, and everyone was wondering what was going on. He spun around and headed back to his office.

The Poe Kats were wondering what was happening, too. I turned around and told the band, "Okay, pack up, guys. We've got to go. He said Al can't be on the stage with us."

"It's okay, Wanda," Al said. "I don't want y'all to miss out on the gig. I'll wait in the car and you just go ahead and finish up."

Not a chance. I said, "Al, you're as much a part of this band as any of us. If you go, then we all go."

He smiled and nodded. "Thank you, Wanda. That means a lot to me."

The guys started taking off their guitars, unplugging their amplifiers, and packing up to go. When that manager saw what was happening, he ran over and said, "Oh no. There's been a misunderstanding. The rest of you can stay. We still want a good show here tonight."

"Look, he's part of our band," I said. If he's not welcome, then none of us are." I asked Al one time, "How in the world do you stand the fact that all of us can go in a place and you can't go with us, or that people make you feel so unwelcome just because of who you are?"

"Well, you know, it hurts," he said. I asked him why he did it and he just grinned really big and said, "For the music."

That was something I could understand. We musicians and singers will put up with an awful lot just to be able to perform. I was really proud of Al in the late 1970s when he started recording for Warner Bros. He put three or four songs into the Top 20 on the country singles chart, which was very exciting to me. He was a warm, wonderful man and a real talent.

When I recorded the *Wanda Jackson* LP, I brought the Poe Kats into the studio to be my backing band. They didn't have a bass player at the time, so we augmented the lineup with Skeets McDonald on bass and Buck Owens on rhythm guitar. Ken Nelson was great to allow that. In Nashville there were studio players and there were live players, and rarely did the categories cross. After Buck Owens transitioned from musician-for-hire to Capitol artist, Ken let him use his own group, The Buckaroos, in the studio. He did the same with Merle Haggard, who brought in his band, The Strangers, to back him on his Capitol sessions. I think one of the things that made Ken such a great producer was that he trusted the vision of his artists. He let us do things that wouldn't have flown in Nashville, and I think it helped us create a distinct sound. When I recorded "Let's Have a Party," for example, I had been playing it in my live shows. The band knew it backward and forward. Even though good studio musicians would have worked up a great arrangement right away, it was nice to record it with the boys who were playing it with me every night. They knew what I wanted and it made for a very good record.

As much as Ken encouraged his artists to be themselves, however, he also had a responsibility to Capitol Records to earn a profit. Ken and Daddy and I were all happy with the material that we were recording, but Ken was getting pressure from above to have me figure out if I was going to be a rockabilly artist or a country artist. The gap had widened between rock and country, and it was almost as if artists were being forced to pick sides. Someone like me who wanted to wholeheartedly embrace both rock and country just couldn't find acceptance in either world.

After not having recorded at all in 1959, Ken called a meeting with me and Daddy. He pointed out that the only success I had experienced as an artist was on the country chart and that my rock material, even though it sounded great, just wasn't going anywhere. He wanted to schedule a session for January of 1960, but suggested that we focus on country material and put our efforts into building the country fan base going forward. It was time to leave rock and roll behind. I didn't like being pigeonholed. I wanted to record whatever I wanted to record, but I also understood that Capitol Records had made an investment in me. They had signed me as a country singer, but I was shooting off all over the place. Every career needs direction, so I decided, "Okay, I'll let them pigeonhole me so they can really focus their efforts and get me solidly established with the country crowd."

We recorded exclusively country songs at that January session, including a twangy shuffle called "Please Call Today" and a crying waltz called "My Destiny." They were released as two sides of a single in the spring of 1960. The rockin' 1950s were over, and Wanda Jackson the country queen was ready to take over the honky tonk world once again.

I was out on the road with the Poe Kats several months later when Ken tracked me down via phone.

"Congratulations, Wanda!" he said.

I didn't know what he was talking about. "Congratulations for what?" I said. He paused for a moment, surprised I hadn't heard.

"For getting back on the charts," he chuckled.

"Oh, Ken," I replied, "I had no idea. Which side is doing well? Is it "Please Call Today" or is it "My Destiny?"

"Neither. It's 'Let's Have a Party,'" he said.

I laughed. "Very funny," I shot back, "a rock and roll song from two years ago that was just an album cut is my new country hit? Now I know you're pulling my leg."

Ken assured me it wasn't a joke. After we'd finally made the tough decision to put rock and roll behind us and focus on country, I was scoring my first Top 40 pop hit with a rock-and-roll song. Apparently, a deejay in Iowa had started playing the song off my *Wanda Jackson* album as the theme to his show. Every time he'd play it, the switchboard at the station would light up and the callers would want to know who it was. This deejay called up Capitol Records, got in touch with Ken, and convinced him to put out "Party" as a single. Around the same time "Long Tall Sally," from that same self-titled debut album, became a hit in Italy. It was a total shock that a two-year-old album was yielding that kind of success, but there I was again, right back up on that fence straddling the line between country and rock.

The success of "Party" prompted Capitol to repackage some of my rockabilly singles together as an album called *Rockin' with Wanda*. Though it was really more of a compilation than anything, that became my second Capitol LP. Suddenly, the focus was shifting once again. After "Party" became a hit, I did Dick Clark's show in November of 1960 and soon found myself on the bill with big pop stars like Bobby Vinton. I was uncomfortable around those artists, and their crowds were what I would call the bubblegum crowd. I was an adult and I was used to adults in my audience. I did not like singing to those little kids. I didn't feel like I was in my element, so I didn't do very many of those kinds of shows.

My newfound rock success did earn me some great bookings in Las Vegas, which I loved. I had already worked the Showboat, but with a new record hitting pretty good on the pop charts, I was invited to do a show at the Golden Nugget. That's when we started calling the band The Party Timers. By that point, Bobby Poe had moved on, and I'd recruited a guy named Billy Graves to front the band on the opening slot. The rest of the Poe Kats stuck with me for a while, but then different musicians came and went. We finally settled down with a pretty stable group, including a blind drummer named Don Bartlett from Kansas. He stood up when he played and didn't use a bass drum. He was also a great singer and added a lot to my show with his vocal backing.

In those days, the Nugget was the coveted gig in Vegas, and you had to have a great band. I brought in a new bass player, Mike Lane, who wound up staying with me a long time. He was a tall good-looking guy who sang great. Even though Don Bartlett was such a great singer, he was handling his duties as a drummer. We decided I needed a new front man who could sing and help me carry the show. I was keeping my eyes open for the right person who would fit the bill. One night I worked a club in the Washington D.C. area. There was a guy there who was the guitarist in the house band, but also performed as a featured act. The manager of the club said, "You ought to watch this guy. He's really something, and he keeps this place filled up." We watched him and he was hilarious. Plus, he was a great singer and he could play the guitar like crazy. That was the first time I became aware of Roy Clark.

We offered Roy the position as lead guitarist and front man for The Party Timers, and he jumped at the chance. It worked out great because he got to sing, do comedy, and he added so much to the group. He was such a good musician that he really sharpened up my band. He made sure we nailed the endings to each song, and he got those arrangements really tight. In the nine months or so that Roy was in the group, he was a real asset.

The hours in Vegas were brutal. We worked five forty-five-minute sets with fifteen-minute breaks between them every night. Once I started playing Vegas, I'd be there for a couple of weeks at a time. I barely knew what to do with myself having to stay in one place that long, but I liked it because it was Vegas. If you wanted a drink you could get it. If you wanted breakfast in the middle of the night, you could do it. You could go to a movie anytime. If you wanted to go to a show or two or three, you just did it. Everything was just wide open all the time. It was my kind of town. Years later, when I went to Branson, I was forced to sit still again. There wasn't much to do there, so I got the heebie-jeebies having to stay put. But Vegas was different. I got to know some of the musicians and other singers. I got to know some of the fans. I also got to party a little more than usual. In Vegas, every night is Saturday night. Every day, too.

RIGHT OR WRONG

In 1961 I hit my commercial peak by finally finding success in both the country and pop fields. In January I released a rock LP called *There's a Party Goin' On,* featuring Roy Clark on some lightning-fast guitar solos. Since the *Rockin' With Wanda* LP that was released the previous year was a collection of earlier singles, *There's a Party Goin' On* was the only proper all-rock album I recorded for Capitol. Later that year, I released two songs that each reached both the Top 10 on the country singles chart and the Top 20 on the pop chart. "Right or Wrong" was released in the spring, while "In the Middle of a Heartache," my highest charting single ever, came out near the end of the year.

I had gone to Nashville in the fall of 1960 for a few days of recording sessions. It was the first time I had made any records there since my Decca days, and Ken wanted to record both country and rock material. We recorded the entire *There's a Party Goin' On* album, which included songs like "Hard Headed Woman," "Tongue Tied," and "Man We Had a Party." We also cut four sides intended for singles. "Little Charm Bracelet" was a country song that was paired with "Riot in Cell Block No. 9" on the flip side. The latter had been a number one R&B hit for The Robins that was written and produced by the legendary team of Jerry Leiber and Mike Stoller, who are best known for writing a ton of Elvis hits, including "Hound Dog" and "Jailhouse Rock."

Neither side of the single charted for me, but I was the first woman to ever record "Riot in Cell Block No. 9," and it went on to become one of my classic rockabilly cuts. The original version had a line that said "serving time for armed robbery." I changed it to "serving time in Tehachapi," which was the location of a women's prison outside Bakersfield. I was at an event in Paris a few years ago, and was seated next to Jerry Leiber. He said, "I don't know where you got that line about Tehachapi, but your version of it was so much better than ours. Don't tell anybody, but yours is the best!"

Those Nashville recordings also turned out to be Roy Clark's first Capitol sessions. After we cut four of my songs one day, we had time left over on the session. Ken said, "Why don't we have Roy do something?" Ken and some Capitol people had seen our opening in Vegas, and they were quite impressed with him. He recorded "Black Sapphire" that day and then cut "Under the Double Eagle" with the leftover time we had the following day. The Capitol brass loved what they heard, and the two instrumentals became the two sides of his debut Capitol single.

I remember telling Hank Thompson one time how I appreciated him for his thoughtfulness in giving me a platform to launch my career. I said, "There's just no way to ever repay you, but I wish there was."

"There's one way," Hank said. "You can do it for someone else."

Hank gave me an opportunity to get started in the business, and I paid it forward by giving Roy a shot. By the time he became a big country star and was co-hosting *Hee Haw* with my old friend Buck Owens, I was bursting with pride. I loved those guys and was glad to say I knew 'em when.

Another of my own singles that emerged from that Nashville trip featured "Funnel of Love" on the B-side. It wasn't really rock or country, but was just a cool song that mixed various influences and has become a fan favorite. Some of those fans include Cyndi Lauper, who covered it in 2016, and Adele, who once told me that she was really influenced by that record. The A-side, however, was "Right or Wrong," which turned out to be my most successful single up to that point.

"Right or Wrong" was a song I wrote at a point when I was feeling kind of alone. I felt like my life and my career were moving so fast that I would probably never find anyone to marry. It sounds crazy now, because I was only twenty-three years old at the time, but girls from Oklahoma married pretty young back then, and I was already starting to feel like the opportunity was passing me by. I couldn't get acquainted with anybody when I was going from one town to the next on tours every night. I might dance with a guy for a song or occasionally go out to get something to eat with someone after a show, but Daddy was always around, and I had no opportunity to start a serious relationship. I was feeling lonesome when I had this thought that if I ever did find someone, I'd stick with them through everything. I'd be devoted. If I was going to commit to a man, I would commit all the way—right or wrong.

While I was thinking about all this, the phrase "right or wrong" stuck in my brain, and I began to formulate a song around it. I like to have an artist in mind when I'm writing a song. I'll imagine who I think might be able to sing it and then write it with their voice in mind. "Right or Wrong" was meant for Brenda Lee, who was experiencing a huge amount of success at the time. "Right or Wrong" just poured out of me like it was bursting from within. It took about five minutes and it didn't feel like work at all. I wanted Brenda to record it in the new country style that was getting popular, where you could layer background vocals and an acre of fiddles to create a lush pop-country ballad like Patsy Cline was doing.

Brenda and I had worked together on the *Jubilee* and several tours. Man, try following her some time! What an amazing performer. Nobody wanted to go after her because she was such a great entertainer, so we'd take turns. We had gotten to be friends by working together, so my plan was to send the song to her. I thought, *Brenda will have a hit with this, and it will make me some money! Even if it just becomes the B-side to one of her hits, I'll do pretty well with songwriter royalties on the sales of the single.*

When we were getting ready for the Nashville session, Ken asked, "Have you written anything recently?"

I shook my head. "Well, I do have this one song," I said, "but it's not for me to record. I'm going to send it to Brenda Lee."

"Okay, well I'd like to hear it anyway, just for fun," he said.

I started playing "Right or Wrong" for him, but he stopped me after about a minute.

"Oh, no you're not sending that to Brenda," Ken said. "That's a hit song and you're going to record it at our session tomorrow." Ken and I both thought it could be a hit, but I had a hard time imagining myself singing it. He convinced me it was the right way to go. "Besides," he said, "Brenda has plenty of hits, so you don't need to give yours away to her, too!" To this day, I don't know if Brenda ever knew I wrote that song for her.

"Right or Wrong" became my first Top 10 hit since my duet with Billy Gray in 1954, and my first as a solo artist. After "Let's Have a Party," Capitol was really pushing me to aim for crossover songs. It was a complete 180 degree turn from the "country only" decision Daddy and I had made with Ken, but unexpected successes have a way of changing plans. They figured, the more often I could cross over to the pop chart, the more records they could sell. Consequently, "Right or Wrong" was kind of a new sound for me with the luxurious bed of backing vocals and strings. It worked, and the song crossed over to hit number 29 on the pop charts. Instead of simplifying things, now I could add "pop ballads" to rockabilly and country as another genre I was attempting to balance.

In the fall of 1961, Capitol released another album, titled *Right or Wrong,* to capitalize on the success of the single. That's still one of my favorite albums because it was the first one I released with country on one side and rock on the other. It captures the range of my musical interests at that time. The cover of the album shows me wearing a corset. I remember when I went to the photo shoot. They put that thing on me and cinched my twenty-inch waist down to eighteen. I said, "Okay, where's the dress?"

"Oh, there's not a dress," somebody said. "We're just going to take some pictures of you in this, which will have a soft and sexy look on the album."

All I could think was, *No dress! No wonder I have a reputation as a bad girl!*

After "Right or Wrong" became a hit single, I realized why that song flowed out of me so easily when I was writing it. I was sued by the publishers of another song that was very popular at the time called "Wake the Town and Tell the People." The whole first line of my song was, note for note, the same as that song. It wasn't at all intentional, but that melody must have crept into my mind because I was hearing "Wake the Town" so much on the radio.

The lawyer from Central Songs, which was my music publishing company, called me and asked me some questions. He said, "Have you ever heard the song 'Wake the Town and Tell the People?'

"Of course!" I said. "It was a big hit. Everybody heard it."

"Well, we can't let this go to trial," he said when we finished. I asked why not and he explained, "Because we'd have to put you on the stand and you're too honest. You can't get up there and admit you ripped off that melody from another song!"

"Aren't you supposed to be honest when you're on the stand?" I said. It was an unintentional mistake, and I wasn't about to lie about it to cover my tracks. In the end, we reached an agreement with the other publisher so that they received the royalties on "Right or Wrong" for a period of ten years.

"In the Middle of a Heartache" was released soon after "Right or Wrong," and climbed to number 6 on the country chart and number 27 on the pop rankings. Some songs come to you in the shower. Some songs come to you in a dream. This is a song that came to me in a different way—in the mail! I would often have people send me things hoping I might record some of their material. One day I got a package of sheet music. I preferred to hear a demo recording rather than have to go pick out the melody at the piano, so I just glanced through the titles. Nothing really struck me. I left them in a stack for Daddy with a note asking him to mail them back to the sender. The next day Daddy came in and said, "I was just about to send these songs back, but I saw this one called 'In the Middle of a Heartache.' That's an interesting title. Let's go to the piano and see what it sounds like." I did and we were both struck by how pretty the melody was.

I played the song for Hank Thompson the next time I saw
him. He said, "That's a really great idea, but it needs to be
stronger and have a tighter structure." Hank and Billy Gray went
off and started straightening it out and then brought me in to
hear what they'd done. The three of us finished it together. That
was the first time I'd ever tried to write a song with anyone
before, but it worked out pretty well for us.

I had originally recorded "In the Middle of a Heartache" in
January of 1960 at the session after we'd decided to focus on country
music. Gordon Terry played fiddle, and it was just a down home
country record. Capitol hadn't had a chance to release it before "Let's
Have a Party" became a hit and we switched our focus to crossing
over to pop success. At that point, they didn't feel like it fit our ever-
shifting direction. Ken and I both knew it was a good song, so he
wanted to try an alternate arrangement in the new country-pop style.

"In the Middle of a Heartache" began crawling up the pop
chart in October, a month before it hit the country chart. I'm
thrilled that it got up to number six in the country rankings, but
I think it might have actually gotten all the way to number one
had we not made a miscalculation with the follow-up single.
At the same time we recorded "Heartache," I also cut "A Little
Bitty Tear." The song was written by Hank Cochran, who is
best known for classic songs like Patsy Cline's "I Fall to Pieces"
and Ray Price's "Make the World Go Away." The idea was that
"A Little Bitty Tear" would be the follow-up single after "In
the Middle of a Heartache." There was a pretty competitive
environment in Nashville in those days in terms of getting the
best songs from the best writers. I was assured that "A Little Bitty
Tear" was reserved for me and nobody else had recorded it.

Apparently, that wasn't really the case. "In the Middle of
a Heartache" was still climbing up the charts when I started
hearing "A Little Bitty Tear" on the radio. Burl Ives had recorded

it, so we rushed out our version to try to get the hit. It turned out not to be the right move. "Heartache" had not really run its course yet, but I was suddenly sending the signal to the deejays to play a different Wanda Jackson record. Not surprisingly, Burl wound up with a Top 10 country and pop hit with "A Little Bitty Tear," even though I think I had a better version. My record only reached the lower end of the pop charts with just enough airplay to kill "In the Middle of a Heartache" before it could get to the top. I thought, *Oh no. I fell through the cracks once again.* Whether it was missing out on the hit version of "Silver Threads and Golden Needles" or putting my focus on country when I should have been doing rock, or vice versa, it seemed like I was always falling through the cracks. But I always crawled back out and kept going. I had plenty of successes, but they were all hard won.

It was almost as if nothing could come easily for me. Even though 1961 was a fantastic year for me professionally, I ran into a completely unexpected and unpleasant experience that fall. I was scheduled to begin a new run of shows at the Golden Nugget in Las Vegas with The Party Timers. We did a series of one-nighters across Texas and Arizona on the way out, and finished our last Arizona show on a Sunday night. It was "that time of the month" and I was having a rough go of it. The cramping was going on and on, and I was just miserable. I remember barely being able to stand up straight enough to sing at that Sunday night show. It was a real struggle just to get through it.

We weren't scheduled to start at the Nugget until Thursday, but Capitol Records wanted me in Los Angeles for some promotional activities during the first half of the week. Because I was feeling so terrible, Daddy decided I should fly to California while he drove the car from Arizona to meet up with me later. That way, I could get there quickly and have some time to rest. Of course, that's back when you could just show up at an airport, buy a ticket, get on a plane and go! The band, meanwhile, headed on to Las Vegas to get themselves into trouble for a couple of days.

When I arrived in Los Angeles I checked into the Hollywood Plaza Hotel, which is where I always stayed when I was in town recording. It was very close to the Capitol Tower and was a favorite spot for Tinseltown royalty. Bette Davis lived there at one point, and George Burns once had an office on the top floor. Even Marilyn Monroe stayed there from time to time, so I usually felt pretty glamorous when I checked in.

This particular day, however, I felt anything but glamorous. I went up to my room, practically doubled over in pain. I had never had cramps that bad before. Most hotels used to have doctors on call, so I phoned down to the desk, and they got in touch with the hotel doctor for me. They had to track him down at a party, but he called my room and I told him my symptoms. "It sounds like it's probably just gas or something," he said. "Have the bellboy go get you some milk of magnesia, take a couple of aspirin, and call me again tomorrow to let me know how you're doing."

By that time I was really wishing Mother was there. I wanted to be at home in my own bed where I could talk to my own doctor. I called the front desk and asked them if they could send someone to the drugstore. The kid they sent came up to my room with a small bottle of milk of magnesia. I thanked him, but shut the door and rolled my eyes. I was thinking, *This is not going to be enough.* I was disgusted that he didn't really get me what I needed, but was too embarrassed and in too much pain to raise a stink about it. I drank that whole bottle and got back in the bed. I felt bad all night, but finally drifted off to sleep.

I awoke suddenly the next morning absolutely doubled over. I was hurting so bad I couldn't even get dressed. Daddy was somewhere out on the road and I didn't know what to do. I called Ken Nelson at Capitol, and he sent someone over to

take me to a hospital. When we got there the doctor assessed
my symptoms and told me my appendix was about to burst. I
told him about the milk of magnesia and he said, "Wanda, you're
lucky just to be here. That's the worst thing you can do for
appendicitis. If you had had more of it that appendix could have
ruptured and filled your system with poison." Suddenly, I was no
longer annoyed at the bellboy for bringing the small size!

I had never had surgery in my life, but the doctor scheduled
the emergency operation right away. Eventually someone was
able to contact Daddy. He called Mother and she got on a plane
immediately. In fact, she even got to Los Angeles before Daddy did.

The doctor made it clear that I would be recuperating for a
good while, so the Vegas dates were out of the question. With two
days until show time, Daddy had to scramble to find another singer
to front the band so we could keep our commitment. He recruited
Vickie Sallee, an Oklahoma girl who later released a single on the
Reprise label. Kudos to her for getting to Vegas, rehearsing with the
band, and being ready to go at a moment's notice!

Somebody can have major surgery today, and they'll boot you
out of the hospital before the sun sets. In the 1950s, though, they
were very protective. I was probably in the hospital for seven days.
By the time I was released, I was still in a lot of pain and not ready
for the discomfort of a long cross-country car ride. God bless Ken
Nelson, who came to my rescue. He owned a house in Sherman
Oaks, but he and his wife, June, lived in a different area. The
Nelsons were kind enough to let me, Mother, and Daddy stay for
a few days in Sherman Oaks. That was such a big help because it
allowed us to take our time and afford to stay in town for a little
bit without having to pay for hotel rooms and other expenses.

I might have been unlucky in medical emergencies and knowing
the right time to release a new single, but 1961 was still a great year.
In fact, it turned out to be the year I got very lucky in love.

Mother, Daddy, and me in
Los Angeles, 1943

Back in Oklahoma in my "cowgirl" days

A budding local radio star appearing as a guest on Wiley & Gene's show

My first public performance with Hank Thompson at the Trianon Ballroom

Performing on my daily KLPR radio show, 1954

Learning new songs in my parents' living room

With my first boyfriend, Leonard Sipes

My first professional
publicity photo, 1952

My first Nudie suit, with then
boyfriend A.G. Lane

An afternoon rehearsal with
Merl Lindsay and band

Oklahoma cowgirl all the way!

Decca promo photo with Billy Gray, 1954

I am where I am today thanks
to Hank Thompson!

Billy, me, and Hank on one of my earliest
tours with Hank and his band

My senior prom dress that I
designed and Mother sewed

Me and Mother by my first car,
a Pontiac. I paid cash!

With Mother's help I embraced a more glamorous image for the stage.
The photo on the right is a fan favorite, but it's always bothered me that
two rhinestones are missing on the dress. See if you can spot 'em!

Visiting an Arkansas radio station

A photo I took of Elvis on his pink Cadillac

Daddy, at the end of a long tour

Daddy eventually grew
to like Elvis a lot

Rock and roll attitude and plenty of exposed shoulders! Bottom right is onstage at the Terrace Ballroom in Newark, New Jersey, November 10, 1957.

With Daddy and Little Jimmy Dickens, 1956

With Gene Vincent at a DJ Convention in Nashville

Backstage with Ricky Nelson, 1958

With Porter Wagoner at the *Ozark Jubilee*

Norma Jean (upper left) and I loved to take "pin-up" style photos in the mid to late '50s.

Rehearsal for a Japanese TV show, 1959

Japan is the only place I ever felt tall!

The 1960s were a time of transition when I honed my style and worked with some fantastic musicians, such as Roy Clark, who fronted my band (lower left, photo courtesy of Thomas Sims Archives).

Performing with Bob Wills and his Texas Playboys in Las Vegas

One of the 1960s incarnations of my band, The Party Timers

**Family became very important in the '60s when our
daughter, Gina, and son, Greg, appeared.**

As the '60s progressed,
the skirts got shorter...

...and the necklines got lower.

With Rev. and Mrs. Paul Salyer, our
wonderful pastor in the early 1970s

There was a different dress code
once we got into the gospel field!

Jann Browne and Rosie Flores,
two gals who reintroduced
me to rockabilly audiences

Wanda Jackson Day in Maude, OK, 1989

The whole family joined me and Wendell at the 2000 Oklahoma Music
Hall of Fame induction. On the left side is my daughter Gina's family,
including her older daughter, Jennifer, and younger daughter, Jordan,
along with their dad, Jimmy. On the right side is my son Greg and his wife,
Patti, along with their daughter, Jillian. Mother is standing next to me.

Some of the many important girls in my life, including Adele (who took me on tour with her); Miranda Lambert; my granddaughter (and now manager), Jordan (backstage at the Grand Ole Opry); and my first great-granddaughter, Nellie, who got to meet Wendell shortly before he passed

Chapter 16

YOU'RE THE ONE FOR ME

One of my buddies at the *Ozark Jubilee* was Porter Wagoner. He was so funny and everybody loved him, thanks to his goofy mannerisms and great stories. Porter's steel guitar player on the show was Don Warden, who was also his manager, and later Dolly Parton's longtime manager. We were all out doing a show one time when Don married his wife, Ann. They needed someone to stand with them, so the four of us went out to a preacher's home somewhere in one of the Carolinas, I believe. Porter stood with Don while I stood with Ann. That was my introduction to being a bridesmaid, but it definitely wasn't my last. Over the next several years, it seemed like all my friends were getting married. It's an old cliché, but I soon found myself always a bridesmaid, but never a bride.

Technically, I did have one suitor. Smokey Smith was a promoter in Des Moines, Iowa, who booked me fairly often. When I'd go up there to play, Daddy didn't go because I could stay with Smokey and his family at their home. He and his wife had a little four-year-old boy named Leon, who decided he loved me. His mother told me Leon was in Sunday School one time when the teacher had the children go around the room, announce their name, and say that they loved Jesus. All the little kids did it, but when it got to Leon he said, "I'm Leon Smith and I love Wanda Jatten!"

"That's nice Leon, but do you love Jesus?" the teacher said.

"No, I love Wanda Jatten!" he said.

I had been casually dating a disc jockey in Oklahoma City on the rare occasions when I was at home, and Leon must have overheard some conversation about it. I arrived at the Smith family's door one afternoon and was met by Leon, who was red-faced and mad.

"Wanda Jatten! Are you gonna marry that jitt jockey?!?!?!" he demanded.

"No, Leon. I probably won't marry him," I said. He narrowed his eyes and put his hands on his hips.

"Okay," he replied. "You better not!"

My closest friend on the *Jubilee* was Norma Jean Beasler, who later became known in country music circles as "Pretty Miss Norma Jean." She was also from Oklahoma City and was one grade behind me in school. Norma Jean and I first got to know each other at KLPR, where we were both appearing during the local talent portion of Jay Davis's radio show. Even though we went to the same school and were performing on the same shows and contests, we weren't real close back then. Norma Jean was shy, and we just didn't really connect on a deep level. By the time we were both out of school and pursuing our music careers, however, we got to be good friends. After I was hired at the *Jubilee* I told them, "I know a pretty blonde in Oklahoma City who sings real good." They auditioned her and hired her for the show.

Norma Jean and I liked to go out together and have fun. One time she invited me to a New Year's Eve dance to ring in 1961. I was booked in Las Vegas playing a show at the Nugget, so I wasn't able to join her. Several days later I called Norma Jean to wish her a happy New Year and to find out if she had fun at the dance.

"It was great," she told me. "I wound up going with a guy I met recently, but I wasn't really interested in him. Then, this other good-lookin' guy just boldly came right up and asked me to dance. My date was pretty shy, so he said it would be okay."

I laughed, imagining Norma Jean juggling her options on the dance floor. "Well, look at you," I joked. "It sounds like you've just got too many guys to handle."

"Oh, and that's not all," she continued. "This new guy was there with a date of his own. We kind of just forgot all about who we came with. We must have danced three or four songs together before somebody came out to the dance floor and said neither of our dates seemed too thrilled they'd been left waiting at their respective tables for us. We just lost track of time, I guess. He was so handsome that it wasn't hard to do. But he made sure he got my phone number. His name is Wendell Goodman, and he's picking me up for a date tonight."

I wished her luck, promised we'd talk again in a few days, and hung up the phone wishing I could have been there for Norma's latest adventure on the dance floor.

I was playing at the Golden Nugget most of January, so I didn't talk to Norma Jean again for a couple of weeks. I finally called to catch up. "Hey, how was your date with that good-looking guy from New Year's Eve?" I asked. "What was his name? William?"

Norma Jean chuckled and said, "No, his name's Wendell and he's here with me right now. Would you like to say 'hi' to him?"

"Yeah, sure," I said, not thinking much of it. When Norma Jean put Wendell on the phone and I heard his voice, my knees buckled. I started stuttering and had difficulty getting my thoughts together. It sounds crazy, but it was as if I instantly fell for him, just from hearing his voice. I couldn't wait to meet him. I wanted to see what this guy looked like, if just talking to him on the phone had that effect on me!

I returned to Oklahoma City at the end of the month on a night when Norma Jean happened to have a date with Wendell. I called her and said, "Come by the house later. I want to see you and meet your new boyfriend." As soon as they came into the house and I saw Wendell, that was it. It was love at first sight. I'd had it. I thought, *How in the world can I ever be with this guy when he's with my best friend?* Little did I know that as soon as Wendell saw me, he was thinking, *How am I gonna get rid of Norma Jean so I can date Wanda?*

Every time I'd come in from the road I'd call Norma Jean. I was with Daddy day and night when I was touring, so the last thing I wanted to do was sit around the house with him when I was home. I wanted to go out with my friends, but they were all getting married and having kids. Norma Jean was my reliable single friend, but it seemed like maybe I was losing her, too. It got to the point where every time I'd call she'd say, "Well, I've got a date with Wendell tonight, so I guess we can't do anything."

"I don't want to sit here all night," I said. "Ask Wendell if I could go along with y'all. I'll pay my way if you go to a movie or whatever." She asked him, and he said it sure seemed strange, but he said okay because he had his eye on me and I had mine on him. I wanted to be around him. Poor Norma. We used her, I guess. Wendell said he was the most popular guy in town. He had a blonde on one arm and a brunette on the other. We'd go out to eat or go dancing, and Wendell ended up paying for both of us. He wouldn't let me pay for anything.

If I'm honest, I was beginning to get a little jealous that Norma Jean had found such a great guy. I had had a heartbreak along the way here and there that just made me kind of cynical about relationships. I remember one time I got in the car with

Norma and Wendell. I was mad because Daddy had been talking to me about something. I got in and said, "I know the secret now. You have to just work, work, work, and make all the money you can. You can't have any other kind of life. I'm not going to do anything but work from now on!" I just felt left out of life. I provided the entertainment and watched while other people had a great time. But *I* wasn't having a great time. I was working. If I was upset or in pain, I still had to work. I had to make that job. There was no time for love and romance for Wanda, and I was afraid my best friend was about to run off with the guy of my dreams.

Around that time things were changing at the *Ozark Jubilee*. ABC didn't think a country music show could hold its own if they didn't bring in some pop performers. They brought in Don Cherry as the pop singer, as well as Pat Boone, who was Red Foley's son-in-law. That always irked us a little bit. We country folks started the show, and it was getting more and more popular. Why did we need pop artists to come in to help us or make us more legitimate? Well, we didn't! They were all nice people, so it wasn't anything personal, but the spirit of the show changed over time. After a while, it began to feel like it just wasn't really going anywhere. We stopped getting the really good country guests when the flavor of the show changed, and I was also getting tired of making that long drive between Oklahoma and Springfield. I could see the handwriting on the wall and decided to leave. I think the show was taken off the air not long after that.

During this period, our friend Porter Wagoner had established a solid career thanks to his appearances on *The Ozark Jubilee*. He had several big hits in the 1950s, including "A Satisfied Mind" and "What Would You Do? (If Jesus Came to Your House)" that earned him an invitation to join the cast of the *Grand Ole Opry*. He decided to leave the *Jubilee* and head to Nashville. He eventually had the opportunity to launch his own television show. Porter always had a "girl singer" on his TV program and, even though

Dolly Parton was the best known, she wasn't the first. When he was just getting his show off the ground, Porter asked Norma Jean to leave the *Jubilee* and join the cast of his show in Nashville. It was a great opportunity for her, but it would mean leaving Oklahoma City—and her new boyfriend, Wendell—behind.

Norma decided to take the job with Porter. Right before she left, she pulled me aside and said, "Wanda, I don't think Wendell has a lot of friends here. It hasn't been that long since he moved up from Texas, and he's not really settled yet. He mostly works with older people at his job, and I just hate leaving him all alone. Would you be willing to look after him?"

Would I? That was just the chance I'd been looking for! "Okay," I told Norma. "I'll be sure to take care of him." That gave me a license. Norma Jean left in March, and the way was clear for me and Wendell. I wanted to call him the minute she pulled out of town, but I managed to restrain myself for about a week. Finally, I called him up and asked him out for a date. Girls did not do that in 1961, but I just wanted to be with this guy so bad. We both liked to bowl, so I suggested we go bowling that night. He jumped at the chance. Once we got there we talked about Norma Jean. But that only lasted for about five minutes before we quickly moved on to other topics.

Being with Wendell seemed like the most natural thing in the world. I was gone a lot, but whenever I was at home we were together. When I was on the road we talked on the phone whenever possible. I had always enjoyed dating and had a thing for handsome guys, but this was something different. After Elvis and I drifted apart my girlfriends would ask, "Why didn't you latch on to him?" I had a crush on him, but something told me that what I had with Elvis just wasn't meant to last. I wasn't in love, even though Elvis was great. Or maybe I just wasn't that serious about wanting to get married at the time. With Wendell it was completely different. There was just a connection between us, as if we were designed to be together.

Wendell told me later that he fell in love with me the first time he heard the song "Right or Wrong," even though he didn't know me then. It's funny, because I realized later that I had written that song about Wendell, even though I hadn't met him yet. It was about the kind of relationship I was looking for, and the one I found with him.

About a month after we started dating, Wendell came to see me play at the Trianon Ballroom in Oklahoma City. I was wearing a beautiful dress that night that Mother had made for me. In fact, it's the same dress I'm wearing on the cover of the second CD box set that Bear Family Records released of my recordings. After my set we were out on the dance floor together when Wendell told me he loved me. Up to that point I would usually say "love ya" when I'd tell him goodbye or write it in notes and things. But when he said "I love you" it was different. The sincerity of his words almost caught me off guard. I probably didn't give the right response. Instead of saying, "Oh, Wendell, I love you, too," I wound up saying, "Are you sure?" I don't know what prompted me to say that. I knew he was sure. I was sure, too. I knew it was real, and I knew I loved him, too.

My relationship with Wendell felt like just the right fit. Somehow, we both knew we'd spend the rest of our lives together. About four months after we started dating, I was playing a show in Minneapolis. I was in my motel room talking on the phone with Wendell when he said, "Your mother was wondering if you wanted to register for some nice dishes for our home."

"Well, wait a minute," I said. "Y'all are moving pretty fast, don't you think? You haven't even asked me to marry you yet!" Wendell kind of laughed to himself.

"I haven't? Well, Wanda, I was wondering if you'd make me the happiest man in the world by becoming my wife. Will you marry me?"

He asked me right then and there on the phone! Of course, I said yes. We both just knew. In fact, we knew it so deeply that Wendell truly hadn't realized that he'd not actually asked me yet!

Even though I was engaged, I wasn't the stereotypical twenty-three-year-old bride-to-be you would find in 1961. I never did want a big wedding. That didn't even enter my mind. I was a bridesmaid for cousins and friends with all the to-do, and I would think, *Why would anyone spend all that money? Just go marry the boy and live happily ever after!* It finally dawned on me that I didn't have to have my special day, because I already had it all the time. I always had the spotlight, so I didn't need a fairy-tale wedding. That part of me was already fulfilled. I'm sure that made Daddy and Wendell happy when it came to the planning.

I was out on the road most of the time, so Mother and Wendell took care of arranging everything. I had all these dates booked, so we had to find a small window of time when we could get married. I only had two requests. I said, "I will be married in a Baptist church, and Mother and Daddy will be there." They found a little time in my schedule for us to get married in early November, and it was Mother who helped Wendell pick our first apartment and furnish it in preparation for our new life together.

Mother, Daddy, Wendell, and I drove two hours down to Gainesville, just across the Texas border, where we were married in the fall of 1961. We had been dating for eight months. We went to Texas because you didn't have to wait a week to get married after getting a blood test. I was hardly ever in one place for a week, so that wasn't going to work! We went to the Justice of the Peace to get our license, then headed to a Baptist church. The preacher took us in his office and had a little talk about marriage and whether or not we were ready to commit. We were ready! We drove back to Oklahoma City that night and stopped along the way to have a spaghetti dinner to celebrate. The next day I hit the road for a tour with Johnny Cash, and Wendell took two weeks off from his job with Admiral Oil to come along. Not exactly a romantic honeymoon on a beach, but we were just thrilled to finally be married.

I was still living with Mother and Daddy when Wendell and I met, and he was still living with his parents, too. Neither of us had ever lived on our own or even had a roommate! We were both ready to get out of our parents' houses, but it hadn't been feasible for me before that point. Daddy took care of all my business and Mother took care of the clothes, so they wanted me there with them. Once Wendell and I moved into our first apartment, however, it seemed like we'd always been married. I felt like I was *home* with him.

Because we were equally inexperienced with living on our own, we did have to overcome a few little snags that most new couples have to deal with. Wendell had to shame me into hanging my clothes up, which was something Mother battled with me about forever. I had to get onto him about hanging the bathroom towels up. He'd throw them somewhere while they were damp and they wouldn't dry out. We fought over where to squeeze the toothpaste tube for years. I don't know why it didn't occur to us to just buy separate tubes!

When Wendell and I got married, I don't think I'd ever washed a load of laundry in my life. I didn't know how to do that kind of stuff! After a couple of weeks, Wendell said, "Hon, what are you going to do about the laundry? I'm running low on socks."

"Well, I don't really know how," I said.

"Call Tom and he'll help you," he said.

So I called Daddy and asked if he'd ever done laundry before. He said, "Sure, I can show you." He came over and we hauled this big old bag of wash to the laundromat together. Daddy opened up the bundle and pulled out a piece. He said, "Okay, this one goes here," and started a stack. "This one goes over here," he said as he started another pile. He went on and on like that and was just sorting everything into three stacks.

Finally, I said, "What are these stacks for, and how do you know what goes where?"

"Well, I don't know, but your mother always makes two or three stacks, so I think that's what you're supposed to do," he said.

Needless to say, our stacks had no rhyme or reason to how they were sorted. Wendell's black socks all wound up with fuzzy white towel lint on them, and he was probably one of the first men to ever wear pink underwear after I turned all the whites different colors!

I definitely couldn't cook! I had a little time off from the road soon after we were married, and decided I would make Wendell a nice meal. I didn't even know where to start, so I called my friend Beverly, who was already married and had started a family. She said, "I'll tell you what. I'll come over and help you." When she got there I watched her cook a great dinner with fried chicken, gravy, and all these wonderful sides. She got out of there by 5:15, so when Wendell arrived home from work at 5:30, I had the feast spread out on the table. He had no idea Beverly had been there. After we ate, he just bragged and bragged on the meal, going on about how great it was and what a wonderful job I'd done. I didn't have the heart to tell him that it was all Beverly's doing. You'd think it would have occurred to me that it was going to be hard to keep up the ruse very long, but I didn't think that far in advance. I'm sure Wendell wondered why the quality of my cooking dramatically declined by the next meal.

I didn't even know how to mix a martini. I'd heard about having a drink before dinner. Mother didn't approve of drinking, so that never happened at our house. But it sounded very grown up to me, so we got some bottles and made sure that we had a cocktail and a cigarette before dinner. There I was, Mrs. Wendell Goodman, embarking on a new life that felt unbelievably natural, even though it was entirely different from anything I'd known before.

Chapter 17

Mr. and Mrs. Wendell and Wanda Goodman: our wedding photo.

A WOMAN LIVES FOR LOVE

When Wendell and I met he was an IBM Supervisor for a chain of grocery stores called Humpty Dumpty. He took care of the programming and installation of their computer systems, and ran various facets of bookkeeping and accounting back in the days when a computer took up an entire room. He worked for Humpty Dumpty for seven or eight years before leaving to take a job with Admiral Oil Company, which was preparing for a major installation of new IBM equipment. He was overseeing the programming and set-up for that system when we first married, while I was out on the road playing shows all over the country. Wendell's job was reliable and paid well, but he was definitely firmly planted in the traditional nine-to-five career path, while my life was anything but conventional.

Daddy continued to go out on the road with me as my manager and driver after I married. I appreciated his company, but it was hard being away from Wendell so often. Of course, we talked on the phone pretty much every day, but we got married to be together, not in separate cities talking long distance.

It wasn't working to have me traveling and Wendell staying at home. One night I said, "Wendell, you know I love my career. I love getting on that stage and singing for people, and there's almost nothing in the world that could make me give that up. But there is one thing I love more, and that's you. We're pulling in opposite directions, and something's gotta change. You have a good career, and I'm willing to give it up so I can stay home, we can be with each other all the time, and I can just focus on being your wife." He was quiet for several seconds.

"I don't know what the answer is," he sighed, "but I don't want to ask you to sacrifice something that means so much to you. Let's think about it for a little while before we make any quick decisions."

In early 1962 I was booked for another extended run out in Las Vegas. Wendell and I were talking one night when he said, "I miss you, Wanda. I'm just going to fly out there this weekend so I can see your face." That was great news. He came out, and having him in my world for a couple of days reminded me how much I missed him when we were apart. He was just about to fly back to Oklahoma City when I offered, once again, to give up my career for him. He shook his head. "You know what?" Wendell replied, "Your job seems a lot more exciting than babysitting a bunch of computers all day. I love being around your world and I think I like the show business life. Plus, your parties are a lot more interesting than mine. Why don't we try your life, with me helping you out, and see what happens? As long as I can be helpful, I'll be there. I'm not going to just tag along, but if I can make a real contribution and we can be partners, I think we can make it work."

Wendell called Admiral Oil and submitted his two weeks' notice. They said, "We wondered how long it would be before you gave up this job to be with Wanda. We even had bets going about it!" That made me feel good because it meant that others could see the devotion that Wendell and I had to each other. Wendell worked alongside Daddy for a little while learning the ropes of the business and life on the road, and he eventually took over all the business side of my career. He never did just tag along. Though I was the one with the spotlight, Wendell was as important to the operation as I was. And we did it that way for five-and-a-half decades.

At first, Wendell primarily handled the driving. Over time, he started taking over more and more of the responsibilities of a road manager. There were several places where I could count on drawing good crowds, so there were a handful of venues that I returned to regularly. Wendell picked up on Daddy's practice of going out in the audience each night to make sure that the sound mix was right and that I could be heard. As we passed through the same cities multiple times, Wendell began to get acquainted with the various club owners and promoters.

Jim Halsey was still my booking agent at the time. I was the second client he signed after Hank Thompson, but by the 1960s Halsey was one of the most powerful agents in country music. He was an innovator and a visionary who knew how to get exposure for rising stars. But he had a lot of things going by then, and I was beginning to feel like the forgotten stepchild of his organization. He wasn't pushing me and Hank into new territory, like he was with some of the other acts he handled.

He was just booking the reliable dates, so it felt like we were on autopilot. After Wendell took over he said, "You know, Halsey is just booking you in the same places all the time. He doesn't know these people. I'm the one out there meeting them and talking with them. I can start doing it myself and we'll save the commission we're paying him." I don't remember exactly, but it was about 10% or 15% that came off the top from our bookings that we would be able to keep. I thought it was a great idea, and I knew Wendell had the right kind of business sense for handling bookings. Jim Halsey served his clients well, and I'm proud that he learned his skills through working with me and Hank. Times change, however, and different business relationships have their seasons. We knew it was time to move on, so Hank Thompson and I both pulled out around the same time and struck out on our own. With Wendell by my side, I knew it would work out just fine.

Not only did Wendell take on the responsibility of booking the shows, but he also managed everything related to the band. Now that was a job! He had to keep up the car so they could make the dates, make sure to pay their child support, and generally keep an eye on them. There were a few times we had to bail them out of jail so they could work a job. I always had pretty good guys working with me, but they were just boys drinking and having fun and getting into trouble.

It always gave me a great sense of satisfaction that my dad got a second chance to live out his musical dreams vicariously through my career. When Wendell took over, though, Daddy was kind of lost. He couldn't go back to barbering, since his feet gave him so much trouble. Both my folks always had a knack for finding work, so he jumped in and found different things to do. He worked with a guy selling used cars for a while. He loved people, so he enjoyed that kind of work and was pretty

good at it. I know he missed the music and being on the road.
Eventually, the guy who managed the Trianon Ballroom in
downtown Oklahoma City left and went to Nashville for some
other opportunity. When Daddy heard about it he jumped at the
chance to be around music again. He took over that job and was
back in his world again.

Even though I think Daddy was happy at the Trianon, I know
he was a restless soul. He eventually started drinking more heavily,
just because it was something to do. I don't know if he was an
alcoholic, but he liked to drink and he liked to go out every
night. He was a party guy. Mother wouldn't allow any drinking in
the house, so he'd go out and get a nip from his stash in the glove
box of the car. He always wanted to go out to some honky tonk
or a bar somewhere so he could drink and tell jokes and have
fun with the guys. Maybe with the women, too. That caused my
folks some problems. They hadn't been around each other much
because they sacrificed their time together for six years so Daddy
could travel with me and Mother could take care of everything
on the home front. That life must have been lonely for her, even
though she always stayed busy. It was a difficult adjustment for
him, and I always felt a little guilty that those circumstances
changed for him.

Even though there were plenty of changes in my personal life,
it seemed like things were running smoothly by 1962. I had just
experienced two Top 10 hits with "Right or Wrong" and "In the
Middle of a Heartache." And even though things didn't work out
with "A Little Bitty Tear" after the Burl Ives debacle, the follow-
up single, "If I Cried Every Time You Hurt Me," performed
fairly well on both the country and pop charts. Capitol followed
up the *Right or Wrong* album with another LP, *Wonderful Wanda,*
that was well received. That year I was ranked the third most
popular female act in the country, right behind Patsy Cline and

Kitty Wells. Loretta Lynn was number four. The year would bring yet another change, however, that would require some big adjustments.

Motherhood was not something I'd ever dreamed of when I was growing up. I never did babysit when I was a teenager, and—with the exception of maybe posing for a fan photo—I had never even held a baby up to the point when Wendell and I married. He wanted to have at least two children, which I knew, but family planning wasn't as widely discussed in the early 1960s as it is today. Although it was a surprise (a *good* surprise that I prefer to think of as God's timing), our daughter Gina was born in the summer of 1962.

When I found out I was pregnant, I thought, *Oh my gosh. Now what? What's gonna happen with my career?* It makes me sound terrible to say that, but that was my initial reaction. Being a small person, I got big pretty fast. It got harder and harder to travel, and especially to play music. I had to start holding my guitar off to the side when my baby bump got too big to work around. I performed up until the last couple of months of my pregnancy, but I had some trouble. I nearly lost Gina in Las Vegas during a run at the Golden Nugget. The dressing rooms were upstairs and the showroom was downstairs, so I was going up and down all night, which was not good for the baby.

Another time, I started hemorrhaging. I called my gynecologist and he said, "You must get off your feet for at least thirty-six hours." I was working at Charlie Genova's Chestnut Inn, which was a place in Kansas City where I could depend on drawing a good crowd.

Wendell called and said, "Wanda won't be able to make the show. It's doctor's orders. I'm sorry."

"On, no," Charlie said. "She's got to be there." Wendell reiterated that it would not be possible. Charlie called back and said, "How about this? I've arranged for a hospital bed, and we can have it out on the dance floor area."

Wendell had to put his foot down on that idea. Can you imagine that? Me in a hospital bed with my guitar trying to entertain a crowd? My gosh. I think old Charlie would have had me do it, too! Those were the moments when I was glad to have Daddy and Wendell in my life so they could step in and get tough on some of these promoters and club owners who had some unrealistic ideas.

When I finally took a break from touring, I continued to record. We did the *Love Me Forever* album, while I was eight or nine months pregnant with Gina. That LP had a bunch of classic pop songs on it, which I really enjoyed singing. I don't know how I did it, but somehow I was able to get those notes out, and *Love Me Forever*—which was released in 1963, several months after we recorded it—is still one of my favorite albums to this day.

I took two or three months off after Gina was born. We had recently moved into our first house at 2213 Laneway Drive, and I was doing my best to play the part of the domesticated woman. I didn't know the first thing about being a mother, but I knew I was in love. Ken Nelson came and visited us and the new baby when he was in town on some other business. Capitol also sent a little savings bond and a sterling silver piggy bank, which was very thoughtful. It felt like my real family and my Capitol Records family had come together in harmony. At least that's how it felt until it was time to hit the road again. Leaving Gina in someone else's care was extraordinarily difficult, but there was no other choice.

Wendell was as head-over-heels for the little bundle as I was, and he was ready to grow the brood immediately. I was an only child, so I wasn't so sure, but he thought having both a boy and a girl would make for the perfect family. I thought maybe we should at least space it out a little bit. I guess birth control pills had just started to get popular around that time. I started taking them after Gina was born, but every time I took one I would get morning sickness as if I was pregnant. That was strange because I had never gotten morning sickness when I actually was pregnant. Needless to say, those pills didn't last for very long. Natural consequences being what they are, I was pregnant again less than a year after Gina came along.

My son, Gregory Jackson Goodman, was born January 1, 1964. Wendell always jokes that he missed his tax deduction by just three hours. He tells people, "I had Wanda running around the football field and doing sit-ups, but Greg just refused to come in 1963." It sounds hard to believe, but the minute we clinked our glasses together to toast the New Year at midnight, I clutched my stomach. My labor had started!

I didn't have much of a breather between the two babies, and having two children certainly didn't make it any easier on me and Wendell to have to be away so often. The kids had several nannies, but Ms. Willis was the one who was with us the longest. She became part of the family, and we were also very blessed to have actual family nearby. Both my parents and Wendell's parents were local, so they could stop in whenever they were needed. Once Greg came along we moved once again to 8400 Charlotte Drive, which wasn't far from our previous house. That was the first home we actually built, and we have some great memories of our young family in that house.

As much as I loved my kids, pregnancy was not easy on me either time. I had them both via C-section, but I had to go through a good bit of labor. In fact, it was shortly before I became pregnant with Gina—when I had my appendix removed—that the surgeon told me I would have trouble with pregnancy and would need to have children via C-section should I ever get pregnant. I don't know what he saw when he was poking around in there, but I was glad to find out the information when I did. Once Wendell got his boy, I was off the hook. I wouldn't have to endure the unpleasant part of the process again, so we decided to go ahead and officially cap the Goodman family head count at four. I couldn't have asked for two better children, so I knew we weren't going to top ourselves!

Because they were close in age, Gina and Greg always had each other to rely on when their parents were off traveling. They got along remarkably well for siblings, and I was grateful that they were always close. Even though they were buddies, their personalities were very different. Gina never wanted anyone to know that her mother was Wanda Jackson. She wanted to make her own way in the world and be appreciated on her own merits. She wasn't going to use my name to get a part in the play or attract friends. Greg, on the other hand, headed off to kindergarten with one of my LPs under his arm and announced to the class, "This is my mother!" We've always had a good time kidding him about that!

Often, when Wendell and I were traveling for weeks at a stretch, I'd open up a suitcase to discover that Gina had slipped one of her toys in our luggage to go along with us. It was so sweet, but that just broke my heart. I knew she wanted to be the one to stow away to be with her mom and dad, so she was sending an ambassador in her place. When the kids got a little older, we would turn some of our summer tour dates into family vacations. If I was working at fairs, we could bring them along to ride the rides and have cotton candy and that kind of thing. I knew it wasn't a normal childhood for them, and I've always carried a little guilt about that.

Mother kept Gina and Greg on the weekends, so she practically raised both my kids. She was always there for us, and

I was so grateful for her steady and consistent influence in their lives. All the grandkids and great-grandkids eventually started calling her Bobo (pronounced Bob-oh). That came from my mom's niece, Naomi. Mother's side of the family called her Nellie Bob, which was a nickname her dad started calling her when she was a kid. Naomi couldn't say that when she was a little girl, so it just came out Bob. And it stuck. Bobo was the matriarch, and a pretty important person in our family. As it turned out, Bobo was more like a mother to my kids than I was. Even when I was home it was hard to be fully present. There was always some kind of demand like, "I've got to go get this outfit finished for the show next weekend," or "I need to go to this photo shoot," or "I've got to rehearse with the band." I always had stuff to do, so I didn't even really know all the kids' friends. I don't think I was a very good mother. My kids say that's not true. They say they understood what I was doing, but it couldn't possibly have been easy on them. I look at what parents they turned out to be and wonder where they got it. I feel like I didn't do anything right!

Chapter 18

With Otto Demler (left) and his engineer at Electrola Studios in Germany.

SANTO DOMINGO

After "If I Cried Every Time You Hurt Me" faded from the charts in 1962, I couldn't get back into the Top 40 to save my life. Capitol released several singles, including "I Misunderstood," "The Greatest Actor," "One Teardrop at a Time," "But I was Lying," "This Should Go on Forever," and "Let Me Talk to You." None of them, however, hit the *Billboard* charts.

I was just coming off my most successful couple of years as an artist, but I was having a lot of trouble holding on to it. One of the big reasons that it often felt like an uphill climb for me was because I chose to remain in Oklahoma City. I knew the best songwriters were in Nashville, and I knew how they operated. If they wrote a great song, they wanted someone to record it immediately. Why would they be motivated to sit on a potential smash hit by holding it for me when there were plenty of popular singers right there in Nashville who were available to record it right away? The harsh reality is they couldn't get those songs to me, and if they could get them to me, I couldn't set up a recording session on short notice. The other girls who were based in Nashville got the first crack at the best songs. I often got the dregs, and I probably missed out on some hits because I wasn't in the middle of the action. As they say, you must be present to win.

I have to admit that moving to Nashville was pretty tempting, but there was no way we could do that. We had our family nearby to help take care of the kids, which we wouldn't have had in Tennessee. Wendell and I discussed it on several occasions, but choosing not to go to Nashville was a sacrifice we decided to make for our family. Our children's lives were unstable enough as it was. We weren't about to rip them from the only consistent support network they had and throw them into an even more chaotic life. It wasn't an easy decision, in terms of my career, but I have no doubt it was the right decision for us and our family.

I finally caught another break in 1965 and found myself back on top with another number one single. But I had to go outside the Nashville system to make it happen. In fact, I had to go pretty far. Capitol Records asked me if we'd be willing to go to Germany to record some songs for Electrola Records, which was their German distribution partner. To make matters more interesting, they told me they wanted me to sing *in German*. I'm a country girl from Oklahoma, so I have enough trouble with English! I said, "How in the world am I going to sing in German?"

I was told that Electrola was interested in working with me because my voice was "very pleasing to the German ear." The idea was that they would write material especially for me and

then coach me on how to sing it. I was pretty intimidated at
the prospect and, even though I've faced plenty of challenges,
sometimes my first instinct is to run the other direction. I was
wary, but Wendell talked me into it. We decided it would be a
good opportunity to travel together on someone else's dime. We'd
never been to Europe. In fact, at that point, Wendell had never left
the US, and the only international trip I'd ever taken was my tour
of Japan. Plus, we figured there was nothing to lose in giving it a
try.

In March we flew to Cologne, where Electrola was based,
and where they had their big pressing plant. When we went to
the studio we met Otto Demler, an Austrian producer who was
assigned to oversee the sessions, as well as a German vocal coach
who was recruited to help me with my pronunciation. They
hadn't sent me the songs ahead of time, so I was feeling pretty
uneasy. "Where are all the musicians?" I asked after we spent a
few minutes getting to know one another.

"Oh, don't worry about that," Otto smiled. "We've already
recorded the instrumental tracks for you. We'll just add your
vocals."

By that point I was getting *really* nervous. I said, "How in
the world can you have an arrangement made and the tracks
recorded when you don't know what key the songs should be in
for my voice?"

Otto chuckled. "Oh, we've done our homework," he said.
"Our writers studied your recordings and they know your vocal
range."

I shot a glance at Wendell. He nodded reassuringly, but I could
tell he was feeling a little uneasy, too. "Ken Nelson usually counts
on me for the tempo of the songs," I added. "He's always told
me not to let the band set the tempos." Otto put his hand on my
shoulder.

"Trust me," he smiled. "We have just the right tempos for you." I finally decided to just go with the flow.

Otto had four songs prepared, starting with "Santo Domingo." I had to write out all the words phonetically in order to know how to deliver them correctly. We'd record two or three lines and then we'd stop so I could look over the next couple of lines to make sure I could pronounce them right. The vocal coach would get exasperated, grab my chin, and try to move my mouth right. He was giving me fits! I kept getting the words wrong and was getting incredibly frustrated. I would get really mad, start crying, and run out of the studio to the ladies' room. Wendell would have to come in and give me a pep talk to keep me going. I spent six hours at the microphone for "Santa Domingo" alone. There were over thirty musicians on that recording, including the string section, four backup singers, and an opera singer from Berlin who they recruited to sing those high notes. Once I got through my part, the final record just gave me chills. In terms of production and technology, the Germans were ahead of us at that time. It was definitely the most lavishly produced record I'd ever been a part of up to that point. When my part was finally completed, however, we still had three more songs to go!

A long day stretched into a long night, but I got through it. I felt silly most of the time because I didn't really know what I was singing about. I wasn't sure if I was supposed to be sad or happy. One song had a recitation, so that was an interesting moment! In the end, they said I did an excellent job and that my German sounded natural. Of course, I have no way of knowing if that's true or not, but when they released "Santo Domingo" as a single, it became a Top 5 hit on Germany's national chart and reached number one in *Bravo,* which was the country's preeminent teen magazine. I think it's really interesting that the only two number one records in this Oklahoma country gal's career came about in Japan and Germany!

Even though the recording session only took a day, we spent a couple of weeks in Germany. I played shows at several military bases, and we had an opportunity to see the country. All that rich German food wasn't our thing, so we lived on soup, ice cream, Jack Daniel's black label, and Coca Cola. We got through it, but it took some getting used to. We were at our hotel one night and went down for dinner.

"No, you cannot eat here," we were told. "The gentleman must have a dinner jacket and the lady must be wearing a dress."

They said they wouldn't seat us. Wendell blew up. "We're tourists," he said. "We're staying in the biggest suite in your hotel. We are *going* to eat here, so you'll have to figure out how." They finally set up a little hidden-away table where nobody could see us and let us eat.

After our stay in Germany, we headed to Paris, where I performed on a package show with Roy Orbison at the storied Olympia Hall. I don't know if they'd had bad experiences with other artists, but the promoters, for some reason, said, "Whatever you do, don't talk onstage. The audience doesn't understand English. In fact, the band they provided for me didn't speak English, either. When I rehearsed with them I had to tell them the key for each song using the old "do-re-me-fa-so-la-ti-do" scale. It was pretty tough communicating with them! In addition to the ban on speaking, the promoters warned me that the audience would throw things at me if they didn't like my performance. By that point I was scared to death. When it was time for the show, I went out and did several songs in a row without saying a word. Finally, I said to myself, "By golly, I'm the entertainer here. Who are they to tell me how to relate to an audience?" The more I thought about it, the more it just kind of made me mad. So I started talking. I don't know what they thought of it, but, by the end, I got two standing ovations.

After "Santo Domingo" was so successful in Germany, Electrola Records was eager for me to record some additional sides. In October of 1965 Wendell and I returned to Cologne, where I recorded four more German language songs. Immediately afterward, I headed to Amsterdam, where I recorded two songs in Dutch. I might have thought getting the German words right was a tough job, but it was nothing compared to singing in Dutch! That was probably the most difficult recording session I've ever experienced.

For whatever reason, I was suddenly in demand to record in various languages. In February of 1966, I recorded "Oh Blacky Joe" and "Santo Domingo" at Capitol's studio on West 54th Street in Manhattan. That was the only time I ever recorded in New York City and, though I'd cut both songs in German the previous year, this time I recorded them in Japanese. Of all the languages I've sung, Japanese was the easiest. The words are comprised of short and simple sounds that I was easily able to learn. Of course, I had no clue what I was actually saying, but I enjoyed doing it anyway!

It's a funny thing to record songs in a language you don't speak, but I got to where I really liked it. German was the one that ended up being the most successful for me. Between 1965 and 1970, I recorded nearly twenty German-language songs, four or five of which hit the German charts. None of the others were as successful as "Santo Domingo," but I grew to really enjoy the country and its people. I got to where I could sing the guttural German sounds so well that they had to calm me down a little bit. "You don't have to be *that* guttural," they'd tell me. I thought that was pretty funny. I guess that nasty rockabilly voice served me a little *too* well at times!

On one of our trips to Germany, we had a day off, and they asked if we'd like to go into East Berlin. With fear and trembling we said, "Okay." An Electrola promotion man arranged a car and driver and accompanied us across the border. When we arrived at the crossing at Checkpoint Charlie, we had to get out of the car so the guards could search the vehicle. They opened the trunk and the hood and practically tore the car up to make sure we weren't smuggling anything in. Once we were on the other side of the Berlin wall, I was shocked at what I saw. The buildings looked like they had been bombed twenty days before, rather than twenty years before! It was as if someone just pushed back the piles of rubble and left them there. They showed us the bunker where Hitler died and pointed out the "No Man's Land" on either side of the border where you'd be shot on sight if you attempted to approach the wall. We were told to keep our passports close. I nearly squeezed mine to death!

When you crossed the border going in, you had to buy five East German marks, which you were required to spend there. You couldn't bring any of the money back out with you. After some sightseeing of opera houses and libraries and things, the driver decided we needed to go ahead and spend our money before returning. We went to the restaurant of a nice hotel for lunch. When it was time to go, we hadn't spent all that money, so we just piled it up on the table and left it as a tip. The driver said, "You probably just gave that waitress six months' salary!" I'm really glad I got to have that experience because it reminded me to never take for granted the freedoms I enjoy as an American.

One time when we were working in Germany, we got a phone call from our friend Jude, who owned a furniture store and performed as one half of the local Oklahoma country duo Jude and Jody. When Wendell answered, Jude said, "Hey, it's Jude. What are you doing?"

"Are you drunk?" Wendell said. "It's the middle of the night in Oklahoma. Why are you calling us now?"

Jude laughed and said, "No, I'm in the lobby of your hotel."

We invited Jude and his wife, Carol, to come up to the room. They were good friends of ours, and we couldn't believe they happened to be in Germany at the same time we were. She had a brother who was stationed there, so they made a detour to see us while they were visiting him. We got a chance to spend some time sightseeing with our friends, which was a lot of fun. Jude was a big guy and Carol was a big woman who wore furs and gloves and diamonds. She was very flamboyant. Everywhere we went people assumed that she was Wanda Jackson and I was her assistant.

By that point, Wendell and I had gotten pretty comfortable in Germany, so we decided to play a little joke on Carol. Wendell said, "You know, since you're visiting the country for a little while, you should learn a few words in German, like 'please' and 'thank you,' which the locals really appreciate." Carol smiled broadly.

"Oh, that would be a wonderful idea," she replied. "Could you teach me?"

"Sure, I'd be happy to," Wendell said. "'Thank you' is pronounced 'ochsen scheisse,' and any time you can say 'thank you' in German that will go a long way."

Of course, "ochsen" is German for the English word "oxen" or "bull." You can probably figure out what English "S" word would typically follow "bull." We went all around Germany with Carol dressed, fit to kill, in all her finery. Someone would open a car door, and she'd get out with a big smile on her face and nod, "Ochsen scheisse." Wendell and Jody and I could barely contain our giggles.

On some of our later trips to Germany I would sing on television. I couldn't believe they wanted me to lip sync the words to these songs I'd painstakingly recorded line by line. I practiced those songs over and over, trying to make sure I knew how to mouth those words so I wouldn't embarrass myself on TV. Wendell was really patient and helpful in coaching me. I remember there was one line where I would always get tripped up on when we were practicing. Finally, he said, "It sounds like 'fish sticks Magoo.'" After that, I never forgot that line. I think Wendell wound up learning most of those German songs, too, just from having to hear them over and over and over helping me memorize them.

One of the big German TV shows had booked me to appear, but our plane was eight or ten hours late, so we had to go straight from the airport to the television studio. I had my suitcase in a room upstairs with my clothes and makeup. They had some kind of choreography in mind, so I was being pulled in one direction and then another as they showed me the moves. Then the director would say, "Wanda's hair is not showing up. We need to brighten it!" I had no idea what they were doing, and I couldn't speak to them in German. A great big woman who looked like a boxer grabbed me by the hand and took me to the hair and makeup area, where she took a can of silver spray and coated my hair with it. We returned and the director decided he didn't like that. She took me back again and she sprayed a can of black stuff all over my hair. By that point, I had all kinds of gunk built up! Then, they decided they weren't happy with my shoes. I went back to my room and found this big gal pawing through my suitcase, which made me mad.

"You will wear these," she said as she pulled out a pair of flats.

"Oh no. Those are just the flats I wore on the plane. I have heels with rhinestones on them that I brought for the show." But, no. They wanted me to wear those flats. But then they decided the flats weren't shiny enough, so they got some kind of strips to apply to the toe. By then I was tired, jetlagged, and had had enough. I was upset, so I finally let loose. I learned that Germans can be a little headstrong, but if you make a stand or blow up at them, then you become pretty good friends!

In recent years, it has been a German label, Bear Family Records, that has done the most to preserve my legacy. In 1992 they released a deluxe CD box set called *Right or Wrong* that collected all my Decca and Capitol recordings from 1954 through 1962. It was the first time many of my songs appeared on CD, and I was thrilled for them to be digitally preserved and collected in one place. In 1998 they released a second box featuring the rest of my Capitol recordings through 1972. Richard Weize, who founded the label, has always championed my music, and even released a CD of all my German language recordings. In October of 2002, Richard and Bear Family threw me a 65th birthday party in a German castle. It was a really spectacular affair, and it gave me an opportunity to reflect on how thankful I am for finding a second home in Germany during the 1960s, much as I found one in Japan in the '50s.

Chapter 19

KICKIN' OUR HEARTS AROUND

Wendell was my soul mate and the love of my life. We were together for over fifty-five years. And when I say together, I mean *together*. We worked together, parented together, grandparented together, took care of life's responsibilities together, vacationed together, shared all our joys and sorrows together, and did just about everything else you can think of *together*—twenty-four hours a day—for almost six decades! It was hard to tell where one of us stopped and the other began. We were always a team. All the girl singers that I worked with over the years were envious of me over Wendell. They'd say, "Do you even realize what you have?" To have someone who is a cheerleader, supporter, best friend, and ardent defender in your corner is a beautiful thing. And, yes, I always realized what I had. We always said that divorce was never an option for us. Murder, maybe, but never divorce!

When Wendell and I began our lives together, it was almost as if we were two pieces of the same puzzle that finally came together as they were meant to be from the beginning of time. But that didn't mean we didn't have some rocky times early on. When we got married I'd been living with my parents and he'd been living with his. Neither one of us had had a ton or life or relational experience, so we both had some growing up to do.

One of the things that proved a difficult adjustment for Wendell was the way the male fans interacted with me at my shows. It was pretty common for a guy to want to get a picture with me sitting on his lap. Maybe someone would get a little pushy about buying me a drink. Sometimes, if a fan had a few more rounds than he should, he might get a little handsy and refuse to take "no" for an answer. When Daddy was traveling with me, he'd always keep an eye out for that kind of thing, but he'd usually do it from across the room. If a guy got a little belligerent, Daddy would let me handle it. I was pretty good at diffusing those situations with a well-timed comment, but every now and then Daddy would have to step over to intervene. At that point, the guy would almost always back off and we wouldn't have a problem. Wendell handled those situations differently. He had a temper, so he would see that kind of thing and get really jealous. He wouldn't let me handle it calmly, but would step in right away and sometimes cause a scene.

I appreciated that Wendell wanted to leap to my defense. What girl doesn't love a knight in shining armor? But he didn't understand that being a woman in the public eye is different from what most women experience in their day-to-day lives. In the early years of our marriage, his jealousy would spark anger, not only toward some male fans, but also toward me. He didn't

like it when I'd take pictures with men who came to the shows.
If they put their arm around me a little too tight, I'd catch hell
for it later. I'd say, "Wendell, I'm not the one who did anything.
I was just standing there trying to keep it all together and be a
professional. That just comes along with the territory, and you
need to step back a little bit." But that would just get him angrier.

We would sometimes get in serious fights about my
appearance. There are a couple of pictures of me on the cover
of the *Two Sides of Wanda* album that are pretty tame, but some
of the outtakes from that photo session showed me in a sexy
low-cut sweater that revealed plenty of cleavage. The pictures
weren't scandalous and, though a little seductive, were certainly
tastefully done. But when Wendell saw them, he nearly exploded.
"I don't need every man in America ogling pictures of my wife
half-naked," he roared as he slammed them down on our kitchen
table."

"Wendell, if I didn't look like that, you wouldn't have paid a
bit of attention to me when we first met! What do you want?"
Boy, I took all kinds of grief for those photos. Sometimes those
arguments about what I was wearing or how I presented myself
would escalate. Wendell physically tore dresses off me, and there
were a lot of fireworks before we learned how to work out
problems like adults.

Everything came to a head one night when we were at the
Palladium Ballroom in Oklahoma City. I wasn't singing that
night, but Wendell and I were there with my parents. At one
point, Daddy and I headed out to the dance floor. I always loved
to dance with him because he was a great leader and, frankly, we
looked good on the dance floor together. When the song was
over we didn't return to the table where Mother and Wendell
were waiting. In fact, we kept dancing for a couple of more songs.
Finally, Wendell came over, grabbed me by the arm, and pulled

me away. "That's enough," he hissed through clenched teeth. "Come back to the table *now.*" I could understand why he might be upset about me dancing all night with a strange man, but with my own father? Wendell's possessiveness was getting out of control. I was hurt and very embarrassed that my parents saw him behave that way. I didn't say much to anyone for the rest of the evening for fear of bursting out in tears.

Later that night we were driving home when I said, "Wendell, stop the car." He looked puzzled.

"What for?" he asked.

"Just pull over," I said, raising my voice. He could tell I meant business as he steered the car over to the shoulder. I shifted in my seat and turned toward him. "This isn't going to work," I said. "I can't live with you watching over me and counting the number of times I do this or that. You're too controlling, and I can't stand it. I don't want a divorce, but if this kind of behavior continues, that might be where we're headed. You're going to have to let me talk to other people. You're going to have to let me sign autographs and take pictures with fans. You're going to have to understand that when we're out in public, we're going to get interrupted from time to time. And you're damn sure going to have to let me dance with my own daddy if I want to! This has all gone too far!"

Wendell was quiet for a long time. He stared at the steering wheel, shaking his head. "I understand what you're saying," he finally answered, "but I don't like sharing my wife with the whole world. I'm just an ol' boy from West Texas and I'm not used to all this. Where I come from, if a guy has a girlfriend who goes over and sits on another guy's lap and is talking and giggling with him, then you have to do something about it." He said he didn't want to hurt me and that he would try to be more understanding about the demands of my career.

After our conversation that night, I was able to understand Wendell's perspective, and he was able to understand mine. He agreed to work on his jealousy and I agreed to be better about communicating. Instead of just walking off to go talk with male fans, I would let Wendell know where I was going and what I was up to. After hearing each other out, we were both willing to make some changes. One thing I've learned in my years of marriage is that it's good to discuss your problems instead of letting them build up and fester to the point where you wake up one day and discover you don't even like the other person anymore.

One of the hang-ups that took a little longer for Wendell to overcome was my relationship with Elvis. If I talked much about Elvis in an interview, I'd have hell to pay for that, too. I'd say, "Honey, I can't help it. They're asking me questions about him, and I'm just giving them an answer. I don't care if I ever hear his name again, but I can't just ignore the interviewers." I suppose I can understand why it bothered him. Most people don't necessarily want to hear their spouse talk about their teenage flame, but how often would that naturally come up for the average couple? Because of my job, it came up pretty regularly for us, so I see that it was an unusual circumstance. Not only did Wendell have to hear me talk about a previous relationship, but it just so happened to have been with a guy who is universally regarded as one of the most iconic sex symbols of all time. I was never a jealous person. I knew nobody was going to take Wendell from me because I had him, and I was going to keep him. I knew how to do it, and I did. But I guess if Wendell had dated Marilyn Monroe and I had to hear about it regularly, I might not love it. At the time, though, I just could not understand why it bothered him to hear me talk about Elvis. At one point, Wendell told me he didn't want to ever hear Elvis's name again.

Wendell and I had another breakthrough in our relationship that helped heal some of the recurring jealousies. My son Greg was born in 1964. Wendell had always joked, "If you'll have me a boy I'll take you to Las Vegas for a weekend." Not too long after Greg arrived we did, in fact, take off for a getaway weekend in Vegas with another couple we socialized with at the time. When we arrived we checked into the Sahara, freshened up, and headed out for drinks and dinner.

When we went back to the hotel later that evening, the elevator opened on our floor, and there was a big guy in a suit standing there facing us with his arms crossed. "Folks," he barked, "I'm with security and I'm going to need to see your room keys, please."

Wendell fumbled for the key. "What's all this about?" he asked.

"You folks have the only two available rooms on this floor," the guard answered. "The rest of them were rented by Elvis Presley and his entourage, so we have to make sure anyone coming up here is authorized to be here."

I hadn't seen Elvis for the better part of a decade, but my heart stopped. I thought, *Oh no. Given Wendell's feelings about Elvis we might have a scene on our hands.* I looked over at Wendell. His brow furrowed a little. He took a deep breath and smiled at the security guard. "If you're on duty when Mr. Presley returns," he said, "please tell him that Wanda Jackson is here and would like to say hello." The man took a second look at me.

"Wanda Jackson? Oh, my goodness, yes. I'm sorry I didn't recognize you at first. I'll pass along the message, but do you think maybe I could get an autograph first?"

About thirty minutes after we got to our room, the phone rang and someone on the other end of the line asked if it would be okay if Elvis came down to say "hello." In a few minutes there was a tap on the door, and there was Elvis in all of his glory. He was alone with no bodyguards or members of the Memphis Mafia, which is what they called his entourage. He wasn't working, but he was dressed up like you would imagine he'd be. The first thing I noticed was that he seemed so tall. I found out later that's when they were wearing elevator shoes. He didn't need them, since he was already six feet tall, but it certainly added to the sense that he was larger than life.

Elvis came in and I introduced him to Wendell and our friends. He stayed about fifteen or twenty minutes and, even though none of us can remember what we talked about, Elvis was as polite and charming as could be. I realized later that he came down to see us—instead of inviting us to his suite—so he could leave when he was ready. He was smart that way, and that's another show business lesson I picked up from the King. Stay in control of the situation so you can exit when you need to!

What helped Wendell so much is that he could see from our greeting each other that Elvis and I had mutual respect and love for each other, but it was nothing he needed to worry about. That was the last time I ever saw Elvis, but the lasting effect on my marriage with Wendell was far more valuable than any reunion with an old boyfriend could ever be on its own merits. Always a charmer, Elvis won Wendell over, and it helped him move past his jealousy. After that, I would be talking with friends or fans, and Wendell would say, "Hey, tell 'em that story about Elvis."

One of the factors that probably didn't help our marriage as the 1960s progressed was alcohol. Believe it or not, I never had a sip of alcohol until I was of legal age. It was pretty typical for the guys to have an after-party following a show if we didn't have to travel early the next day. I wasn't a part of that when I was on the road with Daddy because he wouldn't allow it. Later on, when I was grown, I could do what I wanted and go to whatever party I wanted. That's when I started drinking more often.

Despite my bad-girl stage persona, I wasn't much of a rebel until I was already an adult. Just before Wendell and I started dating I was getting a little bitter as I watched all my girlfriends get married and have kids. I felt like I was being left out, which made me a little rebellious. I didn't go out and get hooked on drugs and self-destruct, which is the celebrity stereotype today, but I did get into partying and drinking more than I should have. Back in the 1960s there still weren't that many female artists. There might be local girls in bands, but none of them were stars. Promoters usually just wanted one girl on the bill. We were window dressing, I guess. I didn't have the opportunity to work with many other women, so that often meant I was the only female around. Because of that, I always enjoyed the company of men. I never minded being the only girl, and increasingly that meant being more like "one of the boys" to fit in. That was especially true when I was planted in Las Vegas for days on end while performing a string of shows. The after-parties got a little wilder at that point.

I was in Springfield, Missouri, for the *Ozark Jubilee* when I had my first drink on my twenty-first birthday. Norma Jean and her date took me out to celebrate and I ordered a whiskey sour. The two of them got up to dance and, by the time they returned, I was asleep in the booth. I don't know why it had such an effect on me, but I *wanted* to be a drinker. I thought it was the sophisticated adult thing to do. Of course, falling asleep in public isn't all that sophisticated, but I kept trying until I got to where I liked drinking. Being a dedicated Baptist, Mother didn't approve of drinking or smoking. I couldn't indulge around her at first, but I finally broke down and started drinking with Daddy when Mother was around. She would just shake her head.

I started smoking cigarettes before I started drinking. I had just gotten out of high school and, of course, everybody smoked back then. We'd see the movie stars smoking in all the films and it seemed glamorous. I was sitting with some guys from a local band where we were playing a gig one day when one of them lit up a cigarette.

"Don't you smoke, Wanda?" he said.

"No, not really," I said. None of my church friends smoked, so it wasn't a habit I'd taken up at the time.

"You ought to give it a try," he said. "You're a little uptight and it'll calm you down."

Back then there were brands like Winston and Viceroy that would provide small packs with four cigarettes in them that were placed on lunch trays in some cafeterias and restaurants. After that musician made his comment, I took one of those little packs and slipped it into my purse. Every hotel room had ash trays and matches, and I'd seen Daddy do it enough that I knew how to light a cigarette. I fired one up and, even though I didn't know how to inhale exactly, I guess I inhaled enough. By the time I got to the third puff, I was so dizzy I could hardly stand up. I tapped that cigarette out and literally got sick. I had to go in the bathroom to throw up. I drank some water and stretched out on the bed for a while until I felt better. You'd think that would cure me from the desire, but I got up and said, "I'll try it again!"

Now I can't believe what an idiot I was to try so hard to get addicted to something. Once I was on them I became a smoker at heart. It was really hard to quit when the time came, but now I wonder how we lived in that smoke-filled world! The best thing that's happened for singers is being around less smoke.

By the time Wendell and I married, the people that we were around all smoked and drank pretty heavily. That was just the norm in our lives. We would never have admitted it at the time, but our drinking had gotten out of hand. The 1960s was a tumultuous era. Somewhere in all the fighting, drinking, partying, child-rearing, traveling, and career-chasing I drowned out that still, small voice in the back of my head. The things I learned to value in Sunday School and church slipped away as I pursued what *I* wanted.

Chapter 20

On the set of my TV show, *Music Village*.

TEARS WILL BE THE CHASER FOR YOUR WINE

While my priorities were admittedly out of whack for much of the 1960s, I experienced successes and achieved career milestones in that era that I'm still very proud of. One of my personal highlights was when Buck Owens scored a Top 10 country hit with a song I wrote for him called "Kickin' Our Hearts Around." Buck was one of my buddies, going all the way back to when he played rhythm guitar on my first Capitol sessions in the '50s. That was long before he signed his own artist deal with Capitol and, though I liked everybody I was working with in the studio, there are certain folks you just have a rapport with. Buck was one of those guys.

After my first Capitol session in 1956, I was still hanging around the studio after we finished recording. It was the first time I'd ever met Buck, but I felt so sorry for him when I saw him putting his guitar in an old case with broken latches. He'd wrapped white surgical tape around it to hold the case shut so his guitar wouldn't fall out. When he picked it up he had to put it under his arm because the handle was broken. I thought, "Gee, I hope that guy can make enough money to get himself a decent guitar case one of these days." In addition to going on to write and record an endless list of hit records, Buck would become a savvy entrepreneur who bought and sold radio stations, real estate, and various businesses. I once read that his net worth was over $100 million, so I guess he could have bought every guitar case on the face of the earth if he wanted to!

I remember another time we were in the studio and Ken Nelson was wanting me to do something with my vocal performance, but I couldn't understand what he was trying to get me to do. He was trying to change my approach to the song. I went over to Buck, who was stationed nearby, and said, "Buck what does how I'm doing it sound like to you?"

He got a huge grin on his face and replied, "You sound like Wanda Jackson."

I laughed and replied, "Thank you, then I'm going to sing it my way!"

I wrote "Kickin' Our Hearts Around" in Nashville when I was in town for the big DJ Convention they used to have every year. I was in my hotel room one night with nothing to do but flip through a movie magazine. There was an interview with Joan Collins, who was talking about her relationship. She said something like, "I told him we've got to stop kicking our hearts around because we're just hurting each other." When I saw that I thought, *Man, what a title!* I got out my guitar, a pen, and some paper. As I've mentioned, I always liked to have another artist in mind when writing. I thought, *Who would sound good singing those words?* Buck, who had already had several hits by then, just popped into my head. I'd decided I'd make it nice, clean, and simple and hope that Buck would record it.

Not long after, Buck and I were on the same bill for a show somewhere. I told him I had written a song for him, played it backstage in a dressing room, and gave him the lyrics. He said he really liked it and wanted to record it. When I got home I made a recording and sent it to him, but I didn't hear anything else about it.

One day Wendell was outside cleaning the cars at the first little house where we lived. Suddenly he called through the kitchen window, "Wanda, get out here quick!"

I thought something was wrong, so I ran out as fast as I could. I didn't even notice that he had the radio playing. "What is it, Wendell?" I asked breathlessly.

"Listen! Isn't that your song?" he said.

Sure enough! There was Buck on the radio singing his new single, "Kickin' Our Hearts Around." That was one of the most thrilling experiences of my life to have somebody in mind when writing a song and then have them sing it exactly the way I wrote it. Buck didn't change a single line or make the slightest adjustment to the melody at all. I was so happy with that. It's been a great song in my career, and I'm sure glad I didn't have anything else to do that night in Nashville but read magazines!

In 1970 I joined Buck, his son Buddy, the Hager Twins, Billie Jo Spears, and Tex Ritter on the Country Caravan Tour, a string of European dates intended to promote Capitol Records. By that point Buck was the biggest star in country music and had been named Capitol's Artist of the Decade. It was a thrill to get to spend some time with him again. I'm grateful to have had the chance to have Buck play on my early records and to have contributed a song to his impressive string of hits. They might just be a couple of pieces of a very large puzzle, but it means a lot to me to know I had the chance to contribute to Buck's development on his way to superstardom.

In 1966 Buck Owens launched his own TV show called *The Buck Owens Ranch Show* that predated his duties co-hosting *Hee Haw* with Roy Clark. Buck's show was produced by Bud and Don Mathis, furniture dealers in Oklahoma City with whom Wendell and I socialized. The Mathis brothers had a show of their own called *Country Social* that I appeared on several times. A year before they teamed up with Buck, I partnered with them to launch a syndicated program of my own called *Music Village*. We launched the show in the fall of 1965 and managed to place it in several national markets. Other country artists had their own syndicated TV shows at that time. While Porter Wagoner's was the most popular, there were others hosted by Bill Anderson, Arthur (Guitar Boogie) Smith, Ernest Tubb, Flatt & Scruggs, Billy Grammar, and even my old friend Bobby Lord. As far as I know, mine was the only syndicated country music television program hosted by a woman.

The stage set was designed to look like a little town. We had storefronts and a little church down at the end of the street, like you see in the old cowboy movies. I would perform with my band; Bud Mathis would appear; we had a bluegrass gospel group called The Black Mountain Boys; we'd have guests on almost every week; and we even had a comic character, like every country show in that era. We couldn't think of anyone to play the rube, so Wendell decided he'd be the comic relief. He wore overalls and portrayed Lenny, a dumb farm boy, whose character was inspired by Jonathan Winters, who used to play a similar role.

We had six or seven workable sets on *Music Village*. We always started down at the honky tonk and ended up at the church. I particularly liked the introduction. We had a real stagecoach that we got from an amusement park called Frontier City. We'd have everybody line up on one side of the stagecoach with the camera at just the right angle so you couldn't see the line. It gave the impression that we were all packed into this little stagecoach and were emerging, one at a time, like clowns from a tiny car. One time we brought in live horses, but only once! The crew put down some plastic around the set in anticipation of the inevitable. What we didn't count on was how bad it stank under those hot lights!

We had fun on the show, but it was hard work. When we syndicated it we sold it to furniture companies in various markets. I would talk about furniture and then we'd go to the break. The local furniture company would then splice in their own promos. In other words, it was designed specifically for furniture stores to sponsor, since that's what the Mathis brothers did. We'd mail out these huge two inch tapes on a reel to the various markets, but would rotate them. We'd send a tape to market one, and then it would go to market two the next week, and on and on. Once it went to the last market they would return it to us.

Eventually, we ran into some disagreements with Bud and Don. When they started doing Buck's show, it was basically the same kind of show we were doing. It was shot on the same stage and competed for the same market. There was a falling out and we ended up erasing all those tapes! Boy, I sure wish I could have them again. I'd love to see some of that footage after all these years, but it's gone. As tensions escalated with our partners, Wendell and I realized that the show was taking us away from our touring business anyway. It was time to refocus. Eventually, we decided to agree to disagree with Bud and Don and separated as friends. All in all, *Music Village* lasted no more than a year, but I'm proud to have been a female pioneer in country music television.

Our friends Jude and Jody, who were in the furniture business but also worked as entertainers, started out working for the

Mathis Brothers before they struck out on their own. Jude and his wife were the ones we had some fun with when they showed up unexpectedly in Germany. Jody, who I went to a dance with in high school, ended up marrying Norma Jean. Wendell and I actually hosted their wedding in our home. It's kind of funny to think that my best friend ended up marrying a guy I'd dated in high school, and had the ceremony in the home I shared with my husband, who was her former boyfriend whom I'd effectively stolen. She wound up with the guy I'd dated first, and I wound up with the guy she'd dated first. Then my husband and her husband became hunting buddies! Plus, we'd all been in business with Bud and Don Mathis. The local entertainment world was like our own little soap opera, so I guess that was the country music version of *Peyton Place* in Oklahoma City!

One of the things I'm grateful for is that Capitol gave me the chance to record often, so I built up a substantial body of work in the 1960s. In 1964 I released the *Two Sides of Wanda Jackson* album, which featured country on one side of the LP and rock on the other. One of the songs I recorded for that project was "Honey Don't," by my old friend Carl Perkins. I worked with Carl a lot in the '50s and I always enjoyed watching him because he was such a good entertainer. The Beatles also recorded the song, but I latched onto it before they released their version. I guess you could say the Fab Four and I both had good taste when it came to picking songs.

The Beatles, of course, changed everything in the 1960s. The British Invasion marked a turning point in rock and roll as all these bands that had been influenced by Chuck Berry, Gene Vincent, Jerry Lee Lewis, Little Richard, and my fellow American rockers expanded on what we created and took the world by storm. Suddenly, it was hard for us original rockers to compete. Music tends to experience waves of popularity. There have been times when early rock and roll was in vogue, and times when it seemed hopelessly outdated. The same can be said for country. For six decades I've seen these cycles come and go, and was always grateful that my diverse musical interests helped me ride out some storms that might otherwise have been a big challenge to my career. As the 1960s progressed, I became increasingly identified as a country artist, which, of course, was a return to my roots.

In 1966 Capitol released "The Box It Came In," which was my first Top 20 country single since 1961.

That was one Ken Nelson was a little worried about because of the subject matter. The lyrics are written from the perspective of a woman who's been abandoned by her man. He even took her wedding dress, leaving only "the box it came in" in her closet. He gave the dress to another woman, so the lyrics describe that the box he'll soon be in will be lined with satin. I thought it was great, but Ken was always a little scared of courting controversy. I always liked feisty songs, so I convinced him we should do it. The gamble paid off, resulting in a hot streak. Twenty of the next twenty-two singles I released hit the charts, and more than half of those broke into the Top 40.

One that only got up to number 46 was "This Gun Don't Care," which had me warning a woman who might take my man that a gun doesn't care who it shoots. That was another feisty one, which might have reinforced my reputation as the sweet lady with the nasty voice. Wendell and I really thought that one would be a big hit. We flew to Hollywood just to do a photo session of me holding two pistols. Capitol used the photo in an ad in *Billboard*, but it didn't become a big hit. I was surprised when the follow-up single was the one to hit the Top 10. "Tears Will Be the Chaser for Your Wine" was a great song, but I really thought "This Gun Don't Care" would be the one to take off. You can never predict what will or won't catch on, but I was carving out a voice in that era for songs from a strong and fiery female perspective. My rock-and-roll attitude was informing my country success.

Shortly before that streak of hits began, I'd released an album called *Blues in My Heart*. That was my first LP that appeared on the *Billboard* country chart, and it's one of my personal favorites of my albums. I got to sing The Delmore Brothers' "Blues Stay Away From Me" and Marty Robbins's "Don't Worry About Me." I loved those kinds of songs. I had great vocal backing by The Jordanaires and my old friend Marijohn Wilkin from the *Ozark Jubilee*. I look back very fondly on recording that album in Nashville.

By 1969 I was deep into a string of successful country singles that included "Both Sides of the Line," "A Girl Don't Have to Drink to Have Fun," "My Baby Walked Right Out on Me," and "My Big Iron Skillet." That one came from a guy named Bryan Creswell who had gone to school with Wendell. We would see Bryan and his wife, Wilda, at reunions and that kind of thing. We socialized with them occasionally, but when Bryan told us they had written a song I thought, *Oh no*. Everybody's *got a song*. I braced for the worst. But it turned out it was a good song, so I recorded it. I still perform "My Big Iron Skillet" in my shows. Even though the rock audience doesn't know it well, I just mention that you can't understand the full scope of my career if you don't know about the country years. Plus, I love to do that one for the girls, who always enjoy it.

I was enjoying my success in the late 1960s, but Wendell and I were always looking to try new things and push my career into new territory. I had been releasing a steady stream of studio recordings for the better part of two decades, but always felt like I was at my best on stage. One thing I'd never attempted was a live album. In 1969 Ken Nelson and I decided to give it a shot. We booked two nights at a club called Mr. Lucky's in Phoenix, where I always had great crowds. I remember it was the same week that the astronauts first walked on the moon, which everyone was talking about. I brought my own band, but we also added some Nashville musicians, including guitarist Fred Carter and drummer Willie Ackerman, to enhance the sound. Willie was a studio player and was not used to pounding the drums the way I wanted them in a live setting. I want the drums to kick me in the butt! He played his heart out, but we felt sorry for him when he showed up on the second night. His hands were all wrapped with tape because he'd gotten blisters from playing so much more aggressively than usual. I said, "Oh no! Willie, I'm so sorry about your hands." But he didn't care.

"Wanda, I've never had this much fun in my life!" he said. "I don't normally get to cut loose like this." He was so happy. And so was I.

The only thing I wasn't happy about, in terms of my career, was that I was working with Ken Nelson less and less in that era. He came and produced the live album at Mr. Lucky's, but for the two years prior to that, I'd been assigned to producer Kelso Hurston. I had always been so comfortable with Ken and trusted his judgment, so it was a big change to get used to someone else being in charge in the studio. I liked Kelso fine, but, to me, Ken Nelson *was* Capitol Records.

By 1970 it seemed that Capitol was regularly changing A&R men on me. I never knew who was going to be overseeing my sessions. After Kelso, George Richey became my producer. He's best known for writing songs like "The Grand Tour" by George Jones and "Till I Can Make It on My Own" by Tammy Wynette. He later married Tammy and became her manager. George was a hot producer in the early '70s, but I felt like he was more interested in the musical tracks than in my performance. He wasn't making any suggestions, paying me any attention, or giving me any feedback. That just made me mad. Even though I had a Top 20 single with "A Woman Lives for Love," a song George produced and co-wrote, I said I didn't want to work with him anymore.

After George I was assigned to Larry Butler. He produced several of my sessions, including the one that spawned "Fancy Satin Pillows." It fell just shy of the Top 10 and was my last country single to land in the Top 20. Larry was talented, but it was a struggle to recapture the feeling I had working with Ken. Maybe the times were changing and producers, in general, were becoming stars in their own right, but it wasn't the world I was used to. Ken Nelson had faith in every artist he worked with and let us shape our own destinies in terms of selecting and arranging songs. He listened to us because he trusted our instincts. He had an uncanny knack for signing artists for who they were and letting them follow their own voice. That's why he had so much success with Hank Thompson, Buck Owens, Merle Haggard, and so many others.

I might have been mourning the loss of working with Ken on a regular basis, but I was being recognized by the industry during the 1960s in a way that was gratifying. In 1965 I was nominated for a Grammy award for Best Country Vocal Performance for the *Two Sides of Wanda Jackson* album. My second Grammy nomination came several years later for "A Woman Lives for Love." I had the chance to perform at the show in March of 1971. That was really exciting. I got a beautiful gown, and Wendell and I went to Hollywood for the live telecast. Charley Pride had the male nomination, but they had me perform his song and him perform my song. I was disappointed. I did, however, enjoy getting to meet some of the other celebrities there. John Wayne was a part of the show, as was Aretha Franklin. I remember meeting The Jackson 5 backstage. When I found out their name was Jackson, I had to meet them. That was the day the future King of Pop met the Queen of Rockabilly! Though I was riding high with my career, a big change was coming later that year that I could never have imagined.

Chapter 21

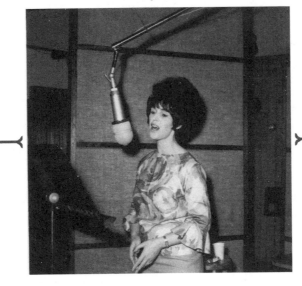

I SAW THE LIGHT

By 1971, I'd had seventeen Top 40 hits on the *Billboard* charts and had traveled the world. Wendell and I had been married for a decade, had two wonderful children, and lived in a beautiful home. I had all the material things I could possibly want, but I was unhappy with myself. Sometimes I would lie in bed at night with a gnawing feeling in the pit of my stomach that something was missing. I felt restless and anxious. Then I would feel guilty for feeling restless and anxious. After all, I had everything that a person could need or want. But I still couldn't shake that dull but persistent sense of emptiness inside.

Looking back now, I realize our marriage was probably in trouble. I don't think we ever would have divorced, because that's not something that either of us wanted. Yet there was no denying that being away from the kids, the long hours, the late nights, the heavy drinking, and Wendell's jealousy issues had all taken a serious toll on us. I felt like I didn't have a solid footing in my own life, and I knew down deep that the pressures were coming to a head. I felt like maybe I couldn't handle it anymore. That thought scared me. I imagined what it would be like to quit touring, but our entire family depended on my career. Would I be letting them down? How would Wendell react? Would we be okay? I tried to chase away the internal whispers that were telling me something wasn't right, but they never stayed away for long.

Around that time a lot of people were talking about The Living Bible, which was a brand-new paraphrase of Scripture in contemporary language that was easier to understand than a lot of translations. I thought maybe I could find some hope or wisdom from that, so I got a copy and started reading it out loud to Wendell when we were traveling on the road. I would go over several passages and Wendell and I would discuss it together. It seemed to me that there were contradictions in the Bible, and I was having trouble grasping many of the passages. A lot of it just didn't make sense to me, but I *wanted* to understand it. It wasn't until later that I understood that the Bible is God's love letter to Christians. If you're reading it, but you're not a Christian, that's a good thing, but it's almost like reading somebody else's mail. You can't fully understand it. But we were trying.

Mother and I had, of course, started attending South Lindsay Baptist Church when she and Daddy and I first moved back to Oklahoma City from California in the late 1940s. Over the years my church attendance decreased as my career took me out of town most weekends. Mother, however, remained faithful. In fact, she kept my kids, Gina and Greg, most weekends and, just as she'd done with me when I was a little girl, she insisted they attend Sunday School.

A new minister named Paul Salyer came to South Lindsay in 1971, and our kids were very excited about Brother Paul.

They wanted me and Wendell to come meet him and hear one of his messages. We told them we would go as soon as we could, but we never made it a priority. I was glad that my kids enjoyed going to church, but, truth be told, I just wasn't that interested in getting up early and getting myself together to attend. I don't think Wendell was, either. Even though we were open to trying to understand the Bible during those long stretches of interstate, we weren't that anxious to go hang out with a bunch of church people. That wasn't really our crowd.

Brother Paul had been at South Lindsay for about six months when he saw my name on the church roll. He knew who I was and was aware of my singing career. He knew my mother came, but noticed I was never there. Paul asked some folks around the church about me, and they explained that I was traveling a lot and they didn't see me often. For whatever reason, he and some of the members of the church decided to start praying for me and Wendell. Of course, it wasn't until later that I figured it out, but now I realize that those prayers coincided with that period when I was feeling something stir within me. I now understand that those were the early rumblings of God working in my heart and drawing me toward Him.

One day Brother Paul called our home seemingly out of the blue. None of the other preachers who had served at the church had gone out of their way to talk to me. He called and said he'd like to take us to lunch. I'm kind of surprised that we accepted, but we did, and we were amazed at how much we liked him right away. There was just something so easy and simple about talking with Brother Paul. He made us feel really comfortable, asked good questions, and gave us the space to talk about our lives. He'd sprinkle some spiritual references into the conversation, but he didn't pull out a giant Bible and beat us over the head with it. He wasn't judgmental and he certainly didn't tell us we were going straight to hell or anything like that. It seemed like he genuinely loved us, even though we'd only just met.

Paul said a couple of things during lunch that stuck with me. Maybe I'd heard these concepts before, but there was something about the way he explained them that really resonated. First, he said, "Everyone needs Christ, no matter who you are." Then he said, "Sometimes people are afraid to admit they need Christ, and they're afraid to turn to Him because they feel like they're not good enough or they've done some things that make them feel like God couldn't possibly love them. But He does. He loves every single person and, in order to know Him, you don't have to change anything about your life. You don't have to give up anything. You just come to Christ as you are and then, if there are changes that need to be made, He'll make it clear to you, and then He'll give you the strength to change them." That made so much sense to me, and I walked away from that lunch feeling like the answer to my restlessness was starting to come into focus.

After our lunch with Paul, Wendell and I headed out for a two-week run of shows in Alaska. Every day we were there I felt God pulling on my heart. Later I learned that Wendell was feeling it, too. We didn't talk about it. We didn't know *how* to talk about it. Subconsciously, we were probably scared at the prospect of surrendering our lives to God. Instead of embracing the lure of His love, we tried to make it go away. All I remember about Alaska was drinking. Everywhere we went we tried to drink the place dry. We were running. Running from the reality that our marriage was suffering. Running from the fear that our lives were unraveling. Running from Brother Paul's words that everyone needs God. Running from facing the hard truth that we needed God, but were ignoring Him. Looking back, the trip was a complete blur.

When we returned home from Alaska, it happened to be a weekend. That was unusual because I almost always worked on weekends. The kids were excited and made us promise we'd come to church to meet them after Sunday School and go to the morning service with them. When Sunday morning came, we were hung over. We thought, *Oh, gosh. The last thing we want to do right now is go to church, but we said we'd meet them there.* We were late getting out the door and, by the time we arrived, Mother and the kids had given up waiting for us. She had gone ahead and taken them home so she could fix a late breakfast for Daddy after church. "The kids are gonna be so disappointed," I said out loud to nobody in particular. "I guess there's not much point in us sticking around." I turned to Wendell. "Let's just head on over to Mother and Daddy's house," I suggested.

Wendell shook his head. "No," he said. "We're here, so we might as well just go ahead and hear Brother Paul preach. He seemed like a nice guy, so we'll listen to him, say hello, and then go get the kids."

I look back on that Sunday morning, and I think God knew just exactly what He was doing. He didn't intend for our children to be there, because He didn't want us to be distracted, and He didn't want us to feel self-conscious about our kids watching us. Instead, He wanted us to hear His voice. I don't even remember the details of Brother Paul's message that day, but I know that when he was done, he invited anyone who felt compelled to come forward and accept God's love into their lives by beginning a personal relationship with Jesus. It wasn't an audible voice, but I heard God speak to my spirit just as clearly as if someone were sitting next to me having a conversation. He said, "Walk with me."

I would have walked through fire at that moment if I had to, but I knew I was giving my life to Christ. I turned to Wendell. I hoped God was speaking to him in the same way and that he would come with me, but, either way, I knew I had to go. I said, "Honey, there's something I've got to do."

"Me, too," he said.

We both stepped out, took one another's hand, and headed down that aisle while the congregation sang the old hymn "Pass Me Not O Gentle Savior." On June 6, 1971, the old Wanda and Wendell were changed. We prayed with Brother Paul and were reborn as God's children. After we got up off our knees everything was different.

That afternoon we went to visit friends of ours who had just moved into a new home and invited us to come see it. As soon as we walked in they said, "What do you want to drink?" Wendell said, "Oh no thank you. I'm going to be baptized tonight." They weren't quite sure what to make of that! As the days progressed and we saw other friends, they all began wondering why Wendell and I were suddenly different people. All of a sudden, friends would come over to discover we didn't have drinks to offer and Wendell's jokes were a lot cleaner. It was as if our thinking, our priorities, and everything just changed so fast.

The first thing we noticed was that God gave us a hunger for understanding His Word, the Bible, and what it meant to live a life of service to Him. We went to church twice a week—on Sundays and Wednesdays—attended conferences and Bible studies, hosted meetings in our home, fasted from midday Sunday until midday Monday, and tried to pray together for an hour every day. It was all just so good and wonderful that I couldn't soak it all up fast enough. I had a lot to learn, but God was teaching me. We were surrounded by some of the greatest people who came alongside us and shepherded us as we grew in our faith. I felt like, at the age of thirty-three, I was just learning what it really meant to live life to the fullest. God didn't just save our souls. He saved our marriage, too, as Wendell and I came together in pursuit of spiritual maturity. Our priorities were realigned and we were both filled with an indescribable sense of peace. My selfishness and Wendell's jealousy and possessiveness that caused so many problems for us early on faded into the past. Wendell joked, "I was so mean and jealous in our early years you should have just shot me!" Thanks to God's healing power now I look back on those days and just laugh about the immaturity we displayed before we let God get a hold of our hearts.

Not only did God shake up my personal life in the best way possible, He also opened new doors of opportunities in my career. I had never really liked gospel music very much, but when I became a Christian I got a gospel album by The Oak Ridge Boys and played it over and over. Then we got an album from The Florida Boys. All of a sudden I was collecting gospel LPs.

I gave my very first gospel concert on October 3, 1971. It was held at South Lindsay Baptist Church, which was fitting. Wendell shared his testimony that night, telling the crowd about how God had changed his heart and his life. Six people dedicated their lives to Christ that evening, and the event was a tremendous success. A week later, I sang four songs at First Baptist Church in Houston, Texas, where John Bisagno was the pastor. Wendell shared his testimony once again and received a standing ovation. We were so warmly received, and we felt like we were doing exactly what God wanted us to do. It was during that trip that Wendell and I both felt like God was calling us to stop working in nightclubs and bars in order to dedicate ourselves to the ministry. At that time, between seventy and eighty percent of our family income came from my nightclub work, so deciding to give it up was a leap of faith, to say the least. We believed it was God's plan for our lives, and we believed God would somehow provide. It was a little scary, but I clung to a favorite Bible verse from Matthew 6:33, which encourages God's people not to worry about material things, since He already knows exactly what we need. In the Living Bible it says, "He will give them to you if you give Him first place in your life and live as He wants you to."

Wendell got on the phone to start canceling some of the shows that were coming up on the itinerary. One of them was at the six-hundred-seat Frontier Room in the White Horse Bowling Academy in Trenton, New Jersey. He explained to the owner, Charlie Fox, that, due to religious convictions and personal changes, we'd have to cancel the date.

"Wendell, you can't do that," Charlie said. "I've got a signed contract and the date is coming up soon. Everything is set and we've been advertising."

"I know it, and I'm sorry," Wendell said. "But if you'll look at the contract down at the bottom, in small print, it says 'This agreement can only be altered or changed due to an act of God.' Well, sir, this is an act of God and we can't come do your show."

"Okay, in that case, Wendell, it's fine," Charlie finally said. "We'll work it out."

We still had some nightclub dates on the books that were coming up too soon to cancel, so I began sharing my testimony on stage. Sometimes that was the easiest thing in the world for me to do, but other times I was a little hesitant about how the audience might react. I remember doing the very last show before we gave up the clubs. It was in Kansas and I recall thinking, *Lord, I don't want to give my testimony tonight.* I was out there in front of the audience, and the decision about whether to talk about my faith or not was weighing on my heart. I was thinking, *Should I or shouldn't I?* I got to the end of the show and never did tell the audience about my conversion. I was just glad to be saying "goodbye" to the honky tonks and was ready to get off the stage and call it a night. I was waving to the crowd as the band was playing my exit music. I went back to the same place where I thought I'd come on stage, but I couldn't find the opening in the curtain. I thought, *Well, maybe it was behind the drums.* There was a little path, so I followed it over there, but still no opening! I literally could not get off that stage. Finally, a lightbulb went off. I realized, "Oh, God isn't going to let me go." That's the moment I realized that God's got a sense of humor. I went back to the microphone and I said, "Folks, I want to tell you why this is the last place I'm working." I explained my new priorities, and I got a lot of applause. Then I just walked off stage, and the opening in the curtain was right there where it had been when I first went on!

At the end of October we participated in our first revival, which was held at the First Baptist Church in Choctaw, Oklahoma. It was a full eight days of singing and bearing witness to what the Lord had done in our lives, and it was such a joy.

Twenty-one people joined the church, and we made so many new friends, including the church's regular pastor, Brother Harold Thompson, and his wife, Mamie. We felt like God was blessing us with new relationships and a spirit of excitement. Being around so many spiritual people helped shape us in positive ways.

When we were home we often participated in church events around our area with Brother Paul. We sang and shared our faith at a revival at Southwest Friendship Baptist Church in early November that drew record crowds. At the end of that month we did a revival with Brother Harold Thompson in Anadarko that drew the largest crowd ever for that church. The next several months were a blur of Baptist church visits, including eight days in Corpus Christi, Texas, a five-day revival at First Southern Baptist Church in Wasco, California, near Bakersfield, an appearance at First Baptist Church of Whitesboro, Texas, near Gainesville, and a pair of concerts at Immanuel Baptist Church in Wichita, where there were record crowds of three thousand people in attendance. It was there that I prayed with someone who wanted to receive Christ for the first time. It was a sixteen-year-old girl named Brenda Dutton, and I was so thrilled to share in the experience of leading her to faith. When I gave a 1972 gospel concert at Red Star Baptist Church in Cape Girardeau, I was reminded of how I'd first met Elvis in that town several years prior. I would always treasure my performances with the King of Rock and Roll, but I was filled with a much deeper joy to be performing for the King of Kings!

Shortly after we were saved I was praying about my smoking. I knew I shouldn't be doing it, but I was worried and afraid I couldn't give it up. I had been smoking for around fifteen years at that point, and I really liked it. On one of our road trips I was trying to fall asleep in the back of our motor home while Wendell was driving. I was praying about that smoking, and I felt like God was saying to my spirit, "Wanda, don't be afraid." After that, I was able to let go. I've come back to that gentle reminder so many times over the years when I'm facing challenges that I know I can't tackle with my own strength.

Eventually we formalized our gospel presentation, calling it "an evening of entertainment and inspiration." I would sing and Wendell would share his testimony, followed by an invitation for others to come forward to receive Christ if they felt God calling them. We traveled together in a van, just the two of us, with our own audio equipment. I didn't carry a band at that point, which would have been too cost prohibitive. Instead, we just used prerecorded tracks, over which I sang live. It was a radical change of lifestyle, but Wendell and I felt happier and more fulfilled than we ever had before.

It was all so different from what I was used to. I had never had stage fright playing in honky tonks, but the first few times I sang at churches, I was so scared I was throwing up before I went on. I hadn't learned a lot of lessons yet. If you really put God in charge, you really don't have to figure it all out ahead of time. I was used to singing for people who were there for a party. It was nighttime, and there was smoke, and everyone was drinking and acting silly and having fun. Suddenly, there I was in a long dress—not a miniskirt—and no fringe and no go-go boots. And it was daylight and everyone was sober! I didn't know how the church folks would react to me.

Not long after my conversion, I was performing at an open-air concert at Disneyland in California. While I was singing it was like a light switch came on and I realized, *Hey, I've got the confidence now that I never had before.* All of a sudden I thought, *I can do anything.* God had a lot to do when He got a hold of me. He had some chiseling to do if He was going to form me into my best self. But I was ready. Wendell and I always said, "If God can use us, He must be desperate!" But if He wanted us, we were all His.

Chapter 22

MY TESTIMONY

In March of 1972 Capitol Records released my 20th album, *Praise the Lord*, featuring a cover photo that was, ironically, taken of me onstage in Las Vegas. Oddly enough, I'd begun recording it in January of the previous year, several months before I gave my life to Christ. I finished up the sessions in December, where I recorded an original song, "My Testimony." I'd never written a gospel song, but I just opened my heart and shared what happened in my life. It's one of the strangest songs I've ever written in terms of the feel and the structure, but it's also one of my favorites because it's pure autobiography.

There's nothing like the zeal of a new convert. After I surrendered my heart to God, I was very enthusiastic. I was so full

of joy because I'd found a very real peace in my spirit. I'd come
to realize that everyone needs Christ. He died for everybody,
but it's up to each person to accept or reject His offer of love. I
was ready to tell that "good news" to anyone who would listen,
and, frankly, my zeal probably got to the point of annoying a few
people. My heart was in the right place, and I never meant to be
pushy, but looking back I realize I could have toned it down a bit.
I confess I was a little impatient when others didn't immediately
share my enthusiasm. Ultimately, my new faith impacted my
relationship with Capitol Records in unexpected ways.

After the *Praise the Lord* album, Capitol released a secular LP
called *I Wouldn't Want You Any Other Way*. It included the songs
"Back Then" and "I Already Know (What I'm Getting for My
Birthday)," both of which had been Top 40 country singles for
me the previous year. They had enough material in the can to
round out the album, so I wasn't back in the studio until October
of 1972. As I was preparing for the session, I told Ken Nelson I
wanted to do another gospel LP. "No," he said. "We can't have
that. Capitol's not in the gospel field and, once we've done a
gospel record with an artist, that's all we need."

Around that time I was approached by Word Records. They
said they wanted to record my gospel material. I still had two
years before the end of my Capitol contract, so I asked Ken if
I could sign with Word to put out gospel music on their label
while fulfilling my contractual obligations to Capitol by releasing
country music for them at the same time. "No," he said. "It
doesn't really work that way. You can't be signed to two record
labels at the same time." We had several conversations about it,
but he wasn't changing his mind. I kept hounding him to at least
let me record gospel for Capitol if he wouldn't let me do it for
Word. The answer was always, "No." We were on the phone one
afternoon when Ken finally said, "I think I know where your

heart is, Wanda. You should pursue a company that specializes in gospel music so you can do what you want to do." Even though I had two more years on my contract, Ken arranged for Capitol to let me out of the deal after recording one final album.

My last Capitol LP was *Country Keepsakes,* which was recorded during two trips to Nashville in late 1972 and early 1973. George Richey produced the first session, while Joe Allison finished the album. Capitol released two singles, "Tennessee Women's Prison" and "Your Memory Comes and Gets Me," but neither appeared on the charts.

In between the two final Capitol sessions I recorded my debut Word album, *Country Gospel.* All my Capitol recordings since the start of 1970 had been cut at Jack Clement's studio in Nashville, which is where we did the Word album, too. In fact, many of the musicians who played on my Capitol recordings were there for the Word sessions, including guitarists Billy Sanford and Ray Edenton, and steel guitarist Weldon Myrick. There were several new faces, too, including Billy Ray Hearn, who was my producer and A&R man at Word.

There's a perception that I turned my back on secular music in the 1970s, but that's not true. Shortly after my conversion I was playing at a little club in Omaha on a double bill with Hank Thompson. Hank was a pilot and flew himself to most of his shows, but his band's bus broke down en route to the performance. I was on first, so I stalled while Hank and one of his musicians, who flew with him, grabbed a couple of guys from the warm-up band and put together an impromptu version of the Brazos Valley Boys. I had already played a full ten song set by the time Hank figured out his plan, so I went back out and played another half dozen songs while he ran through the set list backstage with his new recruits. It wound up becoming a pretty informal performance while I was stalling, and it was actually a lot of fun. I was chatting with the audience members and I told them, "Write your requests down and pass them up to the stage. If we don't know 'em, we'll just make 'em up!"

I realized at that moment that the Lord was giving me a forum to talk about Him with my audience. I loved singing and sharing my story in churches, but I didn't want to run the risk of just preaching to the choir. I also wanted to get out where folks who might never set foot in a sanctuary would have a chance to hear about God's love. I continued to play country music in theaters and club venues, but wanted to avoid the honky tonks and bars where audiences were more rowdy and there was a lot of drinking going on. Wendell and I had given up alcohol in our own lives. When someone experiences such a dramatic conversion, the pendulum can swing in the other direction before striking a balance in the middle. That was true for us, but we also felt like God was calling us to that radical change of direction in our lives at that time. We knew it was a big adjustment, but we wanted to be faithful.

At the same time, the church was becoming more open to fresh ideas and recognized that it needed to change some things if it was going to reach a new generation. When I was growing up there were very strict rules about how one dressed for church and those kinds of things that can become legalistic. The 1970s saw an openness to modern life and a concerted effort to be more welcoming. I remember when I started wearing pants to church instead of skirts or dresses. Daddy, even though he wasn't religious, could not believe it. He was running the Trianon Ballroom at the time and they had a strict dress code. Daddy said, "I'm not having any woman come into that club in pants, and you're wearing them to church!" He didn't understand that the world was changing. When Wendell and I became Christians, Daddy didn't find us much fun to be around anymore. He was happy for us. He knew it was a good thing, but he still didn't think it was for him.

In that same spirit of openness, I didn't see any conflict with recording and performing both secular country music and gospel. In fact, that was my plan all along. If Ken Nelson had allowed me to record both styles for Capitol, I would have stayed as long as they'd wanted me. One of the things that attracted me to Word was that the owner came to our home and told us, "It's a wonderful time for you to sign with us because we want to expand and start doing some country music, too." That sounded good to me. I was voted Scandinavia's most popular female singer in 1971. A country music promotional organization called "The Nashville Sound of Puerto Rico" named my *Salutes the Country Music Hall of Fame* album the "best of the decade" in 1972. That same year I embarked on an international tour as a UNICEF ambassador along with several country stars, including Tex Ritter, Connie Smith, Freddy Weller, Tom T. Hall, and Leroy Van Dyke. I knew people were still interested in hearing Wanda Jackson sing country music, and Word was filling our heads with thoughts of grandeur. We could do both country and gospel and work some big shows. They had all kinds of things in mind.

Just before we signed with them, Word opened a subsidiary imprint called Myrrh, which is probably best known as the label that launched Amy Grant's career. The idea was that my gospel records would be released on Word and my country records would come out on Myrrh. In 1974 I released my debut country album for the new label, which was called *When It's Time to Fall in Love Again*. The label released two singles, the title track and "Come on Home (to This Lonely Heart)." The first didn't hit the country singles chart at all, and the second one just barely crept into the Top 100, peaking at number 98. It would be the last time one of my country singles would chart in *Billboard*.

Around the same time they released my country album, Word signed country legend Ray Price to their Myrrh imprint, too.

Ray scored a Top 5 country hit with "Like Old Times Again," so I had faith that the label could keep me on the country chart once we hit our stride together. I looked forward to trying again, but it turned out that I'd never get another chance to record country for them. The ABC/Dot label purchased Word in the mid-1970s and, after the sale, the folks at Dot didn't know what we were talking about in terms of recording country. Dot was having tremendous country success with Roy Clark, Donna Fargo, Don Williams, and Tommy Overstreet, so they were doing just fine in the country market. They were more interested in Word for the gospel material, so I fell through the cracks once again. Whereas Capitol indulged me with one religious album and insisted I focus on country, the Word/Myrrh folks, after the sale, felt like they'd indulged my one country album and wanted me to focus on gospel. I was stuck, once again, being pigeonholed.

Between 1975 and 1978 I released three more albums for Myrrh, or Word, all of which were gospel. *Now I Have Everything,* from 1975, included "Jesus Put a Yodel in My Soul," while neither *Make Me Like a Child Again* or *Closer to Jesus* are particularly memorable to me. We thought our deal with Word was going to be great, but the ABC/Dot purchase threw a wrench in the plan. At that point I wanted to be a big duck in a little puddle, but Dot had such a powerful roster that I felt like I was getting lost. I just didn't feel at home there.

I had always been outside the mainstream of the country music world in Nashville, and the gospel music community wasn't much different. The Dove Awards, which are the Christian music industry's equivalent of the Grammys, never recognized me in any way. It didn't really hurt my feelings, but it did make me a little mad. Just because I didn't live in Nashville and go to one of the churches there doesn't mean they couldn't have invited me to sing on some program during their annual convention. But I never heard anything from them. At some point I decided, "Okay, I'll just stay out west and do my thing." I was already used to that anyway.

By the late 1970s the Word deal was over, and Wendell and I felt like we needed a change. We started to wonder what God's plan for our lives would be going forward. We were praying about it a good bit, and Wendell felt like God was telling him that it was time for us to quit traveling and quit show business altogether. We were friends with Manley Beasley, who was a prominent Southern Baptist evangelist in Dallas, as well as with an Alaskan businessman named Jerry, who had sold a large piece of property and wanted to use the money for a new ministry endeavor. Wendell, Manley, and Jerry felt God was leading them to build an office building in North Dallas that would be leased to various ministries that could share resources, such as a printing department, marketing department, and office equipment as a way of uniting together and saving operational resources that could be directed into their direct ministry efforts.

Ever since Wendell and I met him, we tried to do what God wanted us to do, and, in 1979, Wendell discerned that this was God's plan for our family. I wanted to be faithful to God's leading, but I didn't want to leave Oklahoma. When the time came, however, we bought a house in the North Dallas area and headed for Texas. There were a lot of tears accompanying our departure. It was especially tough for our kids. Gina was a junior in high school. She was a popular cheerleader with a lot of strong friendships, and it just broke her heart to think that she wouldn't be able to join her classmates for their senior year.

Adjusting to life in Texas was a challenge because we didn't know anyone there. If we needed a doctor or a dentist, for example, we had no idea where to go. Soon, however, we joined the First Baptist Church of Euless, Texas, where Jimmy Draper was the pastor. He was a great preacher and became a close friend. We had a beautiful home down there and, for the first time in my life, I had the experience of being a stay-at-home mom. I got into exercising during that period and also started cooking. I had put on a few pounds in the '70s, but having the time to focus on my physical well-being resulted in a good health kick for our whole family. That part was fun, but I grew restless pretty quickly. All I'd ever known was travel and acclaim and getting patted on the back. Suddenly, all that was gone.

Everywhere I went in Oklahoma City people would know who I was, but that wasn't the case in Dallas. I'd write a check at the grocery store and they would ask to see identification. I recall one time I was in a health food store talking with a girl who worked there. I mentioned that I was a singer.

"Oh, have you been on the Grapevine Opry?" she asked.

That was a local show that featured amateur talent. I said, "No, I haven't."

"Well, honey," she said, "you can go up there and audition, and they might let you on the show!"

Well, that just about did it for me. I can't even remember how I responded, but I know I didn't like it. I knew that my identity was rooted in God's love and not at the bright end of a spotlight, but I also enjoyed the accolades. I don't know if it was ego, but I struggled with not being known because that meant I wasn't out there connecting with audiences. I loved performing so much, and I began to feel like I wasn't living up to the full potential of the talents God had given me.

Meanwhile, every time Wendell would find a piece of property for the Dallas ministry, there would be one hitch or another. It began to seem like Jerry, who was the primary financial backer, vetoed every option, and we began to wonder if he might be regretting getting into the venture for one reason or another.

He had not moved from his home in Anchorage, and our other partner, Manley, already lived in Dallas. We were the only ones who'd uprooted our lives for the endeavor, so we bore the brunt of the pressure to see something materialize. We never lacked anything we needed, but these were leaner times for us than we were accustomed to. We had to rob Peter to pay Paul and shuffle funds around to keep our household going. God blessed us and met our every need, but we had to really trust Him. It didn't come easy.

Wendell finally took a job with a ministry of the Baptist Sunday School Board that brought teaching via satellite TV to every church that had the connection. They used the technology to teach the local Sunday school teachers during a weeknight to prepare them for their classes that coming Sunday. He had to do some traveling for that job, and I was longing to go with him. I didn't like it when he was away, plus I was itching to be back out there on the road, too.

After several months, Wendell and I were left scratching our heads. Why did God lead us to Dallas if the ministry opportunity was going to fall apart? Were we missing something about His plan for our lives? We were frustrated and confused, but wanted to hang in there if that's where God wanted us. We fasted and prayed for three days to seek God's direction. He seemed to be telling us both the same thing, which was, "I really don't care where you live as long as you continue to serve me." That gave us the freedom to go home to Oklahoma, which we did in 1980. Wendell used to say we "got out after eleven months on good behavior."

When we came back to Oklahoma, we built a house in the same neighborhood where we had been living before we moved. In fact, the house we built upon our return is where I still live today. We got back into doing church appearances, but we were also selling Amway products, which is a pyramid sales program. If Wendell and I got into something, we got into it all the way. We'd invite people over for coffee, have meetings at our house, and try to interest them in the program. That experience taught me that I'm not a salesperson. I'm an entertainer!

In the early 1980s I cranked out some country releases for the budget labels Gusto and K-Tel, but they weren't particularly inspired. The material was mostly comprised of re-recordings of earlier hits or covers of songs that had been popular by other artists. I also recorded a couple more gospel albums for a small label called Vine Records, but they didn't get much attention. By the mid-1980s I hadn't had a Top 40 hit in nearly a decade and a half. I wasn't even fifty yet, but I felt like I'd been forced into an early retirement as time had passed me by. It wasn't a good feeling, but I tried to adjust to my new reality and appreciate the fact that I still had the opportunity to sing for church audiences.

Then the strangest thing happened. Wendell and I had gone out of town to perform at a church. We were staying in a hotel suite with a separate living area so I could have an afternoon nap before the evening service, while Wendell got some work done in the other room. At one point he came into the bedroom just as I was waking up. It's hard to describe, but there was almost a glow around him as he walked by the bed. It was so beautiful, but so startling that I couldn't even say anything. Later he said, "Wanda, when you were taking a nap I was praying, and I had an experience that was almost like a waking dream or a vision. It was like our lives were a line. The line was going one way with your country music career, but then it took a ninety degree turn. That represented gospel music. I don't know what it means, but the line continued on in that gospel direction, before taking an abrupt turn again. I don't know what to make of it."

I didn't know what to make of it either, but I knew a change was coming. And I knew that God knew exactly what was in store for us.

Chapter 23

ROCKABILLY FEVER

By 1984 I hadn't played a country show in years. And my rockabilly days were so far in the rearview mirror at that point that I'd nearly forgotten them. I assumed everyone else in the world had probably forgotten them, too. Apparently, at least one person remembered.

Wendell and I received a phone call in the summer of 1984 from Harry Holmes, a Swedish newspaper man who had started his own label called Tab Records. He was a fan of mine who explained that there was a big rockabilly revival going on in Scandinavia and that he'd like me to come over and record an album. He said he could also put together a tour for us while we were there. Going from gospel back to rock and roll was an unexpected turn in my life, but Wendell and I both realized that this was what his vision was preparing us for. God was redirecting us once again for His purposes. I just didn't yet fully understand what that would mean.

We traveled to Sweden, and I was absolutely shocked to go into these little towns and draw sold-out crowds. I didn't know I had any fans in that part of the world, and I was even more surprised to discover that these were the most diehard fans I'd ever met! Kids would come in with stacks of albums for me to sign, and I could barely believe it. Harry put together a wonderful backing band for the tour, and those dates became the first rattle out of the bag in terms of getting back into secular shows after a long gospel era.

In September I went into a studio in the city of Kumla and recorded my first rock material in twenty years. With producer Kenth Larsson and a backing band of Swedish rockabilly fanatics, I did my take on some classic songs like "Stupid Cupid," Buddy Holly's "Oh Boy" and "Rave On," and Otis Blackwell's "Breathless," which was made popular by Jerry Lee Lewis. We also recorded some country sides, and I even squeezed in a disco-tinged gospel track to close out the album called "Ain't It Gospel." The album, *Rockabilly Fever,* was released in Europe and was well received.

Harry hired a photographer to take some shots of me for the album cover. Before long, I was talking about my faith in God and sharing my testimony with this young man. "It's the strangest thing," he commented during the shoot, "when you started talking about God your whole countenance changed. Your face softened and you began to look so happy." He began asking me questions about Christ and we had a really great conversation.

I soon discovered that there was an openness to spiritual conversations in Europe that I didn't find in America. In the

States you can mention God briefly on the radio, and they'll just change the subject of the interview. Over there, however, people are more open to it. I think maybe they're not immune to it because they haven't heard as much about it. I could go on the radio in Europe and give my full testimony. They would ask me all sorts of questions, and we would have nuanced discussions about the meaning of life. That was a new experience for me.

I came to understand that my longing for the spotlight back in Texas wasn't actually self-centeredness. I had struggled to keep those feelings at bay, believing that wasn't the kind of attitude God desired. I had wrestled over my feelings toward some of the gospel performances. I was starting to get tired of having to work with tracks and not having a proper stage a lot of the time. I would fuss at myself, "You shouldn't feel that way. You're doing what God wants you to do." But the truth was I was getting unhappy. Now I see that all those feelings I was fighting out of a desire to live in God's will was actually the process of God drawing me back to the world of secular music. I came to understand that you're not going to win the world to Christ if you're not actually out there in the world. I love the church community, but you can't stay in the four walls of the church if you want to make an impact.

Wendell and I both realized that God was going to use our testimony in places that needed it. It was a tricky adjustment at first. Initially, I felt a little guilty because I'd thought of my secular career for many years as something I'd walked away from out of obedience to God. It was hard to feel right about singing in bars again, but God confirmed in my spirit, time and again, that that's right where He wanted me and that's where I could be most effective. I came to feel like I was in God's will singing my little rockabilly songs and sharing His love. I was ready. I wanted to get back out there!

During that Swedish tour it seemed that nearly every night the audience would start chanting, "Mean, Mean Man." I'd tell them, "I know I wrote the song, but I haven't sung it in so many years, I don't even know the words anymore." One morning we were getting out of the elevator in a hotel lobby when a young man ran up to me with a piece of notebook paper.

"Wanda, here are your lyrics to 'Mean Mean Man.' I wrote them down for you. Please start doing it again. We love it!"

So I did. And it's been on my set list ever since. I still can't believe that people who weren't even born when I was recording those songs know them even better than I do!

I continued to release gospel and country material on the independent Amethyst label in the 1980s as Wendell and I toured Europe on a regular basis. Sweden opened that door for us and, before long, German promoters were calling. That led to all kinds of festivals. There are festivals for everything in Europe. They'll do just about anything as an excuse to enjoy beer and dancing! From there, things opened up for us in the UK. Later on came Spain, Switzerland, Hungary, the Czech Republic, and so on. I was the Queen of Rockabilly in those places, so touring overseas was very successful for us. We would make four or five trips a year, and I felt like I was back where I belonged when I was onstage with a live band.

Discovering my new fanbase in Europe was one of the great joys in my life. Unfortunately, that time period also brought about the saddest moment. I was traveling in Norway in March of 1985 when I found out that Daddy had died. He had been ill with kidney problems and had had several operations, including open heart surgery. His body was breaking down on him. We were just finishing the tour when Gina reached us in our hotel room. Wendell answered the phone and I couldn't tell who he was talking to. When he hung up he said, "Honey, sit down here

on the bed a minute." He knelt beside me and took my hand. "I
hate to have to say this, but you need to know that Tom has died."
I broke down in tears. The young guy who drove us arrived just
at that time to take us to the airport. I ran out to him and sobbed,
"Peter, my Daddy has died!" I cried all the way home. They could
hardly get me through the door at the funeral home. Brother
Paul and Wendell had to help me. I had always put Daddy on a
pedestal and it was hard to believe he was gone.

Despite my grief I took comfort in knowing that Daddy
received Christ just a few days before he died. It was our preacher
who led him to God, but Mother had been praying for him
for forty years. She lived a faithful life in front of him, and after
Wendell and I became believers we tried to do the same. I had
the chance to speak with him afterward from Norway, and I said,
"Daddy, I'll be singing while you're having that operation, but it's
going to be really hard for me because I'll have you on my mind.
Would you pray for me during that time?" It felt so good and
so strange to ask Daddy to pray, but he said he would. He didn't
get to live a Christian life, but I know that he's in the presence
of God today and that I'll get the chance to see him again in
Heaven. That thought brings me great comfort.

In 1986 a US label picked up the *Rockabilly Fever* album and
released it under the title *Rock 'N' Roll Away Your Blues.* By that
point there had been quite a rockabilly resurgence in America.
The Stray Cats were the most popular rockabilly revivalists, but
bands like The Clash, The Blasters, X, and The Cramps blended
rockabilly with punk and created a whole new subculture of
young rockabilly fans who dressed exactly like we did in the
1950s, but added a whole lot of tattoos and piercings to the
equation! I discovered that many of these musicians were fans
of mine. Even country artists were getting into the game by the
late 1980s, including Marty Stuart, who had a hit with "Hillbilly

Rock," and my friend Rosie Flores, who released her debut album in 1987 and became one of my biggest champions.

In 1995 Rosie released an album called *Rockabilly Filly.* I joined her for two songs, "His Rockin' Little Angel" and a cover of my own "Rock Your Baby." She also featured Janis Martin on the album, who had signed with RCA in 1956 and came to be known as "the female Elvis." Like me, she recorded both country and rock material and was also rediscovered in Europe during the rockabilly revival. Even though Janis and I have both been championed as the female pioneers of rockabilly, and even though we both became friends with Rosie Flores, we never actually crossed paths. I regret that I didn't get the chance to meet her and swap stories about our rockin' days in the 1950s. Rosie produced a really good album for Janis, and was glad she took the opportunity when she had the chance. Janis was diagnosed with cancer and died not long afterward.

I give Rosie a lot of credit for my rockabilly resurgence in the US. When she first reached out to me, I wasn't familiar with her. She said she was a fan of mine and she sent me her record. I really liked what I heard. She ended up coming to Oklahoma City and visiting us at our house. That's where we recorded my parts on the songs for her album. I just thought she was wonderful and I was so glad she contacted us. Rosie had a good following and was the one who helped me realize that I did, too. She ended up reintroducing me to the new rockabilly scene and they really embraced me. Wendell and I started to get calls from her from time to time, inviting us to do shows with her. Before long, she arranged for an agency to put together a tour for us. We spent five weeks zigzagging across America and up into Canada. It was like old times being on the road again, except this time I wasn't the only girl on the bill. I had another gal there with me to share the experience.

One of the dates we played was in Nashville. I'd always felt like a black sheep in Music City and didn't think that anyone there would even come out to see me perform. I never did pursue any dates around there. Other than the time I appeared on the *Grand Ole Opry,* the first time I played a show in Nashville was with Rosie. We played one of the clubs there, and the room was packed. I couldn't believe it. I didn't think anybody there even knew me. And if they did, I figured they didn't like me! I was pleasantly surprised to find out I was wrong. In fact, I even donated my Martin D-28 guitar to the Country Music Hall of Fame. I thought it was fitting for them to have the one I was holding on the cover of my *Salutes the Country Music Hall of Fame* album. It was the second good guitar I ever owned, but I'd worn it out over the years. In fact, I felt like I'd made peace with Nashville, and it was nice to feel embraced by the community there.

In some ways that tour with Rosie was a little scary. We'd been in a lot of clubs and honky tonks in our day, but some of these venues she was playing were a whole different thing altogether. Everything was painted black, and I couldn't believe some of the stuff that was written on the walls! In Europe we usually played festivals, so rock clubs were a new thing for us. It was kind of eye-opening. Even though the rooms were a little frightening, the audiences couldn't have been sweeter. They came because they loved the music, and it was just so wonderful and so amazingly unexpected to be embraced by a new generation of kids. It also introduced us to a whole new circuit of venues and booking agents. When I was playing with Rosie, a lot of the managers of the clubs would talk to Wendell about booking me again in the future. Before long, work just began to open up for us in the US. We didn't have to make four or five trips per year across the ocean. We enjoyed traveling overseas, but we were nearly sixty by that point, and it wasn't as easy on us as it had once been.

Even though I would have never imagined myself on some of the stages I've been playing since the mid-1990s, I just absolutely love it. I believe God has given me two deep desires, and He's provided me with the opportunity to fuel them both. First, I love to rock 'n' roll. It's great to get on the stage, feel those drums pounding behind me, and get the audience on their feet. Second, He gave me the desire—and also the courage—to talk about my faith onstage, whether I'm at a church revival or a punk rock club.

Everybody knows the chorus to "I Saw The Light" by Hank Williams. To this day, when I play it for my country audience or the rockabilly crowd, it always goes over well. I like to play that song and give my testimony onstage. It's hard for me not to say more than I do. Here's all these beautiful young people in front of me and I want them to want what I have. I want them to experience the peace and healing that only God can provide. A hush comes over the crowd when I mention that I gave my heart and life to Jesus Christ. In all the years I've been talking about my faith in my secular shows, I've had very few problems with people marking smart remarks or heckling me. Every once in a while, I'll have a drunk girl sarcastically yell out "hallelujah" or something. Some guys have mouthed off a little bit, but the audience will shush them for me, so I don't have to say anything. Now my fans know I'm going to share from my heart, and they don't seem to mind. They listen. As long as I can hold them, I'm going to talk about it. I think my fans respect me, but I also try to be cool and respect them by not talking too long.

The only time I had any problems with sharing my faith onstage was at a big show at the Wimbledon Coliseum in London. The promoter, Mervin Khan, wrote a letter to Wendell afterward saying they'd like to have me back the following year for another show, but I'd have to agree not to make contact with the audience by way of "preaching." I guess I was kind of lengthy that first time! We went back the next year and I said, "I've given my heart and life to Jesus, so this next song I'd like to dedicate to Jesus Christ." I told Mervin, "That was just a song dedication. That's not preaching!"

By the time I returned to secular music, the country genre had gotten so big and so popular that people didn't turn their radios down anymore when someone came to their door or pulled up next to their car. It had become respectable, and nobody was embarrassed to be a country fan anymore. I struggled with feeling some resentment that I didn't get to experience that kind of mass popularity in my heyday. I didn't have the elaborate staging and the top-notch pickers to comprise an unbelievable band. I didn't get to enjoy the better microphones and the great monitors that gave new artists better sound than I could have ever dreamed possible. I didn't have the big light rigs and all that kind of thing in the little dives where I worked in the 1950s and '60s. I was a little resentful that I didn't have the opportunity that was enjoyed by the girls for whom I paved the way. They started getting advertisements and sponsorships as the face of Revlon or the creator of their own perfume line. I was longing for that, but it never happened. But it was okay. I had carved my own path and I was proud of my accomplishments.

Chapter 24

One of the many great bands I've worked with in Germany.

WHOLE LOTTA SHAKIN' GOIN' ON

In the summer of 2003 I cut my first real rockabilly album recorded in the US in decades. Called *Heart Trouble,* it was released by CMH Records, which specializes in bluegrass. Initially, the idea was to do a bluegrass project, which I was really excited about. I love bluegrass, but somewhere along the way the plan morphed into something completely different.

We were going to make the record in North Hollywood, California. When word got out around town that I was going to be recording, the label started getting calls from various people who wanted to be involved. Dave Alvin wanted to play guitar. Lee Rocker, from The Stray Cats, wanted to be part of it. Rosie Flores signed on, as did The Cramps and a band called

The Cadillac Angels. James Intveld wrote a song for the album and ended up recording with us, too. Before long, the bluegrass concept was abandoned and CMH decided to go a different direction. I might have been a grandma, but it was time to rock again!

One of the things I really enjoyed about recording *Heart Trouble* was that we thoroughly rehearsed before we began recording. Boy, that's something that never used to happen back when I was making records in the '50s and '60s. You would just go in, the musicians would come up with arrangements on the fly, and everything would be done very quickly. We look back now on recordings from those days as a lasting document of an artist at a particular time, but, truth be told, we didn't put as much weight on recordings then. A record was just something to help you get more live gigs. We didn't overthink it, and we never imagined that anyone would still be listening to those recordings in a year—much less fifty years down the road! Today, the process is approached much differently, and it was fun for me to take some time thinking about the arrangements and building rapport with the musicians. There's value in both approaches, but I was glad to try the new way of doing things.

We were rehearsing one afternoon when Elvis Costello's drummer, Pete Thomas, stopped by. He said, "Wanda, Elvis plays the DVD of your *Town Hall Party* performances on our tour bus all the time. That's what gets him in the mood to perform a show. Would you like to have him do something with you on the album?"

As I mentioned, Wendell had been jealous about my relationship with Elvis Presley when we first married. He laughed when he heard Pete's question and said, "Well, that's all the hell I need is another Elvis in my life!" He was joking, of course, as he had grown to love my Elvis Presley stories, and we both had great respect for Elvis Costello. I told Pete we'd jump at the opportunity to work with Elvis.

When Pete mentioned it to Elvis, he said he definitely wanted to do it, but he didn't just want to add a vocal part at a different studio later on, which is pretty common for duet performances. He said he wanted to record with me in person. He brought his own band and we did Buck Owens's "Crying Time" together. We had so much fun, and I really liked him immediately.

Elvis invited us to come out to watch the taping of an episode of the TV show *Frazier*, which he was going to be on. We decided to go, and were in the audience when Elvis spotted us after the rehearsal of one of the scenes. He said, "Wanda! I've got to show you something!" He ran to his dressing room and came back with two of my albums. He said, "I found these just the other day! Will you sign them?" Even though he's a big star, Elvis is still a music fan with the enthusiasm of a teenager. I have a lot of respect for the way he uses his platform to celebrate other artists. In fact, I doubt I would have made it into the Rock and Roll Hall of Fame if it weren't for Elvis Costello.

Wendell had been saying for years he couldn't believe I wasn't in the Rock and Roll Hall of Fame. I told him I didn't expect to be because I never had a string of hits. He would always say, "Yes, but you were the first female rock singer. You were the pioneer, and you deserve to be in." Wendell took it upon himself to begin writing the nominating committee every year. For three or four years he'd send a packet to them summarizing my career and demonstrating why he thought I should be inducted. I was charmed by the way Wendell championed me so tirelessly, but I was also a little embarrassed. I didn't think they'd be interested and I didn't want Wendell to be disappointed.

Through Wendell's efforts we got to know Terry Stewart, who was the President of the Hall of Fame for several years. He was a big fan of mine and was always very nice to us. When Elvis Costello found out I wasn't in the Rock Hall, he couldn't believe it. In May of 2005, he wrote them the most wonderful letter:

To Whom It May Concern:

This is to propose that the Rock and Roll Hall of Fame finally nominates Wanda Jackson for induction. For heaven's sake, the whole thing risks ridicule and having the appearance of being a little boy's club unless it acknowledges the contribution of one of the first women of rock and roll.

It might be hard to admit, but the musical influence of several male pioneers is somewhat obscure today. Even though their records will always be thrilling, their sound is not really heard in echo.

Look around today and you can hear lots of rocking girl singers who owe an unconscious debt to the mere idea of a woman like Wanda. She was standing up on stage with a guitar in her hands and making a sound that was as wild and raw as any rocker, man or woman, while other gals were still asking, "How much is that doggy in the window?" . . .

It is strange to find myself a member [of] the Rock and Roll Hall of Fame while there seem still [sic] be a number of notable absentees. I'd like to be able to send the museum some old guitar that I played in '77, with a good heart and clear conscience. Right now I'd be embarrassed to see it on display in a glass case in Cleveland while Wanda is still rocking and still missing from the Hall . . .

Come on you guys. DO THE RIGHT THING . . . HELP INDUCT WANDA . . .

Yours through music,
Elvis Costello

When Terry saw the letter he said, "Wendell, that's the best thing you can do. Get the people who are already in the Hall of Fame to advocate on Wanda's behalf." In December of 2006 Bruce Springsteen and his wife, Patti, came to see me play a show at the Asbury Lanes in New Jersey. The manager came to the dressing room before I went on.

"Wanda, Patti and Bruce Springsteen are here. Would it be all right if they came back and said 'hi' to you?"

I thought he was joking. I said, "Yeah, sure, send 'em on back. When the president gets here, he can come, too!" But he wasn't kidding. After I met them they spent the night out in the audience dancing and singing along with all the other fans, which completely blew me away. Bruce was another person who, like Elvis, spoke up for me and advocated for my induction into the Hall.

Finally, in 2009, I was inducted in the "Early Influences" category. I was thrilled by the honor, but I was even more thrilled that all the hard work had paid off for Wendell and so many of my fans who had lobbied the nominating committee for several years. Wendell found out on a Friday afternoon when Terry called him to deliver the good news. He held the secret in until Sunday when he could invite the whole family over under the guise of watching a football game together. Wendell's brother and his wife were there, and Gina and Greg were both there with their families. I was just enjoying having my kids and grandkids all together. I never imagined anything more was going on.

At halftime Wendell said, "Let's all go into the living room." When I walked in there were a couple of bottles of champagne that had been poured into glasses.

"Wendell, what in the world is all this?" I asked.

"Everybody grab a glass," he said. "I'd like to raise a toast to the newest member of the Rock and Roll Hall of Fame!"

At that moment my granddaughter walked in with a dozen long-stemmed Sonia roses, which are my favorite. The whole family began applauding. My kids were crying and I was crying. I just couldn't grasp it. I thought about all those years, all the long miles on the road, all the triumphs and disappointments, and I thought about Daddy. I wished he could have been there to see the result of what we'd started building together the day he called up Bob Neal in 1955 and arranged to have me play my first show with Elvis. The whole experience was completely overwhelming.

The Hall of Fame asked me to agree on a presenter who would make a speech about my career at the ceremony. I suggested Elvis Costello, but he couldn't do it because he was out on the road and unavailable. The staff at the Hall suggested Roseanne Cash. I didn't think that would necessarily be so great, but it's who they chose, so I went with it. I should have trusted their instincts from the outset. Roseanne called me a couple of times and asked me some questions, like what I most wanted people to know about me. I said, "Number one, I can rock! Number two, I was a lady, and reputations are important, and number three, rock and roll and God are not mutually exclusive!"

When the night of the event came, she gave a wonderful speech. She has a way with words, just like her dad. She was funny and charming, and hit all the right points. She said, "For girls with guitars, myself included, Wanda was the beginning of rock and roll. . . . Every young woman I know, musician or otherwise, worships her as the prototype—the first female rock star. . . . She's vibrant and edgy without being abrasive, and sweet without being saccharine. This is a woman who has rhythm and joy, in equal parts, to the depth of her soul. . . . She's not a red-carpet-celebrity-hang-out-rehab-tabloid kind of person. She's a person of strong religious conviction, deep integrity, a road warrior, and a rock and roll queen. . . . You are, as Wendell always introduces you, the First Lady of Rock and Roll and the Queen of Rockabilly. And now a member of the Rock and Roll Hall of Fame."

I can't say enough about what an excellent job Roseanne did.
I was deeply touched. After I gave my acceptance speech I played
a couple of songs with the house band. Paul Shaffer from David
Letterman's TV show was the band leader, and he was having a
ball. He already knew "Let's Have a Party," so I didn't even have
to teach it to him. We played that and "Mean Mean Man." Scotty
Moore and DJ Fontana, who played with Elvis in the '50s, were
at our table, and it was so cool to be up on that stage playing the
kind of music Elvis encouraged me to embrace, while my old
buddies were cheering me on.

At the Rock and Roll Hall of Fame induction ceremony, I
played my pink Daisy Rock guitar, which has replaced my old
Martin guitars in recent years. The company was founded by
Tish Ciravolo, who was inspired to create guitars that would be
appealing to young girls and help encourage them to get into
playing music. I met Tish in California around the same time I
did the *Heart Trouble* album, and that's where I got her business
card. Daisy Rock ended up sponsoring me and I became an
ambassador for the company. I had a little thing I'd do on stage,
where I'd say, "You see my pretty pink guitar? Well, it's just great
for girls. It's a little bit smaller and lighter, and it's cut down in just
the right spot! Dolly Parton will love this!" Invariably, girls would
ask me, "Is it really cut down differently?" I'd tell 'em that it's
not really, but it makes a good story. Tish said when she saw me
playing that guitar at the Rock and Roll Hall of Fame she was
so proud that she started crying. I just hope her guitars equip an
army of future girl rockers!

My first guitar, the Martin D-18, was stored up in my parents'
attic for several years. About the worst thing you can do with
a guitar is leave it in a hot attic. Of course, it got damaged and
warped by the intense heat and humidity, but Wendell had
it repaired, and we donated it to the Rock and Roll Hall of

Fame so fans can see it on display when they tour the facility in Cleveland.

It's funny, but when people started talking about what an important pioneer I was, I thought, *Really? First I've heard of it!* I hadn't really thought of myself in those terms until these various honors and awards began happening. I received a National Heritage Fellowship from the National Endowment for the Arts in Washington, D.C. I was inducted into the Oklahoma Hall of Fame, the Oklahoma Country Music Hall of Fame, the International Gospel Hall of Fame, and the Rockabilly Hall of Fame. It's always such an honor to be recognized for my contributions, but there's just one piece missing from the puzzle.

I have nothing in the world to complain about, but I've always wished I was in the Country Music Hall of Fame, too. Country was where I started, and I had far more commercial success— nearly thirty charting singles—in that genre than I ever did in rock or gospel. It's commonplace for a female singer to have a sexy image in country music today—heck, all of 'em have that image!—but I was the first one to do it. I broke that ground and set the template for the girls who came along after. I made it okay for the gals to put a little rock and a little glamour in their country music. Perhaps, when the time is right, I'll be recognized in that way. If it doesn't happen, that's all right, too. I've already had more accolades thrown at me than any one person could ever deserve. But I won't say I don't think about it! That's just human nature, isn't it?

Chapter 25

With my buddy, Jack White.

THUNDER ON THE MOUNTAIN

After my disastrous experience at the *Grand Ole Opry* in 1955, I vowed I would never go back again. But you can't stay mad forever. In January of 2011, I finally returned to the *Opry* stage for the first time in 56 years. The show had moved from the Ryman Auditorium to a much larger venue on the outskirts of Nashville in the mid-1970s, but in recent years they've started going back to the Ryman in the winter months when there are fewer tourists in town. Since it was the off-season, I got to return to the exact stage where I'd been before. This time it was a wonderful experience. I even wore a white fringed blouse with long sleeves, so the ghost of Ernest Tubb wouldn't have to worry about seeing my shoulders. It's not that I learned my lesson, it's just that old age got me! I always say that neck lines go up when you're a little girl, come down when you're a teenager, and go right back up if you become a gospel singer. Now I can wear whatever I want, but you have to ask yourself what looks best for where you are in life.

The man who coaxed me back to the *Opry* stage was singer, guitarist, and producer Jack White. I had just finished recording my fortieth studio album, *The Party Ain't Over,* with Jack, and he suggested we go to the *Opry* with the band he put together for our tour. It was actually the first time he and I performed together publicly, and I'll never forget what a great evening it was.

When we were onstage Jack told the audience the story of what had happened to me the last time I was at the *Opry.* He went into details about how I got in trouble for wearing something too revealing and how I'd been sent back to my dressing room to cover up. He changed the last part of the story and said I finally came strutting out onstage naked, and that's the day that country music embraced the "Nudie suit." I didn't know he was going to say that, but I thought it was pretty funny. The audience whooped and hollered and got a big kick out of it.

I was only vaguely aware of Jack before we worked on that album together. I'd heard his name once when I was over in Europe, and I knew he'd had a band called The White Stripes. But I didn't really know much about who he was. I always try to say I knew of him more than I actually did, because Jack's a big star, and I don't want people to think I'm not keeping up! But if I didn't know much about him at first, I found out real quick.

The idea of working with Jack came to me through Jon Hensley, who was my publicist and manager until he died unexpectedly at the age of thirty-one in 2015. Jon was really great about making sure younger folks knew who I was and appreciated my music. One day he mentioned to Wendell that

Jack White was interested in recording me. Wendell didn't know anything about Jack at the time, so he didn't pay much attention. We were at home one day when he said, "Boy, I keep getting all these emails from this Jack White guy. He must really want to work with you." My daughter Gina was walking through the room and overheard his comment. She stopped right in her tracks. "What did you say, Dad? Jack White is a huge star. You need to write him back *immediately!*"

Once the grandkids found out about it they went nuts. My granddaughter said, "Ma! You don't know Jack White? He's the biggest thing in the world. You've GOT to work with him!" At first I wasn't really sure if I wanted to do it or not. Honestly, I was a little intimidated. Jack was a big rock star, and he seemed to come from a different world than me. I didn't know if we would be particularly compatible or if he would really understand me as an artist. But for the sake of my children and grandchildren, I reluctantly resigned myself to giving it a try.

Jack and I began communicating about song ideas over the phone and via email, but I never actually saw him in person until it was time to record. I went down to Nashville in 2010 and met up with him at his house. He had a beautiful home with about five acres. He showed me around, and I thought he was so cute with that hair hanging down in his face. I never did mind long hair on guys if it was clean and neat. There was a shyness about Jack that kind of reminded me of Elvis. I liked him right away, but there was still a bit of awkwardness between us, since we were virtually strangers.

We went into the control room in his studio, where we sat down to talk and get to know each other. He explained to me that he didn't enjoy digital recording, but preferred to make records on analog tape the way we used to do it. He was excited to show me his vintage tape recorder. He said, "You know what

I call this one?" I shook my head. He said, "Her name is Wanda."
He let out a nervous laugh and I gave him a great big smile. I
was flattered by that. The more we talked the more comfortable
I got. Jack is a genuine person, and I could see that this guy was
really a fan. He could name a lot of my songs, including some of
the lesser-known things, and was obviously very familiar with my
career. I respected him because he knew my kind of music even
better than I did. He had studied it. It was clear that Jack was *for*
me in every way, and I felt honored by the respect he showed me.

After we talked for a little while, Jack said, "Are you ready to
hear some of your playbacks?"

I was a little taken aback. "You've already got playbacks?" It
never occurred to me that he might have already recorded the
tracks before my arrival. I said, "Jack, you didn't ever ask me what
key I sing these songs in."

He kind of chuckled uneasily and said, "No, I'm sorry. I kind
of guessed at it."

Once he started playing the songs I liked what I heard, but
there were a couple of them I couldn't sing. The key was too
high and they were too fast. "Rip It Up?" My gosh, it was so fast!
I said, "Jack we can't use that one. I won't be able to do it."

"Oh, it'll be fine," he said. "I think you can handle it."

"The only way I can sing it is if we lower the pitch, and the
only way to lower the pitch is to slow it down. I'm going to
have to slow it down anyway to get all those words in." Once
we did that, it was still on the higher end. When you hear it on
the album, I sound like I'm about sixteen years old. On the next
song, I sound like an old lady!

I was happy with the songs we picked out for the album.
When Jack said he wanted me to do "Rum and Coca-Cola," I
couldn't believe it. I always loved the version by the Andrews
Sisters since I was a kid, and I'd always wanted to record it. I don't

know why I never had, but it was as if Jack knew exactly what was right for me. That blew my mind.

One of the songs he had pushed me to do was "You Know I'm No Good" by Amy Winehouse. Amy was still living at the time, but I wasn't familiar with her. From the start, I told Jack I didn't really know the song and, truth be told, I didn't even actually try to learn it. I didn't want to record it. I thought maybe we could skip over that one, but when I found out Jack had already brought the band in to create the track, I figured there wasn't any getting out of it. Finally, I told myself, "Wanda, if you're going to work with this young guy, do what he suggests. He has his finger on the pulse and he's got your best interest at heart."

Of course, that didn't make me any more prepared. I was in the recording booth with headphones on. Jack would sing me the notes from the control room. He'd have me sing along with him two or three times, and then we'd go to the next line. He taught me the song right there on the spot. Jack was incredibly patient, which is unusual for a young man. What's funny is that I didn't want to record "You Know I'm No Good," but it has since become one of my favorites. That's one of the songs I regularly do on stage, and I love to sing it. I was so sad when Amy Winehouse died in 2011. She was only twenty-seven years old, and was so talented. I can only imagine how many great songs we missed out on when she left us too soon.

Jack knew that Bob Dylan liked my music, so he called Bob and told him about our session. Jack said, "I want her to do one of your songs. Which one do you think it should be?" Bob didn't pause for a second. He replied, "Oh, 'Thunder on the Mountain.' No question." Bob's song had just come out four or five years earlier, but Jack and I both agreed it was a great song for me. The original version references Alicia Keys and her being born in

Hell's Kitchen. We changed it to Jerry Lee being born in Ferriday, Louisiana. That was a lot of fun to give a little nod to my old friend. We changed some other lines, too, to reference Oklahoma and my song "Funnel of Love," so I like to tell people that Bob Dylan and I are co-writers. Obviously we're not, but it sounds impressive, doesn't it? Bob once famously called me "an atomic fireball of a lady" on his radio show, so I have to do my best to live up to his expectations!

We wound up shooting a video for "Thunder on the Mountain," and Jack just amazed me. He's real feisty onstage. He's all over the place, kidding me and bumping me. I don't know how many takes we did for that, but every single one was like the first one with Jack. He put his all into it each time. One of the things about Bob Dylan's songs is they tend to have plenty of words in them. I hadn't memorized "Thunder on the Mountain," so there were cue cards everywhere on that set. The cameras were trying to keep from showing them, and I think they succeeded. The whole thing was fun and exhausting. I had a blast. Jack brought that old rock-and-roll energy back when I needed it most.

We set up a short tour with three or four shows. They were really more like record release parties, but Jack's name on the bill drew some really big crowds. I had a nine-piece band behind me, plus two background singers, including Ashley Monroe, who has gone on to make quite a splash as a country singer herself. Jack had a horn section, and he had rehearsed that band so tightly that I didn't have to worry about a thing.

We performed "Shakin' All Over" on David Letterman's show a few days after our public debut at the *Grand Ole Opry*. That was so much fun. When we finished, Dave himself came over and called for an encore as the credits rolled. He was really thrilled with it. The next night we did a concert in New York, before flying to Los Angeles for two consecutive shows at the El Rey Theater. *The Party Ain't Over* came out the next day, and we did one more TV appearance on Conan O'Brien's show. We played "Funnel of Love," and then Conan interviewed me and Jack together afterward. I could tell Conan was a true fan of mine.

I remember when we were looking at photos for the album cover, the art director was making comments about how he could make some little tweaks to my appearance. He said, "Okay, I can sharpen the jaw line here," and that kind of thing.

I turned to Jack and I said, "Please have him take out more of those wrinkles."

"No, I don't want that," Jack said. "You've earned those wrinkles. I think you should be proud of them."

Despite my little moment of vanity, Jack was right. I'd like to show the younger girls who do respect me that it's all right to be old. We all have to age gracefully, so we must accept it as part of life, and just do the best we can. I see older women who, to me, are just beautiful with their silver gray hair, the way they dress nicely, and the classy way they carry themselves.

I have many warm and wonderful memories of working with Jack, but it was a bittersweet time in my life. When we were in Nashville rehearsing for our shows, I got a phone call from Gina telling me that Mother, or Bobo as we all called her, was being taken to the hospital. She had turned ninety-seven less than a month before, and it looked like she was near the end. I felt terrible to do it to Jack, but I had to leave to go home. Of course, he was gracious and promised the band would be ready.

I rushed home to be by my mom's side. She hung on for several days, but I had to return for that *Opry* appearance. Gina called me at about three in the morning on the day I was to fly out to Nashville. "Mom," she said, "Bobo's gone." I was devastated. Mother had been in mental decline for about five years at the time she died. In fact, she had to be confined to the lockdown area in the facility where she'd been living. Considering she never was any good at sitting still, it was no surprise that she was always trying to get out. She got her monitoring bracelet off one time and took three or four other old ladies with her. They got out to the road before someone realized they'd made a break for it. She caused all kinds of havoc at that place, but even though she'd not been herself for a while, it was still hard to accept the fact that she was gone.

I was in a complete fog when I received the news, but I had to get up and get to the airport. Oklahoma was covered in ice, so it took extra time to get there. We were late taking off, since the plane had to de-ice. It was a miserable morning, but we got to Nashville, had a chance to rehearse with Jack one more time, and then did the *Opry* the following night.

I headed right back to Oklahoma, where we buried Mother after a beautiful funeral at her beloved South Lindsay Baptist Church. The following day I was performing on David Letterman's show. It was quite a whirlwind to be performing at two of the most important venues in the country with one of the best bands I'd ever played with in between losing and burying Mother. To say it was an emotional rollercoaster would be an understatement.

Even though that period of time is clouded with the memories of losing Mother, I can still say that *The Party Ain't Over* is one of my best albums, and one of my personal favorites. It was a real challenge, which is one of the things I really liked about it. Instead of covering the same old ground once again, Jack pushed me into some exciting new territory and reignited my rebellious rock-and-roll soul at a time when I needed a little fire under me. Like Rosie Flores and Elvis Costello before him, Jack White has been another important champion of my career resurgence who also became a dear friend.

Chapter 26

My favorite photo of Wendell and me together.
We were celebrating our thirtieth anniversary.

IN THE MIDDLE OF A HEARTACHE

I was seventy-three years old when *The Party Ain't Over* came out, but I had no interest in slowing down. I was thrilled when Jon Hensley suggested I work with Jack White, but the album came out so great, and we got such a wonderful critical reception, that I didn't know how I was possibly going to top it. I felt like I'd done my very best, and I would have been happy to say "that's it." I still wanted to tour and play for the fans, but it was hard to imagine I was going to make another record that I would be as proud of.

Jon suggested that I should record at least one more album, and recommended Justin Townes Earle to produce it. I didn't know Justin. I'd heard his name, but didn't know his music. I listened to a few things he'd recorded, and I appreciated his rootsy country style, so I decided to give it a shot. Unfortunately, I was on the road a good bit in 2012 and didn't have much time to think about what material I'd record. Justin sent me some songs, so I made my selections long distance. He sent some good things, and I think he had a good sense of what kind of material would work for me.

When it came time to record, however, I'd just finished up some European dates. I'd been traveling a lot and was tired. We'd worked pretty hard and the album, *Unfinished Business* reflects it. The songs were good and were cute, but my voice just wasn't in top form. The famous horror writer Stephen King wrote the liner notes and said, "There was never a singer quite like Wanda Jackson, one who could hold her own with rockabilly rebels like Gene Vincent and Jerry Lee Lewis any day of the week." I was flattered, but I felt like I was wrung out before we even started recording. Justin was smart to take me back to more of a simple, stripped-down country and rockabilly sound. It wouldn't have worked if he'd tried to compete with what Jack had created for my previous album, but it was also hard to recapture the excitement that Jack had created.

Unfinished Business was not a career high point for me. It's not Justin's fault; it's just that the timing was off. I had fans and critics who were complimentary, but I know I could have done better. Sometimes I like to pull out my albums and listen to them as a way of walking down memory lane. This is one I hardly ever listen to. I suppose the title was meant to suggest that I had more to do and that perhaps that album would be my final recorded statement. Ironically, it actually *left* me with unfinished business. I decided soon after it was recorded that I would make at least one more album before I hung it up for good. I just needed to wait for the right moment.

Wendell and I continued to tour the world, but, despite our best efforts, we couldn't outrun some of the problems that tend to come creeping in with age. The last couple of years, in particular, presented some real heath challenges, and I was starting to feel a little beat up there for a while. There was a stretch when it seemed like I was in the hospital more than I was out!

Nobody wants to hear people complain about their medical problems, but I'll give you just a little background because it's not really a story about my aches and pains so much as it is a story of God's goodness in seeing me through with His healing power.

My issues began after I contracted an infection in my foot that ended up getting into the bone. While I was being treated for that problem, I contracted MRSA, a virus that clings to any metal or alloy. Since I'd had a knee replacement years before, that MRSA just clung to it and would *not* leave my body. The doctors ended up taking out the replacement and I went for weeks without a knee. I had to walk on my tip toes, all the while taking a high-powered intravenous antibiotic, which just about wiped me out.

During that whole ordeal I fell a couple of times, including once at home, where I knocked my shoulder blade out of joint and chipped the bone. I could go on about my arthritis and other ailments, but the point is that, though it was all very difficult, God won't ever give you more than you can take. I knew I'd push through and get back on my feet again. That's what was most important to me.

Finally, after three operations in a row and three rounds of the medication, the MRSA virus was gone and I could walk again. For some reason, however, the doctors discovered that I had some internal bleeding. I was starting to feel like I couldn't catch a break. But God always has a plan, and He knew how He was going to bring my strength and my health back.

My granddaughter, Jordan, who lives in Nashville and works in the music business, was working with a female trio called Bang!Bang! She booked the girls down in Mexico for an event at a hospital in Tijuana called CHIPSA. Jordan started talking with the owner, Ed Clay, and ended up telling him about my various health challenges. He encouraged her to bring me down there for their innovative inpatient program, which focuses on both medical and nutritional therapy.

My trip to Mexico was a transformative experience. I was there for about a month in the spring of 2017, and Wendell was able to be with me, since their "companion stay" facilities are designed for patients to bring their loved ones for support and encouragement. I received a much-needed blood transfusion and went through a series of oxygen treatments in a hyperbaric chamber. I had to drink thirteen glasses of juice every day and take what seemed like a hundred pills a day. I also ate an all vegan diet. That part was awful. I thought, *Oh, Lord, deliver me!* I'm a meat and potatoes gal, so that was rough on me. But I'll be darned if the place didn't turn everything around for me. God brought the right people along at the right time to help restore my health.

After my stay in Mexico, I felt like a new woman. I was ready to get back onstage and remember, once again, what it's like to perform without feeling exhausted. Wendell and I went out in May, 2017, to play dates in Chicago, Nashville, and Birmingham. We were joined at all three shows by Jordan, who in addition to her various music industry pursuits in Nashville, is an integral part of the third generation of family members who make up Wanda Jackson Enterprises. She started out helping with my publicity and began transitioning into handling management responsibilities as Wendell began to slow down a little bit.

As we were dealing with my own health battles, Wendell had begun showing some early signs of dementia. It took us a while to figure out exactly what was going on. I knew he was forgetful, but, heck, I was, too! After a while, it was clear it was more than just age. He wasn't always himself, and that made it difficult for him to stay on top of everything as he once had so masterfully. Having Jordan step in to lend a hand was a real blessing.

On Saturday night, May 20, I performed at Birmingham's Saturn club. Wendell introduced me and escorted me on stage, as he'd done at every show since he took over as my manager back in the '60s. He was feeling a little weak that night, which had become a more common occurrence in the previous year or so. He had quadruple bypass surgery back in 1993, which they say is usually effective for about twenty years. He had been having frequent "spells"—Wendell's term for feeling dizzy, getting headaches, and losing energy—for a few weeks leading up to that night. He was eating nitro pills like candy, and I later learned that he couldn't get down the steps from the stage that evening until he steadied himself on the rail for a moment and took a few of his "dynamite pills." Jordan helped him to a table and they sat together in the audience for my show.

As I looked out on the two of them, it occurred to me that I couldn't even remember the last time Wendell had been out in the crowd to watch my entire show from beginning to end. Usually he was running around taking care of all the business, but with Jordan in tow, it freed him up to sit down and enjoy the performance as a spectator. "Wanda, you sounded terrific tonight," he beamed when we got back to the hotel room after the show. "Your voice is sounding so strong, and it's so good to see your energy and your strength up there. You're back!"

The next day Jordan dropped us off at the Birmingham airport and headed back to Nashville. While we were waiting to fly home to Oklahoma City, Wendell passed out. The paramedics worked on him for forty-five minutes at the airport, but couldn't revive him. An ambulance transported him to the emergency room, where they continued to work on him. After what seemed like hours, the doctor came out to the waiting area and told me they couldn't save him. He'd had a heart attack. I felt my mouth go dry. I hadn't been without Wendell in over fifty-five years. He was eighty-one years old, but I couldn't believe he was gone so quickly.

Nothing really prepares you for that moment, but the people in Birmingham were so good to me. They treated me like family. In fact, an employee from Delta Airlines and another employee from American who saw what happened came to the hospital, prayed with me, and took care of all the logistics. Neither one of them knew I was an entertainer or had any reason to take an interest in me other than pure compassion. God sent those women to be my angels that day. Despite my profound sense of loss, I was also filled with love, comfort, and a peace that passes all understanding.

I realize now that Wendell was sicker than he let on. Maybe he didn't want to admit that his strength was failing. He'd always been my rock and my knight in shining armor. I can certainly understand why he might not want to face the reality of the changes in his life. I know I certainly didn't. When you're young you think you'll live forever. Maybe it never really gets any easier to deal with your own mortality as you age. But none of us can escape the inevitable.

Even though I'm sad not to have Wendell by my side anymore, I do have hope. I know I'll see him again. I know we'll spend forever together in Heaven. Wendell is no longer in his earthly body, but he's waiting for me in eternity. And he's free. He doesn't have to take those nitro pills. His mind isn't betraying him. His body isn't slowing him down or holding him back. He is in the presence of God and he is whole. As I've thought about it, I'm glad that the Lord chose to take him when he did instead of having him suffer through a long, slow mental decline.

We had a service for Wendell at Southern Hills Baptist Church in Oklahoma City on May 26. My next show was scheduled for June 3 in Seattle, but I couldn't imagine how I could possibly go back out there and do what I do without Wendell there in his dependable role as manager, encourager, organizer, and number one cheerleader. We'd been partners in marriage, parenting, music, business, and life for so many years! It felt like I'd lost an appendage or two (at least), and a great big chunk of my heart. Was I even capable of carrying on without him?

I was trying to go to sleep that night, but a million thoughts were floating through my mind. I was feeling restless and started thinking about Wendell. My mind drifted back to a recurring conversation we'd been having in recent months. I had been talking to him about making a plan for when we should retire. I guess I could see that his dementia was getting worse, and I thought maybe it would be better for him if we stopped traveling. But he wasn't ready. He would always say, "Wanda, I think we should give it at least a couple more years."

As I lay there in the dark, replaying those conversations in my mind, something just told me "I'm going to give it at least a couple more years, and I'm gonna do it for Wendell." At that moment, I realized that the best thing for me is to get right back out there and do what he knew I loved to do. Now I'm on that stage to honor Wendell's memory and to bring glory to God as I share the story of my faith and the story of the kind of love and commitment a couple can have when they build a lasting relationship on the right foundation.

Jordan met me in Seattle for that next show, and everything worked out perfectly. They had a beautiful three-room suite for us, provided transportation to and from the venue, and even took us to a great barbecue restaurant to eat afterward. It was a sweet experience, and everyone was so kind. But I have to confess I was a little nervous before going onstage that night. What if I started thinking about Wendell and got so teary eyed I couldn't sing? How would the crowd react? Would I just end up embarrassing myself?

As it turned out, I felt strong. I felt like the Lord and Wendell were up there watching me with great big smiles on their faces. Maybe they called Daddy and Mother over, too, to enjoy the show. I thought about the old song "May the Circle Be Unbroken" and I felt like I was living out those lyrics in that very moment.

The only time I faltered was halfway through "Right or Wrong." That has always been my special song for Wendell, ever since he told me he fell for me the first time he heard me sing it. I've thought of it as a declaration of my commitment to him and a testament to our love ever since he and I first met. I broke down a little bit during that one, but Jordan swears it wasn't obvious. Whether it was or not, I felt good to be back up there, with my health back where it ought to be, doing what Wendell loved to see me do.

Two weeks later I appeared on the *Grand Ole Opry*—for the third time ever—and sang "Right or Wrong" for Wendell once again. My son, Greg, and his family were there that night with me. In fact, after all my years in the music business, it was the first time Greg had ever been to Nashville! Of course, Jordan was there, too. Since Wendell passed, my entire family—including my daughter, Gina, who's living with me now—has made me feel so treasured and supported. I can say that grief is real, but so is the love of a good family, the faithfulness of God, and the sweet promise that we'll all be reunited again one day.

Chapter 27

TREAT ME LIKE A LADY

Even though my health problems are now behind me, I'm still watching myself getting older and older, and it's a real killer. There's a lot of pressure on women and on entertainers to live up to a certain standard. Add those two together, and you've got a real recipe for defeat. I don't know why, but it seems to me that men's bodies hold up better to the rigors of life as an entertainer. I didn't realize how hard all the traveling and one-nighters can be on a woman when I started out. I look at someone like Merle Haggard, and it seems like his voice sounded so consistently good right to the very end. It's like it was effortless. I feel like we gals get hit twice as hard by the accumulation of the years, which means we have to work twice as hard to keep giving our all.

Despite the temptations, I decided a while back that I was not going under the knife. I understand that plenty of women do it, and I understand why. I don't judge them for that, but kids have respected me all along for being different and not trying to be like everybody else. That's that same message that Daddy drilled into my head from the very beginning: "Don't follow the crowd; find a way to do things your own way."

That spirit has kept me saying, "I'm going to do the best I can, or at least the best with what I have to work with." Trying to be beautiful all the time is a young woman's pursuit, and that's not where I find my worth today. But I won't pretend that the aging process is fun. I'm worried about my balance, and sometimes I can't stand for an entire hour-and-a-half concert, so I'll lean on a stool for a while. 1usually just say something funny about it. I want the audience to know, "Hey, I know what I'm doing and it's perfectly all right."

Not only am I embracing the aging process, I'm also embracing new opportunities and adventures! That includes an approach to songwriting that's different for me. Somewhere along the way I had stopped writing my own songs altogether. During the latter part of my Capitol days, I'd had enough country hits that some of the really good Nashville writers were sending me material. I had better songs to choose from than I'd had in the past, so if I had three or four solid potential hits for a recording session I didn't feel much of a need to contribute my own songs. I didn't really purposefully get away from writing, but between already having access to good material and the fact that my life had gotten so busy, it just kind of happened.

I used to like to be totally alone when I was writing. When I wrote, I'd generally sit down at the piano and try out various things in complete solitude, where nobody would be watching or listening to my process. I'd occasionally written some things while traveling, but preferred being at home with just the piano and total silence. Balancing a career, a marriage, and motherhood made it tricky to really find the time and space to write. Over the years, that part of my life just kind of drifted away.

That all changed recently, thanks to my granddaughter, Jordan. That little squirt is working me to death! She called me not long ago and said, "Ma, I've set up some co-writing sessions for you in Nashville." I said, "Jordan, I haven't written with other people very much, and I don't think I could do that. The country songs I hear on the radio today have changed a lot, and I just don't know if I could write that kind of song." Even as I was protesting, it occurred to me that I'm often thinking of song titles in my head. I can be driving along and formulate a whole verse and a chorus of a song, but I quit writing them down a long time ago. Some of those ideas were starting to gnaw at me again, but fear was holding me back. Jordan suggested that I just go to Nashville and sit in on a songwriting session to see how it works these days. I agreed, even though I was scared. I thought, *My gosh, I don't know what I'm getting myself into here.*

Since I promised Jordan I'd give it a shot, I headed down to Nashville, where she introduced me to Sonia Leigh and Vanessa Olivarez. Sonia is an artist who has written a couple of number one hits with Zac Brown, and Vanessa was a successful contestant on *American Idol* who's written for Sugarland and other big country artists. She's also in the group Bang!Bang! that Jordan works with. I felt like those gals were operating in a world that's a million miles from my experience, but I liked them immediately. The four of us were just sitting around talking, and I was telling the girls that, even though I have a reputation for being a wild or strong woman, I was proud of the fact that I'd always stayed a lady. Before you know it, we were writing a song called "Treat Me Like a Lady." It was the most natural experience, and so much fun. That's when I decided I'd do some more of that co-writing that the Nashville folks do so well.

I'm eighty years old now, and I'm enjoying my newfound career as a Nashville-style songwriter. God works in mysterious ways, and when you're following Him, life is an adventure. You just never know where He's going to lead you, and I'm thrilled that He's opened up this new door for me at this stage of life.

Of course, once I got back into writing I was ready to get to that unfinished business and do some more recording. The opportunity recently came about to work with Joan Jett, and I'm so happy we get to collaborate with each other. She's been producing some tracks for me, and we are working on a full album together. She tells me that I was influential in sparking her desire to sing. Plus, we have a lot in common, just being girl rockers. And she's a *real* girl rocker! I might have gotten things started, but she took it from there! When I hear people like Joan, Cyndi Lauper, or Adele talk about my influence on their careers, it just amazes me and flatters me to no end. I consider them all a part of my extended rock-and-roll family.

I value the opportunity to keep doing the job I love. Shows are different now than they used to be. They're longer and there are fewer acts on the bill. Now, if people come to the show, they're probably coming to see me. They're already fans. At one point, I'd be part of a bill with a list of other entertainers, and I always viewed it as a challenge to win over the audience. I tried to bring the right style and charisma to get them in the palm of my hand before the show was through. That's where Daddy would say, "They're still talking all around this bar and back in that area. You've gotta grab 'em." That was my mission, and I learned pretty well how to do it, even if they weren't there to hear my songs. I wanted to pull everybody in and make sure they were all having a good time. I would always talk with the audience and make little changes based on the feeling in the room. My shows weren't the same every night, and that uncertainty was exciting.

By now, I know how to keep an audience interested. I feel sorry for some artists today who are superstars, but have only done a few shows. They know how to sing, but they don't know how to entertain yet. Some of these kids need all the dancers and the costumes because they've never had to go out and win anyone over on raw talent alone. And that's fine. It's just a different type of show. It's another thing to be on a stage with just you and your music, figuring out how to hook that crowd. I have young adults come up to me and say, "That was the best show I've ever seen." That's a jaw-dropper to me because I don't have any goodies. There are no dancers or crazy lights or fog machines or video projections behind me!

One of my favorite shows on TV is *The Voice*. Oh my gosh, the sets are just fabulous, but it makes the performance harder to listen to. The singer is just one part of this whole show. I don't have all the bells and the whistles and the fluff. For me, that would just clutter everything up. It's the difference between spectacle and really connecting with people, and connecting is what I learned over a lot of years.

I don't know what the future holds, but, looking back, I don't think there's much I would change about my journey up to this point. Oh, maybe there are a few little nit-picky things. I'm not business minded, but if I had been, I might have fought a little harder for more elaborate stage sets and things I wanted that I thought I couldn't have. I probably had some low self-esteem early on and didn't think I was qualified to ask for some of the things I wished I had. Maybe I would be a little bolder if I had a do-over, but the training with Daddy was, "You do what your employer wants you to do." I wish I'd been more of a take-charge person, but I wasn't and never could be. That's just not my personality. So, given who I am and who God made me to be, I wouldn't really change anything about my career.

If I could have a do-over in my personal life, there are things I would find the time for that I never had the opportunity to experience because of the demands of my career. Would you believe I've never planted a flower? I think I would enjoy it. I wish I'd gone to art classes and learned to paint. I wish I'd learned to be a great cook and experiment with some interesting culinary creations. When your work is your life, it's hard to make room for those kinds of simple pleasures.

The biggest change I would make, if I could go back in time, is that I would be home for more of the special things in my children's lives. I was a bit selfish in that regard. Or maybe a lot selfish. As an only-child with a strong father, and then a strong husband, I never had to share things with anybody. My career was still number one, even when the kids came along. I felt like I wasn't really ready to be a mom. I hadn't even been around kids or held them or anything. I think it hurt my children that I missed plays and piano recitals and that kind of thing. That's so important to kids to have their parents there for those experiences. That wasn't as much the case when I was young. Mother worked all the time, so she was never at any of my school-related events. PTA was out of the question, and it was the same for me. I was not interested, but that just wasn't right. I should have taken more of an interest. I should have recognized that times were changing and the other parents were engaging in new ways. That's something I regret and wish I could go back and fix.

I love my children so much, and am so proud of who they've become as adults. Wendell and I were so fortunate that they turned out okay. We never had to get them out of jail or pick them up from the hospital or that kind of thing. Greg and Gina have both done such a fantastic job of parenting with their respective families. I just watch in amazement. They've really got it together, and my children and grandchildren have enriched my life in ways I wish I'd fully appreciated earlier on. When I look at my grandkids—Jennifer, Jordan, Jillian, and Chandler—my heart bursts with pride. Jennifer recently had a baby in March of 2017, officially making me a *great*-grandmother! They named her Nellie Rose, after my mother, and one of the things I treasure is that Wendell had the chance to hold her and dote on her before he passed away. We couldn't have been more proud.

I am a blessed woman. The love that Wendell and I shared only deepened and matured over the years, and I look forward to seeing him again. I've been through a lot of changes and many great adventures, but, for now, I'm still here. I have the love of God, the love of my fans, and the love of a great family fueling me to continue on as a rock-and-roll great-grandma. I have many stories left to write, which means I've got some more songs inside me that are ready to come out. I hope you'll come see me when I stop in to perform them in your town. We'll have one heck of a Saturday night together!